Praise for
Understanding SCA
(Service Component Architecture)

"Jim Marino and Michael Rowley have been involved with SCA from the start and know it as well as anyone. They have great hands-on experience with the Fabric3 open source SCA project. This book also tackles the subject and its broad issues head on, and in addition to the clear and concise technical descriptions of SCA, they provide excellent sidebar perspectives on Java, Java EE, Web services, and SCA's relationship to them all."

—Eric Newcomer, Progress Software,
Coauthor of *Understanding SOA with Web Services*,
and Author of *Understanding Web Services*

"It was really worthwhile reading this book. It not only introduces a powerful technology, but also provides comprehensive coverage of supporting technologies. The authors have paid plenty of attention to practical issues including performance and thoroughly understand the ways that SCA can leverage state-of-the-art technologies such as JPA."

—Tim Holloway, Forum Moderator,
The JavaRanch

"SCA is a nice, conceptually and technically sound advanced component framework. This book enables easy access to this exciting technology for software developers."

—Dr. Steffen Becker

"*Understanding SCA (Service Component Architecture)* delivers the details for how to effectively use SCA leveraging open source tools such as Fabric3."

—Dave Hendricksen, Software Architect

Understanding SCA
(Service Component Architecture)

Understanding SCA

(Service Component Architecture)

Jim Marino

Michael Rowley

✦ Addison-Wesley

Upper Saddle River, NJ • Boston • Indianapolis • San Francisco
New York • Toronto • Montreal • London • Munich • Paris • Madrid
Cape Town • Sydney • Tokyo • Singapore • Mexico City

The publisher offers excellent discounts on this book when ordered in quantity for bulk purchases or special sales, which may include electronic versions and/or custom covers and content particular to your business, training goals, marketing focus, and branding interests. For more information, please contact:

> U.S. Corporate and Government Sales
> (800) 382-3419
> corpsales@pearsontechgroup.com

For sales outside the United States, please contact:

> International Sales
> international@pearson.com

Visit us on the Web: informit.com/aw

Library of Congress Cataloging-in-Publication Data:

Marino, Jim, 1969-
  Understanding SCA (Service Component Architecture) / Jim Marino, Michael Rowley.
    p. cm.
  Includes bibliographical references and index.
  ISBN 978-0-321-51508-7 (pbk. : alk. paper) 1. Application software—Development. 2. Web services. 3. Computer software—Reusability. 4. System design. I. Rowley, Michael. II. Title.
  QA76.76.A65M339 2009
  005.3—dc22
                              2009021249

ISBN-13: 978-0-321-51508-7
ISBN-10: 0-321-51508-0
Text printed in the United States on recycled paper at R.R. Donnelley in Crawfordsville, Indiana.
First printing July 2009

Editor-in-Chief
Karen Gettman
Executive Editor
Chris Guzikowski
Senior Development Editor
Chris Zahn
Development Editor
Susan Brown Zahn
Managing Editor
Kristy Hart
Project Editor
Jovana San Nicolas-Shirley
Copy Editor
Water Crest Publishing
Indexer
Erika Millen
Proofreaders
Seth Kerney
Apostrophe Editing Services
Publishing Coordinator
Raina Chrobak
Cover Designer
Sandra Schroeder
Compositor
Gloria Schurick

Contents

Acknowledgments

We would like to thank the reviewers of our book who provided invaluable comments, feedback, and suggestions: Dr. Steffen Becker, Dave Hendricksen, Tim Holloway, and Dave Ennis. We would also like to extend our appreciation to Raina Chrobak, Susan Zahn, Jovana San Nicolas-Shirley, and everyone at Addison-Wesley who guided us along the way.

Service Component Architecture (SCA) was the outgrowth of a truly collaborative effort. We send a special thanks to the original SCA cohorts— Graham Barber, Michael Beisiegel, Dave Booz, Mike Edwards, and Martin Nally.

Special acknowledgment goes to two individuals who selflessly gave their time, assistance, and encouragement throughout the course of writing this book: David Chappell and Ed Cobb. We are truly grateful for the extraordinary efforts they made on numerous occasions.

Jim would like to express his personal thanks to Niccolò, Jim, Kathy, Michelle, Paolo, Anna, and, in particular, Lia, whose love and support made this book possible.

Michael would like to thank Jim for the opportunity to work with him on this project. Michael would also like to thank to his wife Elise, for whose unfailing love, support, and encouragement he is eternally grateful.

About the Authors

Jim Marino, Ph.D., is Principal at Metaform Systems, where he provides strategic planning, architecture assistance, and training to clients worldwide. Jim is also one of the architects of the Fabric3 SCA runtime. Prior to joining Metaform Systems, Jim was Director of Technology at BEA Systems, where he was involved with the development of Service Component Architecture from its inception.

Michael Rowley, Ph.D., is the CTO of Active Endpoints, Inc. He has been involved in the development of SCA from early in its development and has contributed to 12 of the 15 SCA specifications that were published as part of the Open Service-Oriented Architecture (OSOA) collaboration. He was also an original member of the Open Component Service Architecture (OpenCSA) steering committee, which is the OASIS steering committee that oversees the work of the various SCA technical committees. Before joining Active Endpoints, he was a Director of Technology at BEA Systems where, in addition to working on SCA, he also helped develop the BPELJ extension to BPEL and was involved in the early development of BEA's event processing and service bus products. Michael received his Ph.D. in computer science from UCLA in 1994.

Preface

What is Service Component Architecture (SCA)? What are the key SCA concepts? How will SCA impact technology choices my organization will need to make in the near-term? How should SCA fit into my enterprise architecture? How can I make the best use of SCA in my projects?

Answering these questions is fundamental to understanding SCA. The goal of this book is to help answer those questions by providing the background necessary to use SCA effectively.

Who Can Benefit from This Book

SCA is a technology for creating, assembling, and managing distributed applications. However, this book is not intended solely for developers. Our aim is to benefit "technologists"—developers, but also architects, analysts, managers, and anyone who has a stake implementing information systems—by connecting SCA to broader technology trends.

In this book, we attempt to strike a balance between the "big picture" and the detailed coverage essential to developers. We also endeavor to achieve this balance in a way that is engaging, accurate, and complete.

Both of us have been involved with SCA since its inception, when it started as an informal working group composed of individuals from IBM and BEA (where both of us worked). We were directly involved in shaping SCA as it went through various iterations and changes.

Rather than simply provide a tutorial, we have sought to explain the history and reasoning behind important decisions made during the development of SCA.

Lest we be accused of operating in the "ivory tower" of technology standards, we have also attempted to be informed by practical experience. We have been key contributors to the open source Fabric3 SCA runtime. In addition, while at BEA and now in our current positions, we have had the opportunity to be involved in the development of several large-scale systems built with SCA. We have tried to reflect this experience and lessons learned throughout the book in the form of best practices and implementation advice.

Finally, while we strive for completeness and accuracy, there are inevitably things a book must leave out. SCA is a vast technology that spans multiple programming languages. We have chosen to concentrate on those aspects of SCA that pertain to creating and assembling applications using Java. Although we touch on BPEL, our focus remains on Java, as the latter is a cornerstone of modern enterprise development.

How to Read the Book

Reading a book is like listening to an album (or CD): Both are highly personal experiences. Some prefer to read thoroughly or listen from beginning to end. Others like to skip around, focusing on specific parts.

Understanding SCA is designed to be read in parts but also has a structure tying the various pieces together. The first chapter, "Introducing SCA," provides an overview of SCA and how it fits into today's technology landscape. The second chapter, "Assembling and Deploying a Composite," continues the overview theme by walking through how to build an application using SCA.

Chapter 3, "Service-Based Development Using Java," and Chapter 4, "Conversational Interactions Using Java," respectively, turn to advanced SCA programming model topics. In these chapters, we detail how to design loosely coupled services and asynchronous interactions, manage stateful services, and provide best practices for developing with SCA.

Having explored the SCA programming model in depth, Chapters 5–9 cover the main SCA concepts: composition, policy, wires, bindings, and the domain. In these chapters, we explain how to develop modular applications, use transactions, configure cross-application policies such as security and reliability, integrate with external systems, deploy applications, and structure corporate architectures using SCA.

Chapter 10, "Service-Based Development Using BPEL," demonstrates how to use BPEL with SCA to provide applications with long-running process capabilities.

The final two chapters round out application development with SCA by focusing on the data and presentation tiers. Chapter 11, "Persistence," details how to use Java Persistence API (JPA) with SCA to read and write data from a database. Chapter 12, "The Presentation Tier," demonstrates how to integrate web applications, in particular servlets and JSPs, with SCA services.

1

Introducing SCA

Service Component Architecture, or SCA, is a technology for creating services and assembling them into composite applications. SCA addresses the perennial question of how to build systems from a series of interconnected parts. In SCA, these parts interact by providing services that perform a specific function. Services may be implemented using different technologies and programming languages. For example, a service can be implemented in Java, C++, or in a specialized language such as Business Process Execution Language (BPEL). Services may also be collocated in the same operating system process or distributed across multiple processes running on different machines. SCA provides a framework for building these services, describing how they communicate and tying them together.

We once heard a witty definition of a technology framework that is appropriate to bring up in this context: A technology framework is something everyone wants to write but no one wants to use. Indeed, the industry is replete with frameworks and programming models promising to solve problems posed by application development in new and innovative ways. In the 1990s, the Distributed Computing Environment (DCE) was superceded by Common Object Request Broker Architecture (CORBA) and Distributed Component Object Model (DCOM). Java Enterprise Edition (Java EE) and .NET emerged as the two dominant frameworks in the early

2000s, supplanting the latter two. Open source has also been a center of innovation, with Spring and Ruby on Rails emerging as two of the more popular frameworks.

This raises the question of why SCA? What problems with existing programming models is SCA trying to solve? The sheer scope of SCA as a technology and the fact that it is supported by a diverse set of vendors invariably has led to a degree of confusion in this respect. SCA can be initially daunting to understand.

SCA addresses two key issues with existing approaches: complexity and reuse.

SCA addresses two key issues with existing approaches: complexity and reuse. First, SCA provides a simplified programming model for building distributed systems. The dominant programming models today have grown increasingly complex. For example, writing a Java EE application that exposes web services, performs some processing, and interfaces with a messaging system to integrate with other applications requires knowledge of the JAX-WS, JMS, and EJB APIs. This complexity has not been limited to Java EE: The .NET framework has been subject to the same trend. Writing an identical application using .NET 2.0 requires an understanding of the ASP .NET Web Services, Enterprise Services, and .NET Messaging APIs.

In contrast, as illustrated in Figure 1.1, SCA provides a unified way to build applications that communicate using a variety of protocols.

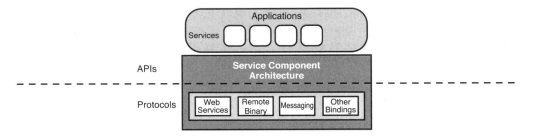

Figure 1.1   SCA provides a unified way to build distributed applications.

Perspective: SCA and .NET

In recent years, increasing complexity has not been limited to Java EE: The .NET framework has been subject to the same trend. Writing an identical application using .NET 2.0 requires an understanding of ASP .NET Web Services, Enterprise Services, and .NET Messaging APIs.

Microsoft has spent significant time addressing complexity in the .NET Framework. Starting with version 3.0, .NET incorporates a programming model that unifies web services, remote procedure calling, queued messaging, and transactions. SCA introduces a uniform way to perform distributed interactions. In SCA and Windows Communication Foundation (WCF), application logic is invoked the same way whether web services, a binary, or a messaging protocol is used (see Figure 1.2).

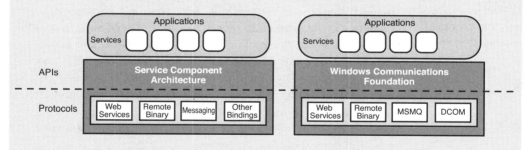

Figure 1.2   SCA and .NET architectures

Adapted from David Chappell, www.davidchappell.com.

This unified approach simplifies development by eliminating the need for application logic to resort to specialized, low-level APIs.

The second problem SCA addresses concerns reuse. There are two basic types of code reuse: within the same process (intra-process reuse) and across processes (inter-process reuse). Object-oriented programming languages introduced innovative features, including interfaces, classes, polymorphism, and inheritance that enabled applications to be decomposed into smaller units within the same process. By structuring applications in terms of classes, object-oriented code could be more easily accessed, reused, and managed than code written with procedural programming languages.

In the 1990s, distributed object technologies such as DCE, DCOM, CORBA, and EJB attempted to apply these same principles of reuse to applications spread across multiple processes. After numerous iterations, the industry learned from distributed object technologies that the principles of object-oriented design do not cleanly apply across remote boundaries. Distributed object technologies often resulted in application architectures that tightly coupled clients to service providers. This coupling made systems extremely fragile. Updating applications with a new version of a service provider frequently resulted in client incompatibilities. Moreover, these technologies failed to adequately address key differences in remote communications such as network latency, often leading to poor system performance.

SCA provides a way to assemble, manage, and control distributed systems.

However, despite the shortcomings of distributed objects, the idea behind inter-process reuse is still valid: There is far greater value in code that is organized into reusable units and accessible to multiple clients running in different processes. As we will explain in more detail, SCA provides a foundation for application resources and logic to be shared by multiple clients that builds on the lessons learned from distributed objects. Similar to the way object-oriented languages provide mechanisms for organizing and reusing in-process application logic, SCA provides a way to assemble, manage, and control distributed systems.

In SCA, applications are organized into components that offer functionality to clients through services.

In order to achieve reuse, SCA defines services, components, and composites. In SCA, applications are organized into components that offer functionality to clients (typically other components) through services. Services may be reused by multiple clients. Components in turn may rely on other services. As we will see, SCA provides a mechanism to connect or "wire" components to these services. This is done through a composite, which is an XML file. Figure 1.3 shows a typical SCA application.

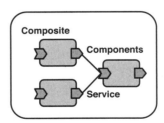

Figure 1.3   An SCA application

SCA and Enterprise Architectures

Unlike Java EE and .NET, SCA is not intended to be an all-encompassing technology platform. SCA does not specify mechanisms to persist data or a presentation-tier technology for building user interfaces. Rather, SCA integrates with other enterprise technologies such as JDBC and Java Persistence Architecture (JPA) for storing data in a database and the myriad of web-based UI frameworks that exist today (servlets and JSP, Struts, JavaServer Faces [JSFs], and Spring WebFlow, to name a few). Figure 1.4 illustrates a typical SCA architecture, which includes the use of presentation and persistence technologies.

SCA does not specify mechanisms to persist data or a presentation-tier technology for building user interfaces.

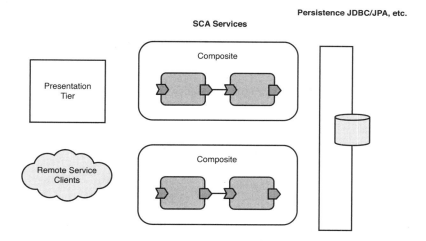

Figure 1.4   Using persistence and presentation technologies with SCA

In Chapter 10, "Service-Based Development Using BPEL," and Chapter 11, "Persistence," we take a closer look at using SCA with some of the more popular persistence and presentation technologies.

Perspective: A New Way to Standards?

Today, SCA is a set of OASIS standards according to the official processes and procedures laid out by that organization. Prior to OASIS, from November 2005 to March 2007, SCA work was done as part of a collaboration of vendors, termed "Open SOA" or OSOA (www.osoa.org).

One of the primary reasons for doing this work outside of an official standards organization was the immaturity of SCA and time-to-market: Standards organizations are bureaucratic and their processes slow things down. This is not necessarily a bad thing, particularly for mature technologies on which many businesses must rely for years. In these cases, stability is an overriding concern.

SCA, in contrast, was a new technology in a rapidly evolving market. Consequently, the collaboration participants needed the ability to make changes relatively quickly, changes that would at times break compatibility with previous versions of the specifications. Even a cursory comparison of the 0.9 version of the specifications published in November 2005 with the 1.0 version in March 2007 quickly reveals significant new features and areas that underwent substantial modification.

In hindsight, this was arguably the correct approach to take. One of the notable aspects of this process is that it diverged from the path taken by many previous specifications, in particular Java EE and CORBA, which were largely designed by official standards committees. In this respect, SCA shares more in common with how web services standards began: as informal vendor collaborations prior to being submitted to an official standards organization.

Given that both web services and SCA efforts have taken the approach of using a collaboration model prior to standardization, the industry may be witnessing a shift in how technology specifications are developed. Although there are certainly upsides to this approach in terms of faster iteration, there are some potentially negative consequences. One of those potential negative consequences is the "smoke-filled room scenario," where a few vendors conspire to create specifications that do not take into account "real" user requirements. We will need to wait and see whether this collaborative approach becomes the *modus operandi* for new technology development and whether it represents an improvement over specifications developed entirely within a standards body.

The remainder of this chapter provides an overview of SCA, covering its key concepts. However, rather than stopping at the customary technical introduction, we attempt to shed light on the things not easily gleaned from reading the SCA specifications themselves. In particular, we consider how SCA relates to other technologies, including web services and Java EE. We also highlight the design principles and assumptions behind SCA, with particular attention to how they affect enterprise architecture.

As with any technology, SCA has benefits and trade-offs. It is an appropriate technology in many scenarios but it certainly is not in all cases. Our intention in this chapter, and ultimately with this book, is to equip readers with the understanding necessary to make intelligent choices about when and how to use SCA.

Perspective: The History of SCA

An outgrowth of vendor collaboration, it is probably more accurate to say SCA has a number of "histories" as opposed to just one. Prior to OASIS and OSOA, the various specification participants worked on precursors to SCA, either as internal projects or in informal cross-company working groups. BEA and IBM, for example, worked together for over a year on component model technologies, even jointly developing code. Some of those technologies, including assembly, would later evolve into core SCA concepts.

What caused these various efforts among the different vendors to coalesce into SCA? There are undoubtedly a number of reasons why this happened, but one common to all the vendors was that each recognized that the Microsoft model of product development was not viable in its market segment. Unlike Microsoft, which is big enough to unilaterally define its own future, none of the original "Big Four" SCA participants—BEA, IBM, Oracle, and SAP—had enough market presence to dictate future technology direction alone. Industry consensus was crucial to achieving individual vendor goals.

In BEA's case, where both of us were employed, this lesson was learned over time. Prior to SCA, BEA developed a proprietary programming model called Workshop aimed at simplifying Java EE. Workshop adopted the Microsoft tactic of eschewing standards in favor of gaining adoption through the introduction of innovative features users wanted. This was perhaps not surprising given that the people behind Workshop came from Microsoft.

Ultimately, the Workshop framework failed at its strategy to gain broader acceptance through innovation alone. BEA's case is, however, not unique: The industry is littered with unsuccessful attempts to push proprietary frameworks and programming models. What happened with SCA was that the various independent initiatives converged as vendors understood the importance of collaboration and consensus.

The Essentials

SCA is built on four key concepts: services, components, composites, and the domain.

SCA is built on four key concepts: services, components, composites, and the domain. Understanding the role each plays is fundamental to understanding SCA. In this section, we provide an overview of these concepts before proceeding to a more detailed look at how applications are built using SCA.

Services

In SCA, applications are organized into a set of services that perform particular tasks such as accepting a loan application, performing a credit check, or executing an inventory lookup. The term **service** has been used in the industry to denote a variety of things. In SCA, a service has two primary attributes: a contract and an address.

Service Contract

A service contract specifies the set of operations available to a client, the requirements for the inputs, and the guarantees for the outputs.

A service contract specifies the set of operations available to a client, the requirements for the inputs, and the guarantees for the outputs. Service contracts can be defined through several mechanisms. In simple cases where a component is implemented using a Java class, an interface may define the service contract. Listing 1.1 is an example of a service contract with two operations defined by a Java interface. The only thing specific to SCA is the `@Remotable` annotation, which indicates that the service can be made available to remote clients (more on this later).

Listing 1.1   *A Java-Based Service Contract*

```
@Remotable

public interface Calculator {

     float add(float operand1, float operand2);

     float subtract(float operand1, float operand2);

     float multiply(float operand1, float operand2);

     float divide(float operand1, float operand2);
}
```

In more complex cases, service contracts may be declared upfront before code is written using a specialized interface description language, such as WSDL or IDL. This "top-down" or "contract-first" development provides a way for organizations to maintain tighter control over the interfaces services provide to clients.

The most common language for top-down development in SCA is the XML-based Web Services Description Language (WSDL). As its name indicates, WSDL is most commonly used to define web service contracts. SCA also makes use of WSDL to specify service contracts. Listing 1.2 presents the WSDL equivalent of the Calculator service contract.

Listing 1.2   *A WSDL-Based Service Contract*

```
<wsdl:definitions xmlns:clc="urn:com:bigbank:util:calculator"
   xmlns:wsdl="http://schemas.xmlsoap.org/wsdl/"
   xmlns:xs=http://www.w3.org/2001/XMLSchema
   targetNamespace="urn:com:bigbank:util:calculator">

  <wsdl:types>
     <xs:schema targetNamespace="urn:com:bigbank:util:calculator">
        <xs:element name="operands">
           <xs:complexType>
              <xs:sequence>
                 <xs:element name="arg1" type="xs:float"/>
                 <xs:element name="arg2" type="xs:float"/>
              </xs:sequence>
           </xs:complexType>
        </xs:element>
        <xs:element name="answer" type="xs:float"/>
  </wsdl:types>
```

Listing 1.2   *continued*

```
<wsdl:message name="calculatorRequest">
   <wsdl:part element="clc:operands" name="operands"/>
</wsdl:message>
<wsdl:message name="calculatorResponse">
   <wsdl:part element="clc:answer" name="answer"/>
</wsdl:message>

<wsdl:portType name="Calculator">
   <wsdl:operation name="add">
      <wsdl:input message="clc:calculatorRequest"/>
      <wsdl:output message="clc:calculatorResponse"/>
   </wsdl:operation>
   <wsdl:operation name="multiply">
      <wsdl:input message="clc:calculatorRequest"/>
      <wsdl:output message="clc:calculatorResponse"/>
   </wsdl:operation>
   <wsdl:operation name="subtract">
      <wsdl:input message="clc:calculatorRequest"/>
      <wsdl:output message="clc:calculatorResponse"/>
   </wsdl:operation>
   <wsdl:operation name="divide">
      <wsdl:input message="clc:calculatorRequest"/>
      <wsdl:output message="clc:calculatorResponse"/>
   </wsdl:operation>
</wsdl:portType>
</wsdl:definitions>
```

In top-down development, after the service contract is defined, tooling is typically used to generate actual code artifacts. For example, tooling will use the Calculator WSDL as input to generate the previous Java interface shown in Listing 1.1.

Service Address

Service addresses are fundamental to reuse: They provide a way for clients to uniquely identify and connect to application logic.

Having seen that service contracts may be defined using Java interfaces, it may be tempting to think of services as simply analogous to interfaces in object-oriented programming. This is true to the extent that services define the set of operations available to a client for a particular component. However, services also have addresses, which distinguishes them from interfaces. Clients obtain a reference to a particular service through a service address. Service addresses operate much like network addresses, uniquely identifying a particular machine on a network. Later in the chapter, we cover the mechanics of specifying service addresses and how applications use them. The important concept to bear in mind is that service addresses are fundamental to reuse: They provide a way for clients to uniquely identify and connect to application logic, whether it is co-located in the same process or hosted on a machine at some remote location.

Components

In SCA, a **component** is configured code that provides one or more services. A client connects to a service via an address and invokes operations on it. This concept is illustrated in Figure 1.5.

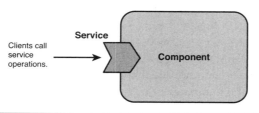

Figure 1.5   Components have one or more services.

Components may be written in a variety of programming languages, including Java and C++, and special purpose languages such as the BPEL.

Creating a component involves two things: writing an implementation and configuring it. Components written in Java are simple classes. In other words, they do not have any special requirements placed on them. Listing 1.3 demonstrates a simple calculator component.

Listing 1.3   *A Java Component Implementation*

```
public class CalculatorComponent implements Calculator {

    public float add(float operand1, float operand2) {
        return operand1+operand2;
    }

    public float subtract(float operand1, float operand2) {
        return operand1-operand2;
    }

    public float multiply(float operand1, float operand2) {
        return operand1*operand2;
    }

    public float divide(float operand1, float operand2) {
        return operand1/operand2;
    }
}
```

When the preceding calculator component is deployed, it provides a single service defined by the `Calculator` interface. Clients connect to the `Calculator` service and invoke one or more of its operations.

Composites

*Components are configured using an XML configuration file called a **composite**.*

The second step in creating a component is to configure it. Components are configured using an XML configuration file called a **composite**. This file can be created by hand or using graphical tooling. The XML vocabulary used to create composites is Service Component Definition Language (SCDL, pronounced "SKID-EL"). Listing 1.3 shows a composite that configures the calculator component using the implementation listed in Listing 1.4.

Listing 1.4   *A Composite*

```
<composite xmlns=http://www.osoa.org/xmlns/sca/1.0

           name="CalculatorComposite">

   <component name="Calculator">
      <implementation.java class="com.bigbank.CalculatorComponent"/>
   </component>
</composite>
```

In Listing 1.4, the `<component>` element is used to define the calculator component. The `<implementation.java>` element identifies the component as being written in Java and the implementation class. The other important item to note is that both components and composites are assigned names, which are used to identify them. This makes it possible to have multiple components use the same component implementation—in this case, `CalculatorComponent`.

A composite may be used to configure more than one component.

All but the most trivial applications will be composed of multiple components. A composite may be used to configure more than one component. Typically, it will make sense to configure related components together in a single composite (therefore the name *composite*, because it is used to "compose" components). Listing 1.5 lists a composite that configures two components: one that processes loan applications and another that performs credit scoring.

Listing 1.5   *A Composite That Configures Multiple Components*

```
<composite xmlns=http://www.osoa.org/xmlns/sca/1.0

           name="LoanComposite">

   <component name ="LoanComponent">
      <implementation.java class="com.bigbank.LoanComponent"/>

   <component>

   <component name =" CreditComponent">
      <implementation.java class="com.bigbank.CreditComponent"/>
   <component>
</composite>
```

As we will do frequently throughout the book, the preceding composite can be represented visually, as shown in Figure 1.6.

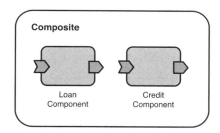

Figure 1.6   A graphical representation of a composite

In the previous example, both `LoanComponent` and `CreditComponent` were implemented in Java. It is also possible to configure components written in different languages in the same composite. For example, if the loan application process required workflow, it may be more convenient to implement `LoanComponent` using BPEL. In this case, the basic structure of the composite remains the same, as shown in Listing 1.6.

Listing 1.6   *A Composite with Components Implemented in BPEL and Java*

```
<composite xmlns="http://www.osoa.org/xmlns/sca/1.0"

           xmlns:bb="bigbank.com/xmlns/loanApplication/1.0"

           name="LoanComposite">

   <component name ="LoanComponent">
```

Listing 1.6   *continued*

```
        <implementation.bpel process="bb:LoanProcess"/>
    <component>

    <component name =" CreditComponent">
        <implementation.java class="com.bigbank.CreditComponent"/>
    <component>
</composite>
```

In changing to BPEL, the only difference is the use of the `<implementation.bpel>` element in place of `<implementation.java>` and pointing to the BPEL process as opposed to the Java class name.

The Domain

A domain consists of one or more cooperating SCA servers, or SCA runtimes, that host components in containers.

Composites are deployed into an environment running SCA middleware termed a **domain**. A domain consists of one or more cooperating SCA servers, or SCA runtimes, that host components in containers. The relationship between a domain, its runtimes, and component containers is shown in Figure 1.7.

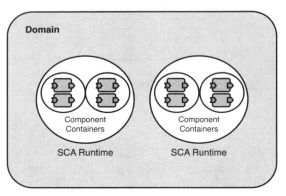

Figure 1.7   SCA middleware: the domain, runtimes, and containers

In an enterprise environment, domains may span many runtimes across distributed data centers.

Figure 1.7 depicts a domain with multiple runtimes. In an enterprise environment, domains may span many runtimes across distributed data centers. But it is also possible for domains to be small. A domain may consist of a single SCA runtime (sometimes referred to as a "server") or may even be confined to an embedded device.

When a composite is deployed to a domain with more than one runtime, its components may be hosted on different runtimes. For example, when the previous loan application composite is deployed, `LoanComponent` and `CreditComponent` may be hosted in processes on different runtimes (see Figure 1.8).

The process of deploying a composite to one runtime or many is vendor-specific. Some SCA runtimes may require additional configuration information identifying target machines. Other runtimes may employ sophisticated provisioning algorithms that take into account factors such as machine load.

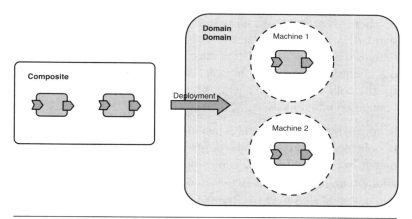

Figure 1.8   A deployed composite

Although the capabilities offered by a domain will vary greatly by SCA vendor (or open source implementation), all domains have several common characteristics. Namely, domains provide management capabilities, policy framework, resource-sharing facilities, and communications infrastructure.

Domains provide management capabilities, policy framework, resource-sharing facilities, and communications infrastructure.

Management

Domains provide common management facilities for composites deployed to them. A domain, for example, is responsible for activating and deactivating components on runtimes as composites are deployed and removed. More sophisticated domain infrastructure may provide additional management features, such as access control, monitoring, and troubleshooting.

Policy

In enterprise systems, basic management needs are often augmented by the requirement to enforce various constraints on how code is executed. In SCA, constraints on the way code is executed may take a variety forms, such as security ("use encryption for remote invocations"), reliability ("provide guaranteed delivery of messages to a particular service"), or transactionality ("invoke this service in a transaction"). SCA domains contain rules that map these abstract constraints to concrete runtime behaviors.

These rules are termed **policy**. Traditional distributed system technologies typically leave the task of configuring policy to individual components or the application. In Java EE, for example, there is no standard way to specify constraints or expectations across systems, such as the type of security that must be enforced on services exposed outside a corporate firewall. Web services define a way to specify policy to external clients but require that each service be configured individually.

A domain provides facilities for the global configuration of policies, which can then be applied to individual components, particular connections between components, or composites.

The domain serves as a repository for application artifacts.

In contrast, a domain provides facilities for the global configuration of policies, which can then be applied to individual components, particular connections between components, or composites. In addition to fostering consistency across applications, global policy configuration simplifies component development. Policies are generally defined using complex specification languages such as WS-SecurityPolicy and WS-Reliability. Global policy configuration means this complex configuration can be done once by specialists—policy administrators—and reused across applications.

Resource and Artifact Sharing

Without a mechanism for sharing resources and artifacts, any reasonably sized distributed system would be unmanageable. A common type of shared resource in distributed systems is a service contract. As we saw earlier, service contracts can be defined using WSDLs or derived from language-specific means such as Java interfaces. In the case where one component is a client of another (the "service provider") and they are deployed to runtimes on different machines, the service contract of the provider will typically need to be accessible to the client. In practice, if both components are implemented as Java classes, and the service contract is defined using a Java interface, the interface must be available to the client process. Components may share additional artifacts, such as schemas (XSDs) that define the structure of messages that are received as inputs to an operation on a service contract. Components may also rely on shared code, such as libraries. The domain serves as a repository for these artifacts, which, as we will see in more detail, are made accessible to components that require them.

Common Communication Infrastructure

Domains provide the communication infrastructure necessary for connecting components and performing remote service invocations. When a composite is deployed, the domain is responsible for provisioning its components to one or more runtimes and establishing communication channels between them (see Figure 1.9).

Domains provide the communication infrastructure necessary for connecting components and performing remote service invocations.

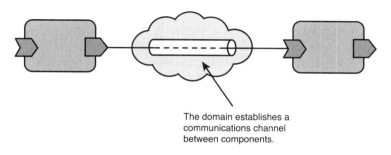

The domain establishes a communications channel between components.

Figure 1.9   The domain communication infrastructure

To support distribution, a domain includes a proprietary communication layer. This communication layer varies by vendor but may be based on web services protocols, a binary protocol, or some other protocol altogether. In this respect, a domain is akin to message-oriented middleware (MOM) systems. Although MOM systems may adopt a standard API such as JMS, their underlying communication protocol remains proprietary.

One advantage that SCA's communications infrastructure has over standardized protocols is that it is in control of both the client and service provider. As a result, users can be general in the way they specify requirements for a wire. This helps reduce complexity, as application code is not required to use low-level APIs.

For example, a user can specify that the wire should deliver messages reliably by marking the end of the wire as requiring reliability.

As we will show in later chapters, this can be done via a Java annotation or in XML configuration. It is incumbent on the infrastructure to figure out how to do this. It could use a JMS queue or it could use web services with WS-ReliableMessaging. If the message sender and receiver are on the same machine and the receiver is ready to receive the message, the message can be delivered to the receiver in an optimized fashion.

Extensibility

Like messaging systems, domains are largely single-vendor.

SCA does not standardize a way to connect runtimes in a domain. Consequently, like messaging systems, domains are largely single-vendor. However, most SCA implementations define a proprietary extensibility mechanism that enables third-party runtimes to participate in a domain.

Is the single-vendor nature of a domain a bad thing? Perhaps, as it creates a "closed" middleware environment. The single-vendor nature of domains does, however, also have practical benefits. Having control over all endpoints in a system allows for communication optimizations. Also, if SCA had standardized a domain extension mechanism, its capabilities would likely have been significantly reduced due to the difficulty in achieving consensus among the different vendors.

Perspective: Is SCA a SOA Technology?

People often ask: Is SCA a technology for Service-Oriented Architecture (SOA)? The answer is, it depends. The problem is that SOA has been hyped to such a degree and means so many different things that it has become virtually useless as a way of characterizing a technology. For some, SOA involves writing applications as discrete units of functionality that *interoperate* regardless of the language they are implemented in. In other words, SOA relies on interoperable web services that are highly autonomous. For others, SOA is a design pattern for organizing an application as units that interact via contracts. Contrary to the first view, these units may not be autonomous.

SCA aligns more closely with the latter than the former. In other words, SCA is a technology for assembling applications from services that are managed by a common infrastructure. To be sure, SCA services may use interoperable protocols and communicate with other services not managed by that common infrastructure, but those are not requirements mandated by SCA. It's likely that many, maybe even most, SCA services will be accessible only by software running on infrastructure provided by the same vendor.

Is this SOA? It depends on your perspective. What really matters is that the benefits and trade-offs associated with SCA are clearly understood. To avoid becoming bogged down in terminology, we consciously avoid the label SOA and simply describe SCA as service-based. As we explain in this section, SCA has a very specific definition of a service, so this will help avoid the confusion caused by the vagueness of SOA.

The Extent of a Domain

Having covered the key characteristics of a domain and its role in SCA, we return to the question of what determines its scope. The number, shape, and size of domains may vary in an organization. An organization could choose to have one domain or many. Two key factors will inform this choice: how information technology (IT) assets are organized and managed, and which SCA implementation is used.

Because a domain is used to manage composites and their compo-nents, it is natural for the domain structure to reflect how an orga-nization manages its technology assets. A small company may have one technology department responsible for managing all of its systems, in which case they would likely have a single domain. A large multinational corporation, on the other hand, may have multiple autonomous technology departments, each responsible for their own systems. In this case, the multinational would proba-bly elect to have multiple domains under the control of each department.

Because a domain is used to manage composites and their components, it is natural for the domain structure to reflect how an organization man-ages its technology assets.

A second factor in determining the size of a domain is the SCA implementation. SCA runtimes are not portable to any domain. That is, there is no standard way to create a domain consisting of mul-tiple vendor runtimes. If an organization uses more than one SCA implementation because it has not standardized on one or it re-quires proprietary features for certain components, it will need to run multiple domains.

This is not to say that a component deployed to a domain will be unable to invoke a service provided by a component in another. As we will see later, SCA provides mechanisms for communicating across domains and with non-SCA services. It does mean, however, that both components will be managed and administered independently.

Perspective: SCA and Java EE—Embrace and Extend, Replace, or Just Confusion?

Various industry pundits have predicted the waning of Java EE as a dominant enterprise development platform, often due to its increasing complexity. Some point to advances in Microsoft's .NET Framework as the death-knell for Java EE. Others highlight the mindshare Spring has gained among Java developers as evidence of Java EE's waning. Among Java EE's more trendy detractors, it has become popular to list Ruby on Rails and other dynamic language-based frameworks as likely successors, which they claim are far more productive. Although it is easy to dismiss the more extreme claims of Java EE's demise (many enterprises have mission-critical Java EE applications that will remain in production for years to come), it is also evident that Java EE does not possess the allure it once did.

Enter SCA into this picture. Is it intended to embrace and extend or replace Java EE? SCA's relationship to Java EE is multifaceted, which is to say there is no simple answer. JPA, for example, provides a nice complement to SCA, which does not specify a persistence technology. Likewise, servlets and JSPs can be used to build a presentation tier for SCA components. However, when it comes to writing application logic, SCA's Java-based programming model offers a single alternative to EJB, JMS, and JAX-WS.

This story is, however, complicated by the fact that SCA also provides support for implementing components using EJB. It may appear as if SCA is schizophrenic. On the one hand, it offers a competing technology to EJB, but on the other, it extends it.

Part of the confusion undoubtedly is a result of SCA being the product of a collaboration among a diverse set of industry vendors and organizations, each with their own view and goals. Some collaborators felt that creating a replacement for EJB and JAX-WS was technically unnecessary or too risky in that it would have difficulty gaining market acceptance. Others, taking the opposite view, argued that a new Java-based programming model was needed because existing technologies did not adequately address the demands of distributed computing. In the end, a compromise was reached where SCA would support a number of different implementation technologies.

The focus of this book is on the SCA Java-based programming model, as opposed to other alternatives such as EJB, JAX-WS, or Spring. Although we endeavor to present an accurate view of SCA, a comprehensive overview of all technology options would be impractical and likely incoherent. Therefore, in places we were left with having to make choices. We chose to focus on the SCA Java-based programming model because, in our opinion, it offers the best option for service-based development using Java.

This view is likely to prove to be controversial, particularly among some of the SCA collaboration participants. However, we consider this position to be pragmatic. Java EE has a number of disparate component models and APIs (EJB, JMS, JAX-WS, and even JSF!) that are not particularly easy to use or well-suited to service-based development. The SCA Java-based programming model represents a unified approach that was designed from the ground up to serve these purposes. It offers a far more productive environment for developers who do not need (or want) to deal with the complexity of Java EE's lower-level programming model APIs.

Moving forward, it is our opinion that Java EE will be viewed less as a platform than as a collection of technologies. Developers will "Balkanize" Java EE by picking and choosing specific technologies to complement SCA. Although developers have been selectively using Java EE technologies since its inception (few use the entire set of Java EE APIs), it will increasingly be the case that Java EE does not offer a complete solution to mainstream development requirements.

In other words, SCA will embrace some Java EE technologies and replace others. SCA will likely coexist with technologies focused on the presentation and data tiers, where it does not offer alternatives (in particular, servlets, JSPs, and JPA). In those areas where it overlaps with Java EE—notably EJB and JAX-WS—SCA will eventually serve as a replacement.

Implementing Components

SCA applications are best characterized as interconnected components assembled together in one or more composites, where the components may be implemented in a variety of programming languages. Clients, whether they are non-SCA code or other SCA components, interact with components through the services they

Components may be implemented in a variety of programming languages.

offer. The implementation details of a particular component—what language it is written in, how it is configured, and what things it depends on—are hidden from clients. Having covered the external facts of a component, we now turn to its internal aspects using the SCA Java programming model.

The Component Implementation

Writing components using the Java programming model is straight-forward—SCA does not mandate any special requirements. As the example in Listing 1.7 illustrates, components can be implemented by ordinary Java classes with a few optional annotations.

Listing 1.7   *The Component Implementation*

```
public class LoanComponent implements LoanService {
    private String currency;
    private CreditService service;

    @Property
    public void setCurrency(String currency){
        this.currency = currency;
    }

    @Reference
    public void setCreditService(CreditService service){
        this.service = service;
    }
    public void applyForLoan(LoanApplication application){
        // ....
    }

    public int checkStatus(String applicationID){
        // ....
    }
}
```

Now, let's examine what the annotations in Listing 1.7 mean.

Properties

Properties define the ways in which a component can be configured.

Properties define the ways in which a component can be configured (see Figure 1.10). As an example, a loan application component may have a property to calculate values in euros, U.S. dollars, pounds sterling, or yen.

Properties are manifested differently depending on the implementation language used for components. In Java, a property is defined by placing an `@Property` annotation on a method; as we will see in following chapters, fields and constructor parameters may also be properties (see Listing 1.8).

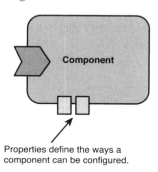

Properties define the ways a component can be configured.

Figure 1.10   Properties are used to configure components.

Listing 1.8   *A Component Property*

```java
public class LoanComponent implements LoanService {
    private String currency;

    @Property
    public void setCurrency(String currency){
        this.currency = currency;
    }

    // …
}
```

The actual property values are specified in a composite file, typically as part of the component definition. When a component instance is created, the runtime it is hosted on will set all properties configured for it. For `LoanComponent` in Listing 1.8, the runtime will set the currency to a string specified in the composite, such as "USD" or "EUR."

Properties assist with reuse but, more importantly, they allow certain decisions to be deferred from development to deployment. A typical case is components that must be configured differently in development, testing, staging, and production environments: For example, a component that is configured to connect to a database differently as it moves from development, testing, staging, and finally into production.

Properties assist with reuse but, more importantly, they allow certain decisions to be deferred from development to deployment.

References

Components also have **references**. A reference is a dependency on another service, which the component connects to at runtime (see Figure 1.11). The loan component may have a reference to a service that returns a rate table stored in a database. The rate table service could be offered by another component whose purpose is to hide the intricacies of querying and updating the database.

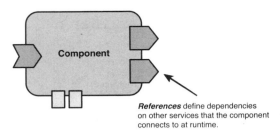

References define dependencies on other services that the component connects to at runtime.

Figure 1.11   A reference is a dependency on another service.

Similar to properties, references are manifested differently depending on the language in which the component is implemented. In Java, a reference is defined by placing an @Reference annotation on a method. (Fields and constructor parameters are also supported.) The type of the method parameter corresponds to the contract of the service requested, as shown in Listing 1.9.

Listing 1.9   *A Reference*

```
public class LoanComponent implements LoanService {
    private CreditService service;

    //…

    @Reference
    public void setCreditService(CreditService service){
        this.service = service;
    }

    // …
}
```

Unlike tradition programming models, SCA component implementations do not look up their service dependencies using an API such as JNDI. The target of the reference—that is, which specific service it points to—is configured as part of the component definition in a composite file. References are made available to components the same way properties are: When a component instance is created, the SCA runtime will use dependency injection to set a proxy that is connected to the appropriate target services.

The SCA runtime will use dependency injection to set a proxy that is connected to the appropriate target services.

After the runtime has provided the component with a proxy to the reference's target service, it can be invoked like any other object. The component can invoke one of its methods, passing in parameters and receiving a result, as demonstrated in Listing 1.10.

Listing 1.10   *Invoking a Service Through a Wire in Java*

```
public class LoanComponent implements LoanService {
    private CreditService service;

    private String currency;

    @Property
    public void setCurrency(String currency){
        this.currency = currency;
    }

    @Reference
    public void setCreditService(CreditService service){
        this.service = service;
    }

    public void applyForLoan(LoanApplication application) {
        // invokes the service through a wire supplied by
        // the SCA runtime
        int result = service.checkCredit(customerID);
    }
}
```

References provide a level of power and sophistication that is difficult to achieve with earlier component technologies. References can be "rewired" to newer versions of a service at runtime. References can also be used to track dependencies in a system. A management tool that understands SCA metadata could analyze component dependencies in a system to assess the impact of upgrading a component that is used by many clients.

A composite file defines one or more components, sets their properties, and configures their references.

Assembling Composites

A composite file defines one or more components, sets their properties, and configures their references. Listing 1.11 provides the full listing of `LoanComposite` used in previous examples.

Listing 1.11   *LoanComposite*

```
<composite xmlns=http://www.osoa.org/xmlns/sca/1.0

           name="LoanComposite">

   <component name="LoanComponent">
      <implementation.java class="com.bigbank.LoanComponent"/>
      <property name="currency">USD</property>
      <reference name="creditService" target="CreditComponent"/>
   <component>

   <component name="CreditComponent">
      <implementation.java class="com.bigbank.CreditComponent"/>
   <component>
</composite>
```

To recap, the meaning of the XML elements in the preceding composite is fairly straightforward, as follows:

- The `<component>` element defines a component and assigns it a name that is used to reference it at later points in the composite.

- The `<implementation.java>` element indicates that both components are implemented using the SCA Java programming model.

- The `<property>` elements configures the value of a component property.

A wire is a communication channel between the client component and the target service.

The `<reference>` element warrants a more detailed explanation. Reference elements are used to configure target services for component references. In the preceding listing, `LoanComponent` has a reference configured to use `CreditService` provided by `CreditComponent`. When a component instance is created, the SCA runtime connects its references to the appropriate target services via proxies. In the listing, the runtime connects `LoanComponent` to `CreditService` provided by

`CreditComponent`. This connection is called a wire. A **wire** is a communication channel between the client component and the target service (see Figure 1.12).

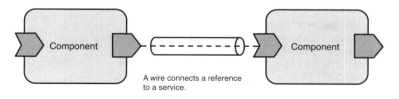

A wire connects a reference to a service.

Figure 1.12   A wire is a communications channel.

Because components can be co-located (in the same process) or hosted in separate runtimes, wires can be local or remote. From the perspective of the client component, however, a wire does not appear any different. In Java, a proxy backed by a wire will look like any other object.

Because components can be co-located (in the same process) or hosted in separate runtimes, wires can be local or remote.

In addition to configuring components and wiring them, composites serve several other important purposes. Developing applications routinely involves interfacing with external systems or services. Similarly, applications must often expose services to external clients. In many cases, these systems and clients will not be built using SCA. Composites provide mechanisms for making SCA services available to clients outside of a domain (for example, available to non-SCA code) and for accessing services outside the domain (for example, implemented by non-SCA code such as a .NET service). Publishing a service or accessing an external service from a component is done through configuration elements in the composite (SCDL file). The process of applying this configuration is termed "binding a service and reference."

Composites provide mechanisms for making SCA services available to clients outside of a domain and for accessing services outside the domain.

Binding Services and References

In SCA, bindings are used to configure communications into and out of a domain. Bindings are assigned to the services and references of a component in a composite file. For example, to expose a service as a web service endpoint to external clients, the web service binding is used. SCA defines bindings for web services, JMS, and JCA. Some SCA implementations also support additional bindings, including RMI, AMQP (a messaging protocol), and XML/HTTP.

In SCA, bindings are used to configure communications into and out of a domain.

Listing 1.12 shows a service configured with the web service binding.

Listing 1.12   *Exposing a Service as a Web Service Endpoint*

```
<component name ="LoanComponent">
      <implementation.java class="com.bigbank.LoanComponent"/>
      <service name="LoanService">
            <binding.ws uri="http://www.bigbank.com/
➥loanApplicationService"/>
      </service>
</component>
```

In the preceding composite, the <binding.ws> element instructs the SCA runtime to expose LoanService as a web service endpoint at the address specified by the uri attribute. When the composite is deployed to a domain, the SCA runtime activates the web service endpoint and forward incoming requests to LoanComponent.

Similarly, component references may be bound to communicate with external services, such as a .NET web service. The code in Listing 1.13 binds a reference to a web service.

Listing 1.13   *Binding a Reference to a Web Service Endpoint*

```
<component name ="LoanComponent">
      <implementation.java class="com.bigbank.LoanComponent"/>
      <reference name="rateService">
            <binding.ws uri="http://www.acme.com/rateService"/>
      </reference>
</component>
```

In the previous listing, the SCA runtime will ensure that the bound reference flows invocations using standard WS-* protocols to the target web service. How this is done is transparent to the component implementation. In Java, the component needs to invoke only a method on an object; transport-specific API calls (such as JAX-WS) are not needed (see Listing 1.14).

Listing 1.14   *Invoking on a Bound Reference in Java*

```java
public class LoanComponent implements LoanService {
    private RateService service;

    @Reference
    public void setRateService(RateService service){
        this.service = service;
    }

    public void applyForLoan(LoanApplication application) {
        // invokes the service through a wire supplied by the
        // SCA runtime
        int result = service.checkCredit(customerID);
    }
}
```

The key point about bindings is that they are handled through configuration in a composite file. This eliminates the need for components to use protocol-specific APIs. Besides simplifying component implementations, this has two important practical effects. First, it allows the actual protocol used to be changed at a later date without having to modify the component implementation. For example, JMS, or a binary protocol such as RMI, could be substituted for web services. Second, it allows services to be bound to multiple protocols. A service could be configured with binding entries for both web services and JMS, in which case it would be exposed to clients using either of those protocols.

Bindings are specified in a composite file.

Composites as a Unit of Deployment

Often, despite the fact that related components may be intended for deployment to different runtimes, it makes sense to manage them as a unit. Applications are typically subdivided into a set of components that depend on one another and cannot operate in isolation. In these cases, composites provide a means to group related components so that they may be treated atomically.

Composites provide a means to group related components so that they may be treated atomically.

When a composite is deployed to a domain, its components will be started. Similarly, when a composite is undeployed, its components will be stopped. In distributed domains, components may be deployed to and undeployed from multiple runtimes. One way to think of a composite, then, is as a counterpart to a Java EE Enterprise Archive (EAR) or .NET Assembly.

A significant difference, however, between SCA and Java EE is that SCA applications are generally more modular than their Java EE counterparts. Experience with Java EE informed much of the design of SCA in this regard. In Java EE, applications are deployed in self-contained archives: EARs or Web Archives (WARs). Although this deployment model works for many applications, for many others it poses severe limitations, particularly when artifacts need to be shared across applications.

SCA applications may consist of multiple composites, thereby making their internal structure more loosely coupled.

SCA applications may consist of multiple composites, thereby making their internal structure more loosely coupled. Each composite can be maintained and evolved independently, as opposed to being part of a single deployment archive. This modularity and loose coupling allow for greater flexibility in maintaining enterprise applications, which must stay in production for years. With SCA, it is possible to upgrade some composites without having to redeploy all the composites in an application.

Deploying to a Domain

The standard contribution format is a ZIP archive, but an SCA implementation may support additional packaging types, such as a directory on a file system.

Components rarely exist in isolation. In all but the most trivial applications, components rely on supporting artifacts, other code such as classes, and sometimes libraries. In SCA, composite files and component artifacts—for example, implementation classes, schemas, WSDLs, and libraries—are packaged as contributions. The standard contribution format is a ZIP archive, but an SCA implementation may support additional packaging types, such as a directory on a file system. Although not strictly required, a contribution archive may contain an sca-contribution.xml file in a META-INF directory under the root. Similar to a JAR MANIFEST.MF file, the purpose of the sca-contribution.xml is to provide the SCA implementation with processing instructions, such as a list of the deployable composites contained in the archive.

Prior to deployment, composites must be installed in a domain as part of a contribution. After a contribution has been installed, its contained composites may be deployed. How installation and deployment is done will depend on the environment. During development, this may involve copying a contribution archive to a deployment directory, where the SCA runtime will automatically install it and deploy contained composites. In a data center, where more rigorous processes are likely to be in place, a command-line tool or management console can be used to install the archive and subsequently deploy its composite (or composites, because a contribution may contain more than one).

Unlike Java EE EARs and WARs, contributions are not required to be self-contained. A contribution may refer to artifacts such as interfaces, classes, or WSDLs in other contributions by first exporting an artifact in a containing contribution and then importing it in another. Imports and exports are done via entries in the sca-contribution.xml manifest. For example, a manifest exports a WSDL for use in other contributions by specifying its fully qualified name or QName (see Listing 1.15).

Unlike Java EE EARs and WARs, contributions are not required to be self-contained.

Listing 1.15   *A Contribution Export*

```
<?xml version="1.0" encoding="ASCII"?>
<contribution xmlns=http://www.osoa.org/xmlns/sca/1.0>
 <!- .... -- >
   <export namespace="http://acme.com/LoanService/>
</contribution>
```

The WSDL is then imported in another contribution by referring to its fully qualified name in an import entry, as shown in Listing 1.16.

Listing 1.16   *A Contribution Import*

```
<?xml version="1.0" encoding="ASCII"?>
<contribution xmlns=http://www.osoa.org/xmlns/sca/1.0>
 <!- .... -- >
   <import namespace="http://acme.com/LoanService/>
</contribution>
```

When the composite in the second contribution is deployed, it is the job of the runtime to ensure that the WSDL and all other imported artifacts are available to its components.

The mechanics of how a domain resolves imports to actual contributions is (thankfully) transparent to developers and administrators: Contribution manifest entries are the only thing required. Typically, under the covers, an SCA implementation will use a repository to index, store, and resolve contribution artifacts, as pictured in Figure 1.13.

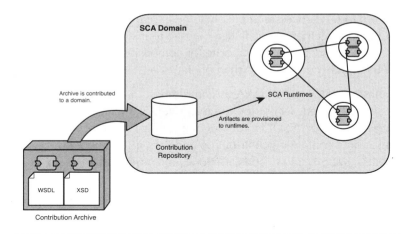

Figure 1.13   Storing a contribution in a domain repository

When a contribution is installed that imports an artifact, the SCA implementation will resolve it against the repository and make it available to the contribution.

The Deployment Process

What happens when a composite is deployed to a domain? A number of steps must take place prior to the point when its components become active. Although various SCA implementations will vary in specifics, we enumerate the general steps involved in deployment here.

Allocation

The loosely coupled nature of composites allows them to be distributed, possibly spanning geographic regions. A composite may contain components deployed in different data centers. When a composite is deployed, its components are allocated to a set of runtimes. In the case where there is only one runtime in the domain, this is straightforward: Components are always allocated to the same runtime. In the scenarios depicted previously, where there are multiple runtimes potentially spread across data centers, allocation will be more involved. A number of factors need to be taken into account by the domain. For example, is a particular runtime capable of hosting a component written in Java, C++, or BPEL? Other factors may come into play as well, such as co-locating two wired components in cases where performance is critical.

Wiring

As components are allocated, the domain must connect wires between them. When two components are allocated to different runtimes, the domain must establish a communication channel between the two. When no protocol is chosen by the user, it is up to the SCA implementation to decide how remote communication should be handled. Depending on the implementation, the actual protocol used could be web services (WS-*), RMI, JMS, or a proprietary technology. One important factor any implementation must account for when selecting a protocol is the policies associated with the wire. If transactions are specified on the wire, for example, the protocol must support transaction propagation. The domain may also select a communication protocol based on the requirements of the client component and target service. For example, when wiring two Java component implementations, the domain may choose RMI as the transport protocol. Or if the target were implemented in C++ as opposed to Java, web services may be selected based on interoperability requirements.

Exposing Bound Services as Endpoints

When the domain has allocated a composite to a runtime or set of runtimes, bound services must be made available as endpoints. For example, a service bound as a web service must be exposed as a web service endpoint. If a service is bound to JMS, the domain will attach the service as a listener to the appropriate message topic or queue (see Figure 1.14).

It is also possible to bind a service multiple times to different protocols. A service could be exposed as both a web service endpoint and JMS listener. The mechanics of how the domain performs the actual endpoint binding are transparent to the developer and deployer.

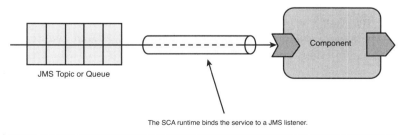

JMS Topic or Queue

Component

The SCA runtime binds the service to a JMS listener.

Figure 1.14   Binding a service as a message endpoint

Domain Constraints

Domains are designed to simplify the tasks of establishing remote communications, endpoint setup, and resource sharing that are left to developers and deployers in traditional programming models. However, with any technology, there are benefits and trade-offs. SCA is no different. Although domains provide a number of benefits, they also impose certain constraints.

A domain cannot be created from multiple vendor (or open source) SCA runtimes in any standard way.

The fact that domain infrastructure is single-vendor means that there is no interoperable way of constructing cross-implementation domains. In other words, a domain cannot be created from multiple vendor (or open source) SCA runtimes in any standard way (of course, vendors could agree to support interoperability in some nonstandard way). This imposes two important practical constraints. First, composites cannot be deployed across multiple-vendor SCA runtimes. The absence of domain interoperability also limits the size of a domain to the component types a particular vendor supports, either natively or through container extensions. If an alternative container is required to host a particular component implementation type, it must be deployed to a different domain capable of running it.

Contrast this lack of domain interoperability to a web services environment where each service is independent and is potentially hosted on entirely different vendor platforms. In this respect, SCA is closer to MOM; there is a one common infrastructure environment, as opposed to many autonomous, but interoperable, islands.

Are the trade-offs between simplicity and common management versus vendor lock-in worth it? There is no way to answer that question in general. However, individual projects can make an informed decision by understanding when SCA may be used effectively and when other technologies are more appropriate. Given the importance of web services, architects and developers will likely be confronted with designing systems using SCA or web services technologies directly.

SCA and Web Services

Both SCA and web services claim to be technologies for building multilanguage, loosely coupled services in a distributed environment. Why not just use web services exclusively to build applications? Recalling that SCA domains are built on single-vendor infrastructure, web services offer a key advantage. They limit vendor lock-in to individual service deployments, as opposed to wider subsystems.

To understand how SCA relates to web services, it is useful to divide web service technologies into a set of interoperable communication protocols (the WS-* specifications) and programming models for using those protocols (for example, in Java, JAX-RPC, and JAX-WS).

At the most basic level, web services deal with protocol-level interoperability. They define how application code communicates with other code in a language-neutral, interoperable manner. Web services make it possible for Java code to communicate with C#, PHP, or Ruby code. Web services achieve interoperability by specifying how service contracts are defined (WSDL) and how data is encoded over particular communications transports (for example, SOAP over HTTP, WS-ReliableMessaging, WS-Security, and so on).

Web services programming models such as JAX-WS define APIs and Java annotations for accessing other web services and making code available as an endpoint. These programming models are specific to web services; their goal is not to provide a communications API that abstracts the underlying transport.

Web services programming models such as JAX-WS define APIs and Java annotations for accessing other web services and making code available as an endpoint.

Perspective: Interoperability and Portability

Standards such as SCA, web services, and Java EE often have quite different goals. The WS-* specifications are about interoperability; that is, providing protocols that different vendor runtimes can use so that software hosted on those platforms can work together.

In contrast, Java EE and SCA are not concerned with interoperability. Java EE does not specify, for example, a protocol for clustering different vendor application servers or a common messaging protocol. Similarly, SCA does not specify a way for different vendor runtimes to operate as part of a single domain.

Rather, the goal of both Java EE and SCA is portability. For Java EE, portability means *application portability*—that is, the ability to run an application on multiple vendor runtimes without modification. Java EE has been criticized for not living up to this goal. Critics have pointed out that application server vendors often interpret the Java EE specifications differently, resulting in runtime-specific behavior. Also, as Java EE critics argue, the specifications don't address many application requirements, forcing users to rely on nonportable, proprietary features of a vendor runtime.

In comparison to Java EE, SCA has adopted more modest portability goals. Much of the initial focus of the specification working groups has been on skills portability, as opposed to application portability. Specifically, the specification authors have concentrated more on creating a common programming and assembly model than on defining strict runtime behavior. Absent the loftier goal of application portability, the thinking went, skills portability would at least shorten the learning curve for developers moving between different vendor runtimes.

This is not to say that SCA is unconcerned with application portability. As the specifications have matured, the working groups have focused more on obtaining this higher degree of portability. For example, when the specifications are finalized in OASIS, conformance test suites that verify common runtime behaviors will be made available.

Taking a slightly cynical view, one could claim that the SCA vendors have purposely downplayed application portability as a way to lock users into their proprietary runtimes. Obviously, vendors have very little interest in complete runtime standardization. If this were to happen, all runtimes would essentially be the same, except perhaps for slight performance differences. There would be no way for vendors to differentiate their implementations by offering unique features.

However, life is more complicated in the standards world. A better argument for why SCA has adopted modest portability goals would account for a number of factors. Certainly there is vendor interest in maintaining proprietary features. Another factor was a practical consideration. Realizing how difficult it is to obtain consensus on new technologies when usage patterns are not clear-cut, and having learned from Java EE's failure to achieve practical application portability, the specification authors adopted less ambitious, but arguably more realistic, portability goals.

That said, as SCA matures and experience using it increases, expect application portability to become an increasingly important goal.

Both at the protocol and programming model level, web services make an important assumption: They were designed for communicating between software that has *nothing in common*. Web service-based architectures consist of "islands of functionality" that interact with one another (see Figure 1.15).

Both at the protocol and programming model level, web services make an important assumption: They were designed for communicating between software that has nothing in common.

Web Services

SCA Domain

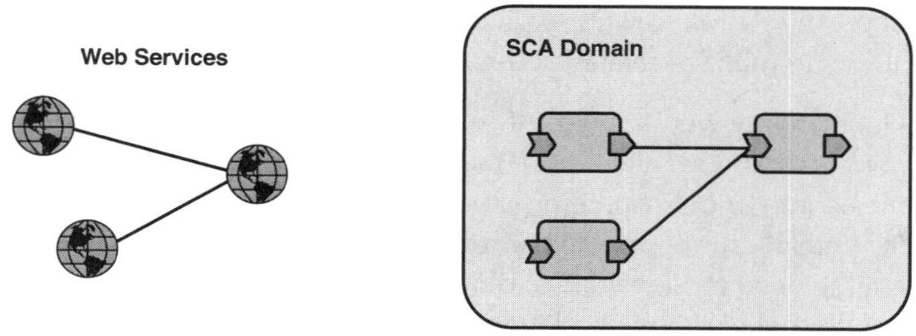

Web services are autonomous "islands" of functionality.

SCA components are managed by a common infrastructure: the Domain.

Figure 1.15   Web service versus SCA architecture

This is not surprising given the array of vendors backing web services standards and their opposed worldviews. However, several consequences follow from this.

First, developing web services can be a complex, labor-intensive process. Sometimes this is necessary. In order to avoid problems with interoperability, top-down development is generally recommended where service contracts are designed upfront in WSDL. Dealing with WSDL is not trivial, notwithstanding tooling designed to alleviate many of the repetitive and error-prone tasks.

A second consequence of web services architecture is that any given service can only make minimal assumptions about the services it interacts with. This limits the degree of management and coordination that can effectively be done across services. It also limits any optimizations that may be done to increase communications performance.

A consequence of web services architecture is that any given service can only make minimal assumptions about the services it interacts with.

Web service architectures certainly have their place when communicating with services from different companies or between autonomous divisions within a company. However, not every component has to integrate with other components as if another

What SCA offers in relation to web services is simplicity, flexibility, and the ability to manage related software components.

company hosted them. Often, components are not independent. They may share common resources, require common policies such as transactionality, or may be capable of using more efficient communications protocols than web services. In these cases, it is useful to have infrastructure that can provide these features and simplify the task of assembling components into applications. What SCA offers in relation to web services is simplicity, flexibility, and the ability to manage related software components.

SCA greatly simplifies the task of writing distributed code by removing the need for developers to use low-level APIs to invoke services.

Unlike many web services APIs, such as JAX-WS, the SCA programming model does not expose the transport binding used to communicate into or out of a component. As we show in ensuing chapters, SCA greatly simplifies the task of writing distributed code by removing the need for developers to use low-level APIs to invoke services. For those accustomed to low-level access, this may seem like a burdensome restriction, but for most developers, it frees them from having to pollute application code with potentially complex APIs.

SCA frees developers from having to configure policy (for example, security, transactions) and transport protocols for every service or component.

Equally important to simplifying application code, SCA frees developers from having to configure policy (for example, security, transactions) and transport protocols for every service or component. Policies can be configured once and reused by multiple components with simple one-word declarations, such as require "confidentiality" on this wire. The intricate details of WSDL, WS-Policy, and the other WS-* technologies (if they are used at all) can be safely avoided by most SCA application code.

Using SCA has another important advantage: It is designed to be dynamic and handle change.

Using SCA has another important advantage: It is designed to be dynamic and handle change. Suppose a new security protocol needs to be introduced between two components. Or consider the case where a new version of a web services standard is introduced. If the components were written against lower-level web services APIs, such changes will likely involve code migration. With SCA, an administrator can adapt the components through configuration changes without affecting code.

A further advantage to using SCA is that it allows protocol swapping without requiring code changes.

A further advantage to using SCA is that it allows protocol swapping without requiring code changes. For example, RMI could be substituted for web services where communication performance between two Java-based components is the most important concern. If a component implementation were coded to a particular API such as JAX-WS, this may entail a near-complete rewrite. With SCA, protocol swapping amounts to a configuration change. In this sense, SCA is protocol-agnostic; it enables users to select the one most appropriate to the task at hand, be it web services, XML/HTTP, RMI, JMS, or some other technology.

Spring and SCA: Wiring in the Small Versus Large

One question that is inevitably raised when explaining SCA to Java developers is how it differs from Spring. Both have a Java programming model and share similar design principles, such as dependency injection. The short answer is that they overlap somewhat (parts of the programming model) but address different problem spaces. Spring, for example, includes presentation- and data-tier technologies, whereas SCA does not. More fundamentally, though, whereas Spring focuses on "wiring-in-the-small" in traditional applications, SCA addresses both that case and "wiring-in-the-large" across loosely coupled, distributed components.

By "wiring-in-the-small," we mean the assembly of components (or "beans" in Spring terminology) in a single address space. In contrast, "wiring-in-the-large" entails component assembly across remote boundaries. To be sure, Spring does have facilities for handling remote invocations and messaging (via message-driven POJOs). However, these are quite different than wiring-in-the-large, which brings to the forefront additional considerations: deployment, resource sharing, policy enforcement, and lifecycle management in a distributed environment, to name a few of the most important.

Wiring-in-the-large introduces a new class of middleware designed to coordinate and run loosely coupled components across multiple hosts. This is a departure from the traditional Java EE two- and three-tier architectures Spring grew out of, which exhibit an essentially silo design.

With this concern on wiring-in-the-large, even in areas where SCA and Spring overlap, there is significantly different focus. In particular, the SCA Java programming model places particular emphasis on designing component implementations using asynchrony and loosely coupled contracts, as opposed to the mostly synchronous interactions of Spring beans.

Summary

Service Component Architecture (SCA) is quickly emerging as a foundation for building distributed systems with significant industry support. Although far-ranging in scope, SCA can be summarized by four core benefits, as follows:

- A simplified programming model for service development
- More efficient and flexible service reuse
- Better management and control of distributed systems
- Simplified policy configuration and enforcement across applications

Having covered how SCA fits into modern application architectures, including its relationship to web services and Java EE technologies, we begin a series of more detailed discussions of its core concepts supplemented with practical examples. Our goal is to provide solid grounding for making intelligent choices about where, when, and how best to employ SCA when building enterprise systems.

2

Assembling and Deploying a Composite

The previous chapter introduced the four core SCA concepts: services, components, composites, and the domain. In this chapter, we explore these in practice by providing a walkthrough of creating a composite and deploying it to a domain. For those wanting to do hands-on development, this chapter also covers using the open source SCA runtime, Fabric3, to deploy and run the composite.

This chapter teaches you the basics of building an SCA application, including the following:

- How to create components that offer services
- How to configure those components and wire them together as part of a composite
- How to expose a service as a web service
- How to package and deploy the composite to a domain

During this exercise, we touch on key SCA design principles and introduce recommended development practices. Subsequent chapters will build on the examples presented here, including designing loosely coupled services, asynchronous communications, and conversational interactions. In these later chapters, we will also cover how to integrate SCA with presentation- and data-tier frameworks.

The `LoanApplication` Composite

Throughout the book, we use a fictitious bank—BigBank Lending—
to construct an enterprise-class SCA application. The SCA application we ultimately will build is designed to process loan
applications from customers submitted via a web front-end and by
independent mortgage brokers via a web service. The high-level
application architecture is illustrated in Figure 2.1.

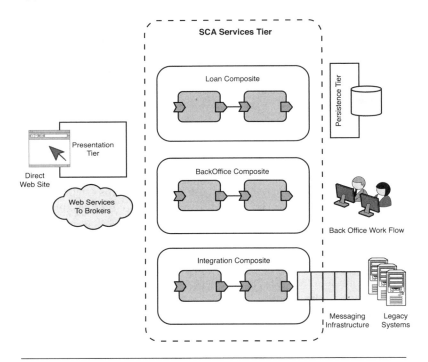

Figure 2.1   The BigBank loan application architecture

The `LoanApplication` composite is the core of BigBank's loan-
processing system. It is responsible for receiving loan applications
and coordinating with other services to process them. In this chapter, we will start simply by focusing on two Java-based components
contained in the composite. `LoanComponent` receives and
processes loan application requests from remote clients using web
services. It in turn uses the `CreditService` interface implemented
by `CreditComponent` to perform a credit check on the applicant
(see Figure 2.2).

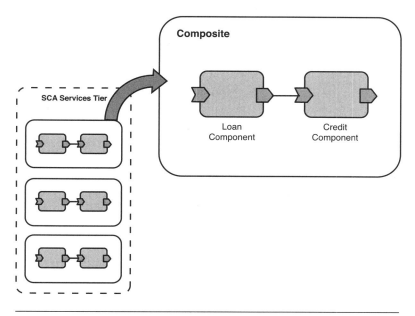

Figure 2.2   The `LoanApplication` composite

The other components—web-front end, data-tier, and integration with external systems—will be covered in later chapters.

▪ Open Source SCA Implementations: Fabric3

Although SCA is an emerging technology, there are already several open source implementations available. Two of the most well known are Fabric3 (http://www. fabric3.org) and Apache Tuscany (http://tuscany.apache.org/). Throughout the book, we use the Fabric3 SCA runtime for hands-on development. Because we (the authors of this book) are involved in the development of Fabric3, you will notice a strong affinity between its capabilities and the topics covered in the book. In addition to support for a majority of the core SCA specifications, Fabric3 provides a number of extensions for popular technologies, including Java Persistence Architecture (JPA) and Hibernate.

Fabric3's design is similar to Eclipse in that it consists of a small core that can be extended through plug-ins. Bindings such as web services, JMS, and RMI are installed as extensions into the Fabric3 core in much the same way that JSP and XML editing support are added to Eclipse. This gives users the flexibility of choosing just what they need and avoids having to deal with the complexity associated with one-size-fits-all approaches.

This design follows a general trend in software modularity popularized by Eclipse. As development environments increased in complexity in the early 2000s, Eclipse introduced an elegant plug-in mechanism based on OSGi that enabled users to configure their IDE with the specific tools they needed to develop their applications. This greatly reduced software bloat and introduced a new level of flexibility for users. This philosophy has now been extended to runtime architectures as well with the introduction of Profiles in Java EE. Ultimately, modularity benefits users by providing a much more streamlined development, deployment, and management cycle.

Later in the chapter, we provide specific instructions for downloading and getting started with Fabric3. If you want to get a head start, you can download the distribution from http://www.fabric3.org/downloads.html. Be sure to also check out the project mailing lists—they are the best way of getting help should you encounter a problem.

Defining Service Interfaces

Recalling from the previous chapter that components interact through services, we start by defining the service interfaces for the LoanComponent and CreditComponent components. Because both components are implemented in Java, we use Java to define their service interfaces. The LoanService interface is shown in Listing 2.1.

Listing 2.1   *The LoanService Interface*

```
@Remotable

public interface LoanService  {

     LoanResult apply(LoanRequest request);

}
```

The `CreditService` interface is presented in Listing 2.2.

Listing 2.2   *The `CreditService` Interface*

```
@Remotable

public interface CreditService {


    int checkCredit(String id);
}
```

`LoanService` defines one operation, `apply(..)`, which takes a loan application as a parameter. `CreditService` defines one operation, `checkCredit(..)`, which takes a customer ID and returns a numerical credit score. Both interfaces are marked with an SCA annotation, `@Remotable`, which specifies that both services may be invoked by remote clients (as opposed to clients in the same process). Other than the `@Remotable` annotations, the two service contracts adhere to basic Java.

Using Web Services Description Language (WSDL)

In the previous example, we chose Java to define the service contracts for `LoanService` and `CreditService` because it is easy to develop in, particularly when an application is mostly implemented in Java. There are other times, however, when it is more appropriate to use a language-neutral mechanism for defining service contracts. There are a number of interface definition languages, or IDLs, for doing so, but Web Services Description Language (WSDL) is the most accepted for writing new distributed applications. Although labeled as a "web services" technology, WSDL is in fact an XML-based way of describing any service—whether it is exposed to clients as web services—that can be used by most modern programming languages. To understand why WSDL would be used with SCA, we briefly touch on the role it plays in defining service interfaces.

WSDL serves as the lingua franca for code written in one language to invoke code written in another language. It does this by defining a common way to represent operations (what can be invoked), message types (the input and output to operations), and bindings to a protocol or transport (how operations must be invoked). WSDL uses other technologies such as XML Schema to define message

WSDL serves as the lingua franca for code written in one language to invoke code written in another language.

types and SOAP for how invocations are sent over a transport layer (for example, HTTP). Programming languages define mappings to WSDL, making it possible for languages with little in common to communicate, as represented in Figure 2.3.

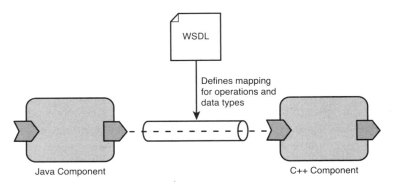

Figure 2.3   WSDL is used to map operations and data types.

Writing WSDL by hand is generally not a pleasant experience; for anything but trivial interfaces, it is a tedious process. Briefly compare the `LoanService` interface previously defined using Java to its WSDL counterpart (see Listing 2.3).

Listing 2.3   *The LoanService WSDL*

```
<?xml version="1.0" encoding="utf-8"?>
<wsdl:definitionsxmlns:ns1="http://loanservice.loanapp/"
xmlns:soap="http://schemas.xmlsoap.org/wsdl/soap/"
xmlns:wsdl="http://schemas.xmlsoap.org/wsdl/"
xmlns:xsd="http://www.w3.org/2001/XMLSchema"
                 name="LoanService" targetNamespace="http://loanser
➥vice.loanapp/">
    <wsdl:message name="applyResponse">
        <wsdl:part element="ns1:applyResponse" name="parameters">
        </wsdl:part>
    </wsdl:message>
    <wsdl:message name="apply">
        <wsdl:part element="ns1:apply" name=
➥"parameters">
        </wsdl:part>
    </wsdl:message>
    <wsdl:portType name="LoanServicePortType">
        <wsdl:operation name="apply">
            <wsdl:input message="ns1:apply" name="apply">
            </wsdl:input>
```

```
            <wsdl:output message="ns1:applyResponse"
name="applyResponse">
            </wsdl:output>
        </wsdl:operation>
    </wsdl:portType>
</wsdl:definitions>
```

Fortunately, SCA does not require WSDL to define service interfaces. Why, then, would someone choose to use WSDL? One scenario where WSDL is used is in top-down development. This style of development entails starting by defining an overall system design, including subsystems and the services they offer, in a way that is independent of the implementation technologies used. WSDL is a natural fit for this approach as it defines service interfaces without specifying how they are to be implemented. In this scenario, an architect could define all service interfaces upfront and provide developers with the WSDLs to implement them.

SCA does not require WSDL to define service interfaces.

Few development organizations follow this top-down approach. Typically, service development is iterative. A more practical reason for starting with WSDL is to guarantee interoperability. If a service is created using language-specific means such as a Java interface, even if it is translated into WSDL by tooling, it may not be compatible with a client written in a different language. Using carefully hand-crafted WSDL can reduce this risk.

Defining service contracts using WSDL promotes interoperability.

A third reason to use hand-crafted WSDL is to better accommodate service versioning. Services exposed to remote clients should be designed for loose-coupling. An important characteristic of loose-coupling is that those services should work in a world of mismatched versions where a new version of a service will be backward compatible with old clients. Because WSDL uses XML Schema to define operation parameters, maintaining backward compatibility requires that the parameter-type schemas be designed to handle versioning. This is difficult to do directly in schema but even more difficult using Java classes. In cases where support for versioning is paramount, working directly with WSDL may be the least complex alternative.

One question people typically raise is if SCA does not mandate the use of WSDL, how can it ensure that two components written in different languages are able to communicate? SCA solves this problem by requiring that all interfaces exposed to remote clients be *translatable* into WSDL. For example, if a service interface is defined using Java, it must be written in such a way that it is possible to represent it in WSDL. This enables a runtime to match a client and service provider by mapping each side to WSDL behind the scenes, saving developers the task of doing this manually.

Given that SCA services available to remote clients must be translatable into WSDL, it is important to note that the latter imposes several restrictions on interface definitions. WSDL stipulates that service interfaces must not make use of operator overloading; in other words, they must not have multiple operations with the same name but different message types. WSDL also requires operation parameters to be expressible using XML Schema. The latter restriction is, in practice, not overly burdensome. Although it might disallow certain data types (for example, Java's `InputStream`), virtually all data types suitable for loosely coupled service interactions can be accommodated by XML Schema. The next chapter will discuss service contract design in detail; for now, it is important to remember these two constraints for services exposed to remote clients.

■ Services Without WSDL?

Given SCA's heavy reliance on services, it may be surprising that it does not have a canonical interface language. The reasoning behind this decision centers on complexity. Writing WSDL is notoriously difficult. Moreover, previous attempts at defining cross-language IDLs such as CORBA suffered from similar issues. The SCA authors wanted to avoid imposing unnecessary steps in a typical development process. For example, when not doing top-down design, where service interfaces are first defined in a language-neutral format, requiring WSDL is an unnecessary burden, even when tooling can automate some of the process.

When services and service clients are written in the same language, there is no need for a language-neutral representation. In fact, the translation to WSDL can be avoided in some situations where the client and provider are implemented in different languages. For example, languages such as Groovy, BPELJ, and JPython can consume Java interfaces, making WSDL mapping unnecessary. Because distributed applications usually have many components written in the same language, translation into WSDL can usually be avoided.

There are cases where a WSDL-first, top-down design should be used. Sometimes the component implementation technology is not known at the time a system architecture is being designed, or the technology is known but there is a desire to hide it. In those situations, defining interfaces directly in WSDL is appropriate. However, it is a conscious design decision on the part of the SCA authors that a technology should be used only when needed. In the case of WSDL, it is a pragmatic "opt-in" approach to complexity.

Remotable Versus Local Services

Returning to the `LoanService` and `CreditService` interfaces, both are annotated with `@Remotable`, which indicates that a service may, but need not be, accessed remotely. For contracts defined using Java, SCA requires that any service exposed across a process boundary be explicitly marked as **remotable**. Services not marked as remotable—the default case—are **local services**: They are callable only from clients hosted in the same process. In contrast, service interfaces defined by WSDL are remotable by default. This makes sense given that most contracts defined by WSDL are likely to be intended for remote access.

For contracts defined using Java, SCA requires that any service exposed across a process boundary be explicitly marked as **remotable**.

Requiring service contracts to be explicitly marked as remotable indicates which services are designed to be accessible across process boundaries. The distinction is necessary because local and remotable services have different behavior. The next chapter covers these differences at length, which we briefly describe here.

Remotable Services Must Account for Network Latency

Clients of remotable services must accommodate network latency. This means that remotable services should be coarse-grained—that is, they should contain few operations that are passed larger data sets, as opposed to a number of individual operations that take a small number of parameters. This reduces the degree of network traffic and latency experienced by clients. In addition, remotable services often define asynchronous operations as a way to handle network latency and service interruptions. Local services are not subject to these demands as calls occur in the same process. Therefore, they tend to be finer-grained and use synchronous operations.

Remotable services should be coarse-grained.

Clients of Remotable Services May Experience Communications Failures

Because invocations on remotable services generally travel over a network, there is a possibility communications may be interrupted. In SCA, the unchecked `org.osoa.sca.ServiceUnavailable Exception` exception will be thrown if a communication error occurs. Clients need to handle such exceptions, potentially by retrying or reporting an error.

Remotable Services Parameters Are Passed by Value

Parameters associated with remotable service operations behave differently than those of operations on local services.

Parameters associated with remotable service operations behave differently than those of operations on local services. When remotable invocations are made, parameters are marshaled to a protocol format such as XML and passed over a network connection. This results in a copy of the parameters being made as the invocation is received by the service provider. Consequently, modifications made by the service provider will not be seen by the client. This behavior is termed "pass-by-value." In contrast, because invocations on local services are made in the same process, operation parameters are not copied. Any changes made by the service provider will be visible to the client. This behavior is known as "pass-by-reference." Marking a service as remotable signals to clients whether pass-by-value or pass-by-reference semantics will be in effect.

Table 2.1 summarizes the differences between remotable and local services.

Table 2.1   Remotable Versus Local Services

Remotable Services	Local Services
Are invoked in-process and remotely.	Are always invoked in-process.
Parameters are pass-by-value.	Parameters are pass-by-reference.
Are coarse-grained.	Tend to be fine-grained.
Are loosely coupled and favor asynchronous operations.	Commonly use synchronous operations.

■ Local Services and Distributed Systems

It may seem odd that a technology designed for building distributed applications specifies local service contracts as the default when defined in Java. This was a conscious decision on the part of the SCA authors. Echoing Jim Waldo's seminal essay, "The Fallacies of Distributed Computing," location transparency is a fallacy: Crossing remote boundaries requires careful architectural consideration that has a direct impact on application code. Issues such as network latency, service availability, and loose coupling need to be accounted for in component implementations. This was one of the lessons learned with EJB: Many early Java EE applications suffered from crippling performance bottlenecks associated with making too many remote calls.

To minimize remote calls, distributed applications have a relatively small number of services exposed to remote clients. Each of these services should in turn have a few coarse-grained operations that perform a significant task, such as processing a loan application or performing an inventory check. Moreover, these services should be carefully constructed so that new versions can be deployed without breaking existing clients. Limiting the number of remotable services and operations helps avoid performance issues and facilitates versioning by restricting change to a few areas in an application.

Given the lessons learned from previous distributed system technologies, the designers of SCA were faced with a dilemma: how to support applications built using coarse-grained services that did not repeat the problems of the past. The answer was, ironically, to provide good support for *fine-grained*, local services. If the only way to get the benefits of SCA such as programming model simplicity were to use remotable services, developers would be pushed into making all code remotable, even if it should not be. By providing a model for local services, remote boundaries can be chosen carefully, exposing only those parts of an application that should be accessible to clients hosted in different processes.

Creating Component Implementations

Well-designed service-based architectures typically have a limited number of coarse-grained services that coordinate other services to perform specific tasks. The heart of the LoanApplication composite is LoanComponent, which is responsible for receiving loan application data through its LoanService interface and delegating to other services for processing. The implementation is a basic Java class that takes a reference proxy to a CreditService interface as

Well-designed service-based architectures typically have a limited number of coarse-grained services that coordinate other services to perform specific tasks.

part of its constructor signature. The LoanComponent component uses the service to provide a credit score for the applicant. When reviewing the implementation, take note of the @Reference annotation in the constructor (see Listing 2.4).

Listing 2.4   *The LoanComponent Implementation*

```
public class LoanComponent  implements LoanService {
     private CreditService service;



     public void LoanComponent   (@Reference CreditService service){
          this.service = service;
     }
     public LoanResult apply(LoanRequest request) {
          // ....
     }
     public int checkStatus(String applicationID){
          // ....
     }
}
```

In Listing 2.4, the @Reference annotation instructs the SCA runtime that LoanComponent requires a reference to CreditService. An implementation of CreditService is provided by CreditComponent, shown in Listing 2.5.

Listing 2.5   *The CreditComponent Implementation*

```
public class CreditComponent implements CreditService {

     public int checkCredit(String id){
          // ....
     }
}
```

Although the code has been simplified from what would be typically encountered in a real-world scenario, the implementation— like LoanComponent—is straight Java. Even though both components may be hosted on different machines, the only thing required to facilitate remote communication is the presence of @Remotable on the CreditService interface.

▦ A Note on OASIS and OSOA Java APIs and Annotations

As mentioned previously, prior to moving to OASIS, SCA was part of the Open SOA (OSOA) collaboration effort. While at OSOA, the Java APIs and annotations used throughout this book are published under the org.*osoa.sca* package. As part of the move to OASIS, the Java APIs and annotations will also be published under the *org. oasisopen.sca* package. We have decided to continue to use the OSOA package version because, at the time of this writing, the OSOA annotations are more prevalent.

SCA leaves the heavy lifting associated with establishing remote communications to the runtime, as opposed to application code and API calls. As we saw in the introductory chapter, SCA does this through **wires**. Conceptually, a wire is a connection provided by the runtime to another service. A wire is specified—in this case, the wire between `LoanComponent` and `CreditComponent`—in the composite file, which we show in the next section. For now, we will assume a wire has been specified and describe how an SCA runtime goes about connecting `LoanComponent` to the `CreditService` interface of `CreditComponent`.

SCA leaves the heavy lifting associated with establishing remote communications to the runtime, as opposed to application code and API calls.

In Java, the runtime provides a wire by doing one of the following: calling a setter method annotated with `@Reference` and passing in a reference to the service; setting a field marked with `@Reference`; or passing a reference to the service as a constructor parameter annotated with `@Reference`, as in the example given previously in Figure 2.3.

In actuality, when the SCA runtime injects the `CreditService`, it is likely not a "direct" reference to `CreditComponent` but instead a generated "proxy" that implements the `CreditService` interface (see Figure 2.4).

The proxy is responsible for taking an invocation and flowing it to the target service, whether it is co-located or hosted in a remote JVM. From the perspective of `LoanComponent`, however, `CreditService` behaves as a typical Java reference.

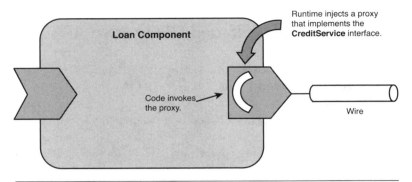

Runtime injects a proxy
that implements the
CreditService interface.

Loan Component

Code invokes
the proxy.

Wire

Figure 2.4   Reference proxy injection

SCA is based on Inversion of Control (IoC), also known as dependency injection.

An important characteristic of wires is that their details are hidden from the client implementation. In our example, `LoanComponent` does not have knowledge of the wire communication protocol or the address of `CreditService`. This approach will be familiar to Spring developers. SCA is based on Inversion of Control (IoC), also known as dependency injection, popularized by the Spring framework. Instead of requiring a component to find its dependent services through a service locator API and invoke them using transport-specific APIs, the runtime provides service references when an instance is created. In this case, `CreditService` is injected as a constructor parameter when `LoanComponent` is instantiated.

There are a number of advantages to IoC. Because the endpoint address of `CreditService` is not present in application code, it is possible for a system administrator or runtime to make the decision at deployment whether to co-locate the components (possibly for performance reasons) or host them in separate processes. Further, it is possible to "rewire" `LoanComponent` to another implementation of `CreditService` without having to change the `LoanComponent` code itself. And, because the client does not make use of any protocol-specific APIs, the actual selection of a communication protocol can be deferred until deployment or changed at a later time.

Injection Styles

In the current version of `LoanComponent`, we elected to define the reference to `CreditService` as a constructor parameter. This is commonly referred to as constructor-based injection. Some developers prefer to inject dependencies through setter methods or directly on fields. The SCA Java programming model accommodates these alternative approaches as well by supporting injecting references on methods and fields. We will take a closer look at each injection style in turn.

Constructor-Based Injection

Constructor-based injection has the advantage of making dependencies explicit at compile time. In our example, `LoanComponent` cannot be instantiated without `CreditService`. This is particularly useful for testing, where component implementations are instantiated directly in test cases. Constructor-based injection also enables fields to be marked as final so that they cannot be inadvertently changed later on. When other forms of injection are used, final fields can't be used. The primary drawback of constructor-based injection is that the constructor parameter list can become unwieldy for components that depend on a number of services.

Constructor-based injection has the advantage of making dependencies explicit at compile time.

In some cases, component implementations may have more than one constructor. The SCA Java programming model defines a rule for selecting the appropriate constructor in cases where there is more than one. If one constructor has parameters marked with `@Reference` or `@Property`, it will be used. Otherwise, a developer can explicitly mark a constructor with the SCA `@Constructor` annotation, as shown in Listing 2.6.

The primary drawback of constructor-based injection is that the constructor parameter list can become unwieldy for components that depend on a number of services.

Listing 2.6   The `@Constructor` Annotation

```
@Constructor
public CreditComponent  (double min, double max) {
   // …
}
```

Setter-Based Injection

SCA supports method-based reference injection as an alternative to constructor-based injection. For example, `LoanComponent` could have been written as shown in Listing 2.7.

SCA supports method-based reference injection as an alternative to constructor-based injection.

Listing 2.7   Setter-Based Injection

```
public class LoanComponent{

    public LoanComponent () {}
```

```
@Reference
public setCreditService(CreditService creditService) {
      // ...
}
```
}

When `LoanComponent` is instantiated, the SCA runtime will invoke the `setCreditService` method, passing a reference proxy to `CreditService`. An important restriction SCA places on this style of injection is that setter methods must be either public or protected; private setter methods are not allowed because it violates the object-oriented principle of encapsulation. (That is, private methods and fields should not be visible outside a class.)

The main benefit of setter-based injection is that it allows for reinjection of wires dynamically at runtime.

The main benefit of setter-based injection is that it allows for reinjection of wires dynamically at runtime. We cover wire reinjection in Chapter 7, "Wires."

There are two major downsides to setter injection. Component dependencies are dispersed across a number of setter methods, making them less obvious and increasing the verbosity of the code because a method needs to be created for every reference. In addition, setter methods make references that potentially should be immutable subject to change, because the fields they are assigned to cannot be declared final.

▪ Setter Injection Best Practices

There are a couple of best practices to keep in mind when using setter-based injection. First, setter methods should not be part of the service interface because they are implementation details. For example, `LoanService` does not define the method `setCreditService(CreditService creditService)`—the fact that `LoanComponent` uses `CreditService` is an implementation detail clients should not be aware of.

Second, avoid making setter methods protected, even though SCA allows this. Doing so makes unit testing difficult because unit tests would need to either subclass the component implementation to override the setters and make them public or use reflection to set them directly. If setter methods are not part of a service contract, there is no risk a client will inadvertently invoke them if they are made public.

Field-Based Injection

The final form of injection supported by SCA is field-based. This style enables fields to be directly injected with reference proxies (see Listing 2.8).

Listing 2.8   *Field-Based Injection*

```
public class LoanComponent     {

        @Reference
        protected CreditService CreditService;

        //....
}
```

Field-injection follows the basic pattern set by method-injection except that they may be private and public or protected. In the absence of a name attribute declared on `@Reference`, the field name is used as the name of the reference. Again, the preceding example would be configured using the same composite syntax as the previous examples.

A major advantage of field-based injection is that it is concise. (Methods do not need to be created for each reference.) It also avoids long constructor parameter lists. The main disadvantage of field-based injection is it is difficult to unit test; component classes must either be subclassed to expose reference fields or those fields must be set through Java reflection.

A major advantage of field-based injection is that it is concise.

The main disadvantage of field-based injection is it is difficult to unit test.

■ Perspective: What's the Best Injection Style?

Several years ago, setter- versus constructor-based injection was an area of contention among advocates of various Java-based IoC frameworks, notably Spring and PicoContainer. Most modern IoC frameworks now support both approaches, as does SCA.

In the process of writing this book, we debated between ourselves about the best injection style. Jim favors constructor injection because it makes service dependencies explicit. Mike prefers field-based injection because it limits verbosity. In the end, like the debates among the various IoC frameworks a few years back, we went around in circles and were unable to convince one another. This led us to agree on an important point: Choosing an injection style is largely a matter of personal preference. Pick the one that best suits the project requirements or the one project developers are used to and stay consistent.

That said, there is one important difference between field and setter versus constructor injection in SCA. Namely, field and setter injection can be dynamic. As we will cover in Chapter 7, field- and setter-based references may be reinjected if a reference changes after a component has been instantiated. In contrast, constructor-based references cannot be changed. If a reference may change, you need to use field- or setter-based injection. On the other hand, if a reference must be immutable, use constructor injection.

Defining Properties

Consider the case where we want to add the capability to set configuration parameters on the CreditComponent component, such as minimum and maximum scores. SCA supports configuration through component **properties**, which in Java are specified using the @Property annotation. CreditComponent is modified to take maximum and minimum scores in Listing 2.9.

Listing 2.9   _Defining Component Properties_

```
public void CreditComponent implements CreditService {

     private int min;
     private int max;

     public CreditComponent (@Property(name="min") int min,
                             @Property(name="max") int max) {
          this.min = min;
          this.max = max;
     }
     // ....
}
```

Like a reference, a property name is specified using the "name" attribute, whereas the "required" attribute determines whether a property value must be provided in the composite file (that is, when it is set to true) or it is optional (that is, it is set to false, the default).

In addition, properties follow the same injection guidelines as references: constructor-, method-, and field-based injection are supported.

Given that most IoC frameworks do not distinguish between properties and references, why does SCA? The short answer is they are different. References provide access to services, whereas properties provide configuration data. Differentiating properties and references makes it clear to someone configuring a component whether a property value needs to be supplied or a reference wired to a service. Further, as we will see in later chapters, references may have various qualities of service applied to them, such as reliability, transactions, and security. The benefits of distinguishing properties and references also extends to tooling: Knowing if a particular value is a property or reference makes for better validation and visual feedback, such as displaying specific icons in graphical tooling.

References provide access to services, whereas properties provide configuration data.

Assembling the `LoanApplication` Composite

Listing 2.10 provides a complete version of the `LoanApplication` composite we first introduced in the last chapter. Let's examine it in the context of the `LoanComponent` and `CreditComponent` implementations we have just discussed.

Listing 2.10 *The `LoanApplication` Composite*

```
<composite xmlns=http://www.osoa.org/xmlns/sca/1.0

    targetNamespace="
http://www.bigbank.com/xmlns/loanApplication/1.0"

    name="LoanApplication">

  <component name ="LoanComponent">
    <implementation.java class="com.acme.LoanComponent  "/>
    <property name="currency">USD</property>
    <reference name="creditService" target="CreditComponent "/>
  <component>

  <component name = "CreditComponent">
    <implementation.java class="com.acme.CreditComponent "/>
  <component>
</composite>
```

Composites include targetNamespace *and* name *attributes, which together form their **qualified name**, or QName.*

Composites include `targetNamespace` and `name` attributes, which together form their **qualified name**, or QName. The QName of the `LoanApplication` composite is http://www.bigbank.com/xmlns/loanApplication/1.0:LoanApplication. QNames are similar to the combination of package and class name in Java: They serve to uniquely identify an XML artifact—in this case, a composite. The `targetNamespace` portion of the QName can be used for versioning. In the example, the `targetNamespace` ends with 1.0, indicating the composite version. The version should be changed any time a nonbackward-compatible change is made to the definition (and should not be changed otherwise).

Continuing with the composite listing in Listing 2.10, `LoanComponent` and `CreditComponent` are defined by the `<component>` element. Both component definitions contain an entry, `<implementation.java>`, which identifies the Java class for the respective component implementations. If the components were implemented in BPEL, the `<implementation.bpel>` element would have been used, as follows:

```
<implementation.bpel process="bb:LoanApplicationProcess">
```

The `<reference>` element in the `LoanComponent` definition configures the reference to `CreditService`, as follows:

```
<reference name="creditService" target="CreditService"/>
```

Recalling that the `LoanComponent` implementation declares a reference requiring a `CreditService` in its constructor, we get the following:

```
public LoanComponent  (@Reference (name="CreditService") CreditService
➥creditService) {
// …
}
```

The `<reference>` element configures the `creditService` reference by wiring it to the `CreditService` provided by `CreditComponent`. When an instance of `LoanComponent` is created by the SCA runtime, it will pass a proxy to `CreditService` as part of the constructor invocation.

Properties are configured in a composite file using the `<property>` element. In the `LoanApplication` composite, `CreditComponent` is configured with `min` and `max` values (see Listing 2.11).

Listing 2.11 *Configuring Property Values*

```
<component name="CreditComponent">
      <implementation.java class=".."/>
      <property name="min">300</property>
      <property name="max">850</property>
</component>
```

The property values will be injected into the component by the runtime when a component instance is created.

It is important to note the naming convention used for configuring references and properties defined on setter methods. In the absence of an explicit name attribute on `@Reference` or `@Property` annotation, the name of the reference is inferred from the method name according to JavaBean semantics. In other words, for method names of the form "`setXXXX`," the `set` prefix is dropped and the initial letter of the remaining part is made lowercase. Otherwise, the value specified in the name attribute is used.

An interesting characteristic of reference and property configuration in a composite is that the format remains the same, regardless of the style of injection used in the implementation. For example, the following component entry

```
<component name="LoanComponent">
      <implementation.java class=".."/>
      <reference name="creditScoreService" target="CreditComponent "/>
</component>
```

configures a reference specified on a constructor parameter,

```
public LoanComponent   (@Reference(name="creditScoreService"
➥CreditService CreditService) {
      // …
}
```

or a setter method,

```
@Reference

public void setCreditScoreService(CreditService creditScoreService){

      //…
}
```

or a field:

```
@Reference

protected CreditService creditScoreService;
```

Binding a Web Service Endpoint

The `LoanApplication` composite would be more useful if its services were made accessible to clients that are outside the SCA domain—for example, to independent mortgage broker systems. In
SCA, services are exposed to external clients over a **binding**.
Bindings are used to specify the communication protocol over
which a service is available, such as web services, RMI, or plain
XML over HTTP (without the SOAP envelope). A service may be
exposed over more than one binding, providing multiple ways for
external clients to invoke it. For example, the `LoanService` could
be bound to web services and a proprietary EDI protocol (see
Figure 2.5).

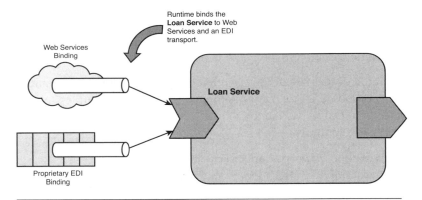

Figure 2.5   Binding the `LoanService`

Moreover, bindings can be added or removed in runtimes that support dynamic updates. For example, after clients have transitioned
to using web services, the EDI binding for the `LoanService` interface could be deprecated and eventually phased out. Alternatively,
a high-speed binary binding could be added for clients requiring
improved performance (such as a binding based on the new W3C
Efficient XML for Interchange format, EXI).

Service bindings are specified in the composite file using a combination of service and binding elements. Listing 2.12 binds the
`LoanService` interface to web services.

Listing 2.12   *Binding the `LoanService` Interface as a Web Service Endpoint*

```
<service name="LoanService">
     <binding.ws>
</service>
```

When `LoanComponent` is activated in the domain, the SCA infrastructure is responsible for making `LoanService` available as a web service.

The exact mechanics of how this binding is achieved are runtime-dependent. However, all SCA implementations must perform the following steps (which will generally be transparent to the person deploying a composite). First, if no WSDL is specified, the runtime will need to generate it based on the `LoanService` Java interface. This will entail creating a WSDL document similar to the one listed at the beginning of the chapter, but also including WSDL binding and WSDL service elements. (The algorithm for generating the WSDL is standardized by SCA.) After the WSDL is generated, the runtime will need to make the service and WSDL available to clients as a web service at the endpoint address listed in the WSDL. Depending on the runtime, this may involve deploying or dynamically configuring middleware such as creating a HTTP listener for the service on a particular machine. Fortunately, SCA hides the complexities of this process, so people deploying composites need not worry about how this is actually done.

Packaging the `LoanApplication` Composite

SCA specifies one interoperable packaging format for composite files and associated artifacts such as Java classes, XSDs, and WSDLs: the ZIP archive. However, to accommodate the diverse range of packaging formats used by various programming languages, SCA allows runtimes to support other formats in addition to the ZIP archive. A C++ runtime may accept DLLs; a runtime may also support various specializations of the ZIP format. Fabric3 also supports JARs and Web Archives (WARs).

SCA ZIP archives include a metadata file, sca-contribution.xml, in the `META-INF` directory. The sca-contribution.xml file provides SCA-specific information about the contents of the archive, most notably the composites available for deployment. In general, one

SCA specifies one interoperable packaging format for composite files and associated artifacts such as Java classes, XSDs, and WSDLs: the ZIP archive.

The sca-contribution. xml file provides SCA-specific information about the contents of the archive.

deployable composite will be packaged in an archive, although in some cases (which we discuss in later chapters), no deployable composites or multiple deployable composites may be present.

A contribution is an application artifact that is "contributed" or made available to a domain.

The name *sca-contribution.xml* derives from SCA terminology: A contribution is an application artifact that is "contributed" or made available to a domain. A contribution can be a complete composite and all the artifacts necessary to execute it, or it might just contain artifacts to be used by composites from other contributions, such as a library, XSDs, or WSDLs. LoanApplication is packaged as a complete composite. Its sca-contribution.xml is shown in Listing 2.13.

Listing 2.13   *A Contribution Manifest*

```
<contribution xmlns=http://www.osoa.org/xmlns/sca/1.0

xmlns:bb="http://www.bigbank.com/xmlns/lending/composites/1.0">

    <deployable composite="bb:LoanApplication"/>

</contribution>
```

The `<deployable>` element identifies a composite available for deployment contained in the archive. In this case, it points to the name of the LoanApplication composite, as defined in the `<composite>` element of its .composite file:

```
<composite  xmlns="http://www.osoa.org/xmlns/sca/1.0"

targetNamespace="http://www.bigbank.com/xmlns/lending/composites/1.0"
            name="LoanApplication"…>
```

SCA does not specify a location for composite files; they can be included in any archive directory.

Unlike sca-contribution.xml, SCA does not specify a location for composite files; they can be included in any archive directory. However, as a best practice, it is recommended that deployable composite files be placed alongside sca-contribution.xml in the META-INF directory so they can be easily found.

Deploying the `LoanApplication` Composite

Composites can be deployed to a domain using a variety of mechanisms. In a test environment, deployment may involve placing the contribution archive in a file system directory. In production environments, where tighter controls are required, deployment would typically be performed through a command-line tool or script.

Conceptually, deployment involves contributing a composite to a domain and activating its components, as depicted in Figure 2.6.

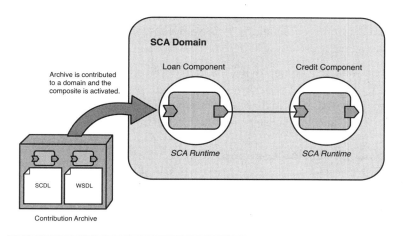

Figure 2.6   Deploying and activating the `LoanApplication` composite

When the `LoanApplication` composite is deployed, the SCA runtime instantiates `LoanComponent` and `CreditComponent`. During this process, because `LoanService` is configured with the web services binding, it is exposed as a web service endpoint. When the `LoanApplication` composite is activated in the domain, its components are available to process client requests.

Using Fabric3

Having completed the walkthrough of assembling and packaging the `LoanApplication` composite, we put this knowledge to practice by deploying a sample application to the Fabric3 SCA runtime.

Fabric3 has a modular architecture similar to Eclipse.

Fabric3 is a full-featured, open source SCA implementation. It has a highly modular design with preconfigured distributions for a number of environments. For example, Fabric3 has distributions that can be embedded in a servlet container, such as Tomcat or Jetty, and specific Java EE application servers, including JBoss, WebLogic, and WebSphere.

Fabric3 has a modular architecture similar to Eclipse. The core distributions implement basic SCA functionality, whereas additional features are added through extensions. This allows Fabric3 to remain lightweight and allows users to include only the features required by their applications. For example, support for bindings such as web services is added as extensions to the core.

To get started with deploying the loan application, you will need to set up Fabric3 and your development environment. We assume that you have JDK 5.0 installed on your machine. To configure your machine, perform the steps outlined in the following sections.

Download Fabric3 `LoanApplication` Sample

Fabric3 provides a `LoanApplication` sample that we use in this hands-on exercise. The sample is a full-fledged version of the loan-processing system covered in this chapter and includes integration with JPA and a web application front-end. It can be downloaded from the same place the Fabric3 distribution is located: http://www.fabric3.org/downloads.html.

The sample contains a utility for downloading the Fabric3 runtime and extensions. Follow the instructions to run the utility and install the runtime.

Verify the Installation

To verify that the server has been successfully installed, go to the `bin` directory where it has been installed and execute `java —jar server.jar`. This will start the server.

Build and Deploy the Application

We are now ready to build and deploy the application. First, follow the instructions for building the sample application. After this is done, start the Fabric3 server by issuing the following command from the `bin` directory where it is installed:

```
java —jar server.jar
```

When the server starts, it activates an SCA domain that is contained in a single process. In a distributed environment, multiple Fabric3 servers participate in a single domain that spans processes.

After the server has booted, copy the loan application JAR that was built in the previous step from the target directory to the deploy directory of the Fabric3 server installation. The server will then deploy the application to the domain.

Invoking the `LoanApplication` Service

After the application has been deployed, we can invoke the `LoanService` interface. The sample application contains a JAX-WS client that can be used to test-drive the service. Follow the instructions for launching the test-client from the command line.

This completes the hands-on walkthrough of building and deploying an SCA application with Fabric3. At this point, it is worth spending some time familiarizing yourself with the application code. As you will see, most of the tedious tasks of generating WSDLs and exposing web services are handled transparently by the runtime. In the following chapters, we expand the loan application by introducing additional SCA features and capabilities. However, the basic structure and simplicity of the code will remain the same.

Summary

We have covered significant ground in this chapter, providing a detailed discussion of key SCA concepts and design principles. Specifically, we have accomplished the following:

- Defined service contracts
- Written component implementations using the SCA Java programming model
- Configured components as part of a composite
- Exposed an SCA service using web services
- Deployed a composite to an SCA runtime

With this foundation in place, we turn our attention in the next chapter to designing and building loosely coupled services using Java.

3

Service-Based Development Using Java

SCA is designed to support applications assembled from services written in multiple programming languages. This chapter provides the background and understanding necessary to implement services in arguably the most important of those languages for enterprise development: Java.

SCA includes a full-featured programming model for implementing services in Java. The primary goal of this programming model is to provide the capabilities necessary in Java to build loosely coupled services. Moreover, it attempts to do so in a way that is simpler to use than existing Java-based alternatives, including EJB and Spring.

SCA includes a full-featured programming model for implementing services in Java.

This chapter focuses on the basics of loosely coupled services, including service contract design, asynchronous communications, and component life cycle. Specifically, this chapter covers the following:

- Designing service contracts
- Implementing asynchronous interactions and callback patterns
- Managing component life cycle, state, and concurrency

After completing this chapter, you will have a solid grounding in implementing Java-based services and an understanding of best practices to apply when designing those services.

Service-Based Development

As we discussed in the first chapter, a key goal of SCA is reuse: Application functionality and code that can be shared by multiple clients is more valuable than functionality and code that cannot.

This goal is far from novel. Many technologies claim to promote code reuse. Arguably, the most successful technologies in this respect have been object-oriented languages, which did much to promote *intra*-process reuse, or calls between code hosted in the same process. By organizing code into classes and interfaces, object-oriented languages allowed complex applications to be assembled from smaller, reusable units that are easier to maintain and evolve.

Yet code would be even more valuable if reuse were not limited to a process or application. In other words, if clients could connect remotely with existing or separately deployed code, the code would be even more valuable. In the 1990s and early 2000s, DCE, CORBA, DCOM, and Java EE attempted to replicate the success of object-oriented technology in distributed applications by applying many of the same principles to remote communications. In particular, these technologies were built around the concept of "distributed objects": units of code that could be invoked remotely to perform a task. The goal of these frameworks was to enable objects to be invoked across process boundaries similar to the way that object-oriented enabled objects could be invoked locally.

One of the key lessons learned from distributed objects is that applications must be carefully designed not to introduce bottlenecks by making too many remote calls or by placing unnecessary requirements on them such as transactionality.

Unfortunately, practical experience highlighted a number of problems with this approach. The most important of these was that local and remote invocations are different and those differences cannot be managed away by middleware. Remote communication introduces latency that affects application performance. This is compounded when additional qualities of service are required, such as transactions and security. One of the key lessons learned from distributed objects is that applications must be carefully designed not to introduce bottlenecks by making too many remote calls or by placing unnecessary requirements on them, such as transactionality.

SCA rejects the notion that object-oriented principles are to be employed at all levels of application design. A core tenet of SCA is that development of remote services is unique. For remote communications, developers rely on the techniques of loose coupling that we describe in this chapter.

Most applications, however, cannot be restricted to remote invocations. In order to achieve scalability, performance, and avoid unnecessary complexity, application code will need to make many more local calls than remote ones. In these cases, SCA stipulates that developers apply principles of good object-oriented design. In addition to loosely coupled remote services, we also detail the facilities provided by the SCA Java programming model for creating services intended for use in a single process, which follow traditional object-oriented patterns.

Protocol Abstraction and Location Transparency

Protocol abstraction and location transparency are commonly confused. Understanding the distinction between the two is fundamental to understanding the SCA programming model. SCA simplifies development by handling the intricacies of remote communications. What it doesn't do is oversimplify the nature of those communications and the impact they have on application code.

Protocol abstraction involves separating the specifics of how remote invocations are performed from application code by requiring the hosting container to manage communications. For example, the following service invocation could be made using web services or an alternative protocol such as RMI—the host container handles the specifics of flowing calls while the code remains unchanged (see Listing 3.1).

Protocol abstraction involves separating the specifics of how remote invocations are performed from application code by requiring the hosting container to manage communications.

Listing 3.1   *Invoking a Remote Service*

```
public class LoanComponent implements LoanService {
// ….
public LoanResult apply(LoanRequest request) {
//… process the request and invoke the credit service
CustomerInfo info = request.getCustomerInfo();
CreditService.checkCredit(info);
//.. continue processing
}
```

*Location trans-
parency allows
code to treat local
and remote invoca-
tions as if they were
the same.*

In contrast, location transparency allows code to treat local and remote invocations as if they were the same. Protocol abstraction does not mean that client code can be written in the same way *irrespective of whether* it is making a local or remote call. Consider the example in Figure 3.1 again where the `LoanComponent` invokes the remote `CreditService`. Because the invocation is remote, the client—in this case, the `LoanComponent`—will need to account for a number of additional factors. Perhaps the most important is network latency, which may result in the call not completing immediately. Second, network interruptions may result in the `CreditService` being temporarily unavailable. In these cases, the SCA runtime may throw an unchecked `org.osoa.sca.`
`ServiceUnavailableException`, and the client must decide whether to retry, ignore the exception and let it propagate up the call stack, or perform some other action. In the example, the client allows the exception to propagate (it's unchecked, so it does not need to be declared in a `throws` clause) and be handled by its caller. If the operation had required a degree of reliability, the `LoanComponent` could have caught the exception and attempted to retry the call.

*Protocol abstraction
does not imply
location
transparency.*

So, protocol abstraction does not imply location transparency. It's also important to note that the converse is also true: Location transparency does not imply protocol abstraction. Programming models that provide location transparency do not necessarily allow communications protocols to be changed. CORBA and DCOM serve as good examples. Both attempt to treat remote and in-process communications in the same manner but support only a single remote protocol. CORBA remains tied to the IIOP protocol. Similarly, DCOM is dependent on its own proprietary binary protocol.

Perspective: EJB and the Myth of Location Transparency

Contrary to conventional wisdom, Enterprise Java Beans (EJB) did not make the mistake of assuming location transparency. In fact, it has long been known that remote objects must be treated differently from local objects. RMI specifically addressed the fallacy that networks are always up by requiring that remotable methods throw `java.rmi.RemoteException`. `RemoteException` was also defined to be a checked exception, requiring clients to handle the exception or rethrow it. In this way, developers were forced to think about the fact that a remote operation is being called. Java EE took this a step further by integrating transaction management, thereby providing more assistance in recovering from the failures that are inherent in distributed systems.

Unfortunately, one fallacy that early versions of EJB did *not* address was the myth that the performance overhead of remote calls is negligible. The result was that developers found themselves creating remote EJBs with fine-grained interfaces. Applications developed in this manner had so many calls through remotable interfaces that performance was degraded. Performance even suffered in cases where the invoked EJB was co-located with its client, because the EJB specification required invocation parameters to be copied in order to simulate remoteness.

EJB also had a complexity penalty. Because remote operations were required to throw `RemoteException`, developers were forced to deal with handling these exceptions even when, in practice, the called object would never be remote. EJB was later revised to include local session beans, which introduced the ability to perform in-process invocations. This concession, however, proved to be insufficient, as EJB never achieved the widespread adoption it was expected to garner.

Having established that the SCA programming model is based on the goal of protocol abstraction rather than location transparency, let's look more closely at what is involved in building remotable services.

Designing Remotable Services

In SCA, remotable services are made available to multiple clients across process boundaries. These clients may be components in the same domain or, if the service is exposed over a binding, another system altogether.

Although the specific qualities of well-architected SCA applications will vary, a common indicator of good design is that an application will have only a few remotable services that expose a set of general operations. Examples of general operations include "apply for loan," "get credit rating," "inventory check," and "place back-order." Think of remotable services as an API. As with a good API,

The SCA programming model is based on the goal of protocol abstraction rather than location transparency.

remotable services should be concise, easy to understand, and limited. Moreover, they should have the following attributes:

- **Remotable services account for the network**—Remotable services should account for the realities of the physical network they are called over, particularly latency and connectivity interruptions. In particular, they should limit the number of exchanges required between a client and service provider.

- **Remotable service contracts take versioning into account**—Remotable service contracts should be evolvable. Rarely do APIs "get it right" in the first iteration. Furthermore, new requirements often arise after an application has gone into production. Barring fundamental changes, it should be possible to version services without breaking compatibility with existing clients.

- **Remotable services limit the assumptions made about clients**—Remotable services should limit the assumptions they make about clients. Most important, they should not assume that clients will be written in the same language they are written in.

SCA relies on techniques of loose coupling developed by integration technologies—in particular, message-oriented middleware (MOM).

To achieve these qualities, SCA relies on techniques of loose coupling developed by integration technologies—in particular, message-oriented middleware (MOM). Loose coupling can take a variety of forms. The two most important forms of loose coupling in SCA are coarse-grained services and asynchronous communications. We deal with designing coarse-grained service contracts in the next section, followed by a detailed discussion of how SCA allows for asynchronous communications via non-blocking operations and callbacks in subsequent sections.

Perspective: How Loosely Coupled Should Services Be?

A common question that arises when designing service-based applications is how loosely coupled remote communications should be. One school of thought says that services should be as loosely coupled as possible and, in order to achieve this, an

Enterprise Service Bus (ESB) should be used to route messages between *all* clients and providers.

ESBs offer the following forms of loose coupling:

- **Target abstraction**—The capability to dynamically route service requests to service providers based on message content or type.

- **Protocol translation**—The capability to transform a service request from a client over one protocol into the protocol supported by the service provider.

These capabilities are provided through a "service bus" that is placed between the client and service provider (see Figure 3.1).

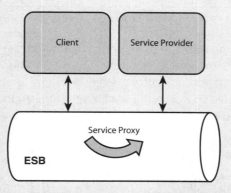

Figure 3.1   A service bus mediates the communications between a client and service provider.

When clients are targeted at the bus instead of the actual service provider, it is possible to change the provider by simply changing the bus configuration. This can usually be done without any programming, typically through an administration console. This gives the added flexibility of allowing the bus to use a different protocol to call the service provider than is used to communicate with the client.

SCA takes a different approach to loose coupling by asserting that services should be no more loosely coupled than necessary. Loosely coupled systems are generally more difficult to write and complex to manage. Moreover, introducing mediation can result in an unnecessary and potentially expensive invocation hop. As shown in Figure 3.2, in an ESB, a message is sent from the client to an intermediary and on to the target service, creating three hops.

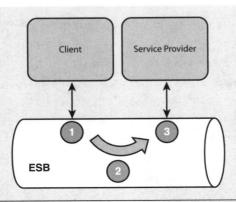

Figure 3.2 ESBs introduce an additional hop.

In contrast, with SCA, the decision to introduce mediation can be deferred until after an application has gone into production (see Figure 3.3). This avoids introducing the performance penalty associated with an extra hop until mediation is needed. If a service contract changes, an SCA runtime can introduce an intermediary in the wire between the client and service provider dynamically that transforms the request to the new format.

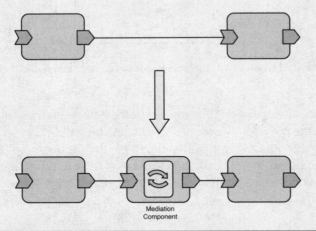

Figure 3.3 SCA and late mediation

Because SCA abstracts the mechanics of remote calls from application code, mediation can be introduced in much later stages of an application life cycle without forcing code modifications.

One area where an ESB has an advantage over an SCA runtime is in target abstraction. SCA provides no mechanism for performing content-based routing where a service provider is selected dynamically based on parameter values. To effect content-based routing in SCA, a client would need to be wired to a component that made routing decisions and forwarded the request to the appropriate service provider.

Coarse-Grained Services

In SCA, remotable service contracts should have coarse-grained operations that take document-centric parameters. Let's examine what this means. Coarse-grained operations combine a number of steps that might otherwise be divided into separate methods. To better understand how coarse granularity is achieved in practice, we start with a counter-example. Listing 3.2 shows a version of the `LoanService` using fine-grained operations.

Remotable service contracts should have coarse-grained operations that take document-centric parameters. Coarse-grained operations combine a number of steps that might otherwise be divided into separate methods.

Listing 3.2   *An Example of a Fine-Grained Service Contract*

```
@Remotable
public interface LoanService {

    String apply(float amount, float down);

    void supplyCreditInfo(String loanId, String ssn);

    LoanResult getResult(String loanId);
}
```

In the preceding fine-grained version, applying for a loan is done through a series of requests to the `LoanService`.

Although a fine-grained design seemingly allows for more flexibility (clients can supply the required information in stages), it can potentially introduce serious performance bottlenecks. Back to Figure 3.2, each invocation of the `LoanService`—`apply`, `supplyCreditInfo`, and `getResult`—entails a separate network roundtrip. This can be extremely expensive, as parameter data needs to be marshaled and unmarshaled when the invocation travels across the network.

In contrast, the `LoanService` version used in the last chapter processes a request using one operation by requiring that all required data be provided upfront (see Listing 3.3).

Listing 3.3   *An Example of a Coarse-Grained Service Contract*

```
@Remotable
public interface LoanService {

    LoanResult apply(LoanRequest request);
}
```

The most important characteristic of the coarse-grained version in Figure 3.6 is that it optimizes network roundtrips, eliminating a potentially costly bottleneck. Instead of the three roundtrips required by the fine-grained version, the coarse-grained `LoanService` requires only one.

Coarse-grained operations are usually document-centric, which means they take one parameter that encapsulates related data.

Another important difference between fine- and coarse-grained interfaces is the number of parameters operations take. With fine-grained interfaces, operations commonly take multiple parameters. In contrast, coarse-grained operations are usually document-centric, which means they take one parameter that encapsulates related data. The `LoanResult.apply(LoanRequest request)` operation shown previously in Listing 3.3 is document-centric because it takes a single parameter of type `LoanRequest`.

Document-centric contracts are recommended for remotable services because they are easier to evolve while maintaining compatibility with existing clients.

Document-centric contracts are recommended for remotable services because they are easier to evolve while maintaining compatibility with existing clients. For example, if BigBank decided to collect additional optional loan information that would be used to offer interest rate discounts, it could do so by adding additional fields to the `LoanRequest` type. Existing clients would continue to function because the additional fields would simply be ignored. In contrast, the fine-grained contract would more likely require modifications to the operation signature, breaking existing clients.

Using coarse-grained operations that take document-centric parameters decreases the amount of inter-process communication in an application. This not only improves performance by limiting network traffic, it also makes writing robust applications easier because developers are required to handle issues related to service unavailability and versioning at fewer places in the application.

However, there is also a disadvantage to the coarse-grained approach—error handling can be much more difficult. In the coarse-grained version of the `LoanService`, applicant-related data is contained in the `LoanApplication` class, which is passed to the former as one parameter. This makes the source of errors in part of the data more difficult to identify and respond to. For example, an invalid ZIP code (postal code) may occur in the applicant's or property address. This requires a mechanism for reporting the source of errors. In addition, the application could have a number of problems with it, requiring a way to aggregate and report them in an exception or result data. Handling errors in this way is more complicated than it is with the fine-grained contracts, but the advantages of loose coupling outweigh the added complexity.

Using WSDL for Service Contracts

Remotable services should be loosely coupled with their clients by making limited assumptions about them. This entails not assuming clients will be written in Java. When defining remotable service contracts, it is therefore good practice to design for language interoperability. One of the key pitfalls in doing so is the translation of data types across languages. In particular, operation parameter types may not map cleanly or at all in different languages. Simple types such as strings and numerics generally do not present difficulties. However, user defined-types, especially complex types such as classes, often pose challenges. To achieve interoperability, it may be necessary to create a language-neutral representation of the service contract that also defines operation parameter types.

As we have seen in Chapter 2, "Assembling and Deploying a Composite," the most common way to do this today is through WSDL. A WSDL document describes a service or set of services and their operations. SCA runtimes and IDEs typically provide tooling that makes it easier to work with WSDL. For example, some tools allow the service contract to be written in Java first as an interface and a WSDL generated from it. This is usually the easiest approach, at least for Java developers. However, some organizations prefer a top-down approach where service contracts are crafted directly in WSDL. This approach, although more time-consuming and potentially difficult, has the advantage of better accommodating interoperability because the contract is defined in a language-neutral way. When starting top-down, Java interfaces that

A WSDL document describes a service or set of services and their operations.

application code uses are created based on the WSDL contract. Fortunately, many tools automate this process by generating the interfaces from WSDL.

WSDL Basics

In this book, we don't explain the details of WSDL. At some point, it is worth becoming more familiar with the technology. The WSDL 1.1 (http://www.w3.org/TR/wsdl) and WSDL 2.0 (http://www.w3.org/TR/ wsdl20-primer, http://www.w3.org/TR/wsdl20, http://www.w3.org/TR/ wsdl20-adjuncts, and http://www.w3.org/TR/ wsdl20-bindings) specifications are options, although they can be tedious reading. For a concise introduction, we recommend *Understanding Web Services* by Eric Newcomer (Addison-Wesley, 2002), which is in the same series as this book. In the meantime, we will briefly summarize the main WSDL concepts that relate to SCA.

In WSLD 1.1, a **port** is some unit of code that is reachable at a given network address over a particular protocol. This unit of code is often referred to as an endpoint. For example, an endpoint may be located at http://bigbank.com/ creditService using the HTTP protocol. A port contains a set of operations that process messages in a given format. The `CreditService` endpoint has a `#rate` operation that takes a customer ID to return a credit rating for. When the endpoint is invoked, it receives a message containing this data via HTTP encoded in a specified format—for example, SOAP 1.1.

Ports are broken down into a number of separate elements. A `portType` defines the set of operations for an endpoint. It is roughly analogous to an interface in Java. A **binding** defines the message format (for example, SOAP 1.1) and protocol details for a `portType` (for example, HTTP). Finally, a port specifies an **address** where the endpoint can be contacted. WSDL separates out these elements so that they can be reused. Two ports can use the same `portType` but different bindings. Two different endpoints would be created that perhaps were available over different protocols but offered the same set of operations to clients.

WSDL 1.1 somewhat confusingly (at least from the perspective of SCA) also defines the concept of a "service," which is different than an SCA service. In WSDL 1.1, a service is a collection of related ports.

In response to limitations and complaints about the complexity of WSDL 1.1, WSDL 2.0 introduced several important changes. Although we will not document the changes here, there are two that you need to be aware of. First, WSDL 2.0 has renamed `portType` to interface and port to endpoint. Second, a service is now restricted to one interface (as opposed to WSDL 1.1, which allowed multiple `portTypes`).

Starting from Java or WSDL largely comes down to weighing the pros and cons of each approach and personal preference. Whether you choose WSDL first or code first, you will also need to account for operation parameter serialization. As we discussed in Chapter 2, remote calls must serialize parameter values over a communication transport. WSDL defines the format for flowing parameter values using XML Schema. If a service provider is implemented in Java, there must be a way of deserializing parameter values into Java objects. How parameter values are deserialized depends on the data-binding technology used by the SCA runtime.

Service Contracts and Data Binding

All SCA runtimes must support a mechanism for serializing parameter types remotely. This mechanism is commonly referred to as "data binding." An SCA runtime may support one or several data-binding technologies, depending on the remote communication protocol used. For example, an SCA runtime may support one data-binding technology for serializing parameter values as XML and another for binary protocols. Some data-binding technologies place special requirements on parameter types that you may need to take into account when designing service contracts. Again, because data-binding technologies are vendor-specific, different SCA runtimes may vary in their approach. Books have been written on the subject of data binding, and we will not cover it in depth here other than to discuss where it fits into remotable service design.

All SCA runtimes must support a mechanism for serializing parameter types remotely. This mechanism is commonly referred to as "data binding."

The most prevalent data-binding technologies when working with XML today are XML Schema-based, including JAXB (part of JDK since version 6), Service Data Objects (SDO), and XmlBeans. Despite their differences, JAXB, SDO, and XmlBeans (and most other data-binding technologies) use XML Schema as the way of defining types for XML in order to map from Java types (for example, classes and primitives) to XML and vice versa (see Figure 3.4).

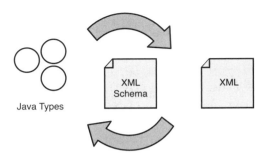

Figure 3.4   JAXB, SDO, and XmlBeans use XML Schema to map between Java and XML.

JAXB, SDO, and XmlBeans specify rules for mapping from schema to Java types and vice versa. These type mappings are used to convert data between XML and Java—for example, mapping `java.lang.String` to the schema type `xs:string`.

An SCA runtime uses a data-binding technology to translate data sent as XML from a client (often written in a language other than Java) to a service. To do so, it uses its schema-based mapping rules to translate the XML data into its Java representation (see Figure 3.5).

An SCA runtime uses a data-binding technology to translate data sent as XML from a client to a service.

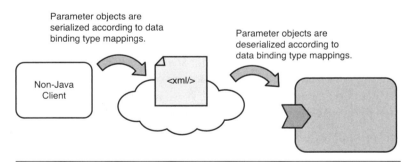

Figure 3.5   Marshaling to XML

Similarly, an SCA runtime uses a data-binding technology to serialize data to XML when a call is made to a remote service.

Fortunately, although data-binding discussions can become complex and esoteric, XML data-binding technologies are relatively easy to use. JAXB, SDO, and XmlBeans all support the "start-from-schema" approach where a combination of WSDL and XML

Schema are used to define the service contract and its operation parameters. In this approach, Java classes are derived from WSDL and XML Schema. An SCA runtime or an IDE may provide tooling that automates this process by generating Java classes.

Some data-binding technologies also support "start-with-Java." In this approach, rather than having to deal with the complexity of XML, developers can define their interfaces in Java and have WSDL and XML Schema generated. An SCA runtime may use one of these data-binding technologies to enable developers to write service contracts entirely in Java. Fabric3, for example, uses JAXB.

JAXB is arguably one of the easiest "start-from-Java" data-binding technologies. Being part of the JDK since version 6, it certainly is the most prevalent. JAXB does a good job of specifying default mappings so developers don't have to. JAXB makes heavy use of annotations to map from Java to XML. For example, to bind the `LoanApplication` type to XML using JAXB, `@XmlRootElement` is added as an annotation to the class (see Listing 3.4).

Listing 3.4   *A JAXB Complex Type*

```
package com.bigbank.message;

import javax.xml.bind.annotation.XmlRootElement;

@XmlRootElement
public class LoanApplication {
        //....
}
```

Perspective: Which Data Binding Should You Choose?

A common misperception is that SCA requires or mandates SDO as its data-binding technology. In fact, SCA is data binding-agnostic and is intended to work equally well with JAXB, XmlBeans, and other like technologies. Selecting a data-binding solution will often be constrained by the runtime, which may support only one or a limited number. In cases where there is a choice, selection should be based on the requirements of an application.

JAXB is particularly well-suited for interacting with data in a strongly typed fashion, namely as Java types. This is perhaps the most common development scenario, as component implementations are generally aware of the data types they will be manipulating in advance. Other major advantages of JAXB are its relative simplicity and its capability to use plain Java Objects (POJOs) without the need to generate special marshaling classes. When combined with SCA, JAXB provides a fairly transparent solution for marshaling data to and from XML. For example, in the following extract, the JAXB `LoanRequest` and `LoanResult` objects can be unmarshaled and marshaled transparently by the SCA runtime:

```
public class LoanComponent implements LoanService {
// ….
public LoanResult apply(LoanRequest request) {
  //… process the request and invoke the credit
  service
  CustomerInfo info = request.getCustomerInfo();
  CreditService.checkCredit(info);
  //.. continue processing to receive a result code
  LoanResult result = new LoanResult();
  result.setCode(code)
  return result;
}
```

A major disadvantage of JAXB is that although it provides strong support for "start-from-Java" and "start-from-schema" development scenarios (that is, generating a schema for existing Java classes and generating Java classes from an existing schema, respectively), it does not handle "meet-in-the-middle" well. The latter is important in situations where existing schemas must be reconciled with existing Java types.

Another feature lacking in JAXB is support for an API to dynamically access XML data. In situations where a component may not statically know about the data types it will manipulate, SDO and XMLBeans provide a dynamic API for introspecting and accessing data.

A significant downside of SDO and XmlBeans is their current lack of support for starting with Java. Both data-binding technologies require Java types to be generated from pre-existing schemas. This introduces another step in the development process (generating the Java types) and slightly complicates application code as SDO and XmlBeans require generated types to be instantiated via factories.

In many cases, JAXB is a reasonable choice given its simplicity and reliance on POJOs. However, application requirements may vary where SDO, XmlBeans, or an alternative technology are more appropriate. Fortunately, SCA is not tied to a particular data-binding solution and can accommodate a number of different approaches to working with XML.

Pass-By-Value Parameters

An important characteristic of remotable services is that operation parameters are **pass-by-value**, as opposed to **pass-by-reference**. The main difference between the two types concerns visibility of operation parameters. When pass-by-value parameters are modified by the component providing a service, they are not visible to the client. When pass-by-reference parameters are modified by a component providing a service, they are visible to the client. In Java, pass-by-reference means a reference to the same parameter object is shared by the client and service provider. Pass-by-value generally entails copying parameters or enforcing a copy-on-write scheme—that is, lazily copying when data is modified. For example, the following example demonstrates the difference between pass-by-value and pass-by-reference:

When pass-by-value parameters are modified by the component providing a service, they are not visible to the client. When pass-by-reference parameters are modified by a component providing a service, they are visible to the client.

```
public class ClientImpl implements Client {
    public void execute() {
        Message message = new Message();
        message.setBody("hello");
        service.invoke(message);
        System.out.println(message.getBody());
    }
}
public class ServiceImpl implements Service {
    public void invoke(Message message) {
        message.setBody("goodbye");
    }
}
```

In the preceding example, assume `ServiceImpl` takes enough time processing the message that the call to `Message.setBody(..)` in `Client` is made before the call to `System.out.println(..)` in `ServiceImpl`. If the `Service` interface is marked with `@Remotable`, `ServiceImpl` will output: `Message is hello`. However, if the `Service` interface is not marked with `@Remotable`, `ServiceImpl` will output: `Message is goodbye`.

In the case where `ClientImpl` and `ServiceImpl` are located in processes on different machines, pass-by-value is enforced as the parameters are marshaled from one process to the other (see Figure 3.6).

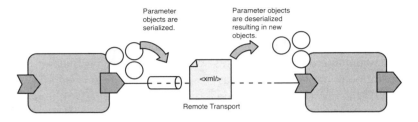

Figure 3.6   A pass-by-value invocation

When both the client and provider are in the same address space, an SCA runtime must also ensure these same semantics. Otherwise, the interaction between two components can drastically change based on how they are deployed, leading to unpredictable results. In order to ensure consistency and pass-by-value, an SCA runtime will typically copy parameters as a remotable service is invoked (see Figure 3.7). This ensures that neither the client nor the service provider is accidentally depending on by-reference semantics.

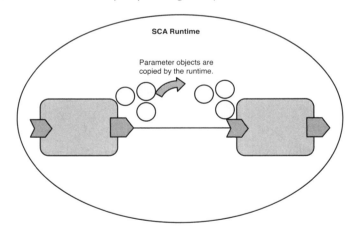

Figure 3.7   A pass-by-value invocation between co-located components

When a client and provider are co-located in the same process, parameter copying may introduce significant overhead.

When a client and provider are co-located in the same process, parameter copying may introduce significant overhead. If parameters are immutable types—for example, Java strings or primitives—the SCA runtime may perform an optimization by avoiding copying because the parameters cannot be modified. However, because parameters are often mutable, it is important to think carefully about the performance impact of defining a service as remotable. Because the `LoanService` must be accessible to remote clients, we are willing to accept the performance penalty associated with pass-by-value parameters.

@AllowsPassByReference

When the client and remote service are co-located, the SCA runtime typically ensures pass-by-value semantics by making a copy of the parameter data prior to invoking the service. If the service implementation does not modify parameters, this can result in significant and unnecessary overhead.

SCA provides a mechanism, the `@AllowsPassByReference` annotation, which allows runtimes to avoid unnecessary parameter copying when an invocation is made between two co-located components. This annotation is specified on a component implementation class or operation to indicate that parameters will not modified by application code. The implementation in Listing 3.5 uses the annotation on the interface, allowing the runtime to optimize all operations when the component is co-located with a client:

SCA provides a mechanism, the `@AllowsPassByReference` annotation, which allows runtimes to avoid unnecessary parameter.

Listing 3.5   *Using @AllowsPassByReference*

```
import org.osoa.sca.annotations.AllowsPassByReference;

@AllowsPassByReference
public class LoanComponent implements LoanService {

    LoanResult apply(LoanRequest request) {
        ...
    }

}
```

Generally, `@AllowsPassByReference` is used on an interface. However, if a service contains multiple operations, some of which modify parameters, the annotation may be used on a per-operation basis.

Asynchronous Interactions

When a client makes a non-blocking invocation, the SCA runtime returns control immediately to it and performs the call on another thread.

Calls to remotable services that take place over a network are typically orders of magnitude slower than in-process invocations. In addition, a particular service invocation may take a significant amount of time to complete; perhaps hours, days, or even months. This makes it impractical for clients to wait on a response or to hold a network connection open for an extended period of time. In these cases, SCA provides the ability to specify **non-blocking** operations. When a client makes a non-blocking invocation, the SCA runtime returns control immediately to it and performs the call on another thread. This allows clients to continue performing work without waiting on a call to complete.

Asynchronous communications are more loosely coupled than synchronous variants and provide a number of benefits that outweigh the additional complexity in many situations.

Asynchronous communications have a long history in MOM technologies and differ substantially from the synchronous communication styles adopted by technologies including RMI, EJB, DCOM, and .NET Remoting. A downside to asynchronous interactions is that they tend to be more complex to code than synchronous invocations. However, asynchronous communications are more loosely coupled then synchronous variants and provide a number of benefits that outweigh the additional complexity in many situations. Because a client does not wait on a non-blocking call, the SCA runtime can perform multiple retries if a target service is not available without blocking the client. This is particularly important for remote communications where service providers may be rendered temporarily unavailable due to network interruptions.

Asynchronous interactions have an additional advantage in that they generally improve application scalability. They do this by enabling clients to perform other tasks while a call is outstanding. Non-blocking operations also let clients make a series of parallel invocations, potentially reducing the amount of time required to complete a request as operations do not need to be performed serially. In addition, particularly in cases where an operation may take a long time to complete, non-blocking operations allow runtimes to hold network resources for shorter periods of time and not have to wait on a response.

To summarize, the advantages of asynchronous interactions include the following:

- They are more loosely coupled.
- They tend to be more scalable.
- Fewer network resources are held for long periods of time.

Although there is no hard-and-fast-rule, non-blocking operations should be used for remotable services when possible. To see how this is done, we will modify the `CreditService.checkCredit()` operation to be non-blocking. Calculating a credit rating may be time-consuming, and by performing this operation asynchronously, the `LoanComponent` component can continue with other tasks. In addition, BigBank may decide in the future to use multiple `CreditService` implementations that rely on different credit bureaus. Making the service asynchronous will allow the `LoanComponent` to issue multiple calls in succession without having to wait for each to complete.

Although there is no hard-and-fast-rule, non-blocking operations should be used for remotable services when possible.

Specifying a non-blocking operation using Java is straightforward: Mark a method on an interface with the `@OneWay` annotation. Listing 3.6 demonstrates a service contract with a non-blocking operation:

Specifying a non-blocking operation using Java is straight-forward: Mark a method on an interface with the `@OneWay` annotation.

Listing 3.6   *Defining a Non-Blocking Operation*

```
import org.osoa.sca.annotations.OneWay;
@Remotable
public interface CreditService {

    @OneWay
    void checkCredit(String id);
}
```

It is important to note that SCA places two restrictions on non-blocking operations. First, they must have a void return type. (We cover how to return responses using callbacks in the next section.) Non-blocking operations must also not throw exceptions.

SCA places two restrictions on non-blocking operations: They must have a void return type, and they must not throw exceptions.

Listing 3.7 shows how the `CreditService` is called from a client:

Listing 3.7   *Calling a Non-Blocking Operation*

```
public class LoanComponent implements LoanService {
    private CreditService creditService;
```

```
public void LoanComponent (@Reference CreditService service){
      this.service = service;
}

public LoanResult apply(LoanRequest request) {
      creditService.checkCredit(request.getId());
      // continue without waiting for the call to complete
      ...
}
```
}

In the previous example, when the call to `CreditService.`
`checkCredit()` is made, the runtime will return control immediately to the `LoanComponent` without waiting for the call to the
`CreditService` to complete.

Why @OneWay Instead of @NonBlocking?

You may wonder why the SCA authors chose to name the annotation that defines
non-blocking operations `@OneWay` instead of `@NonBlocking`. The reason has to do
with the vocabulary used in the world of protocol standards. Message exchange patterns, or MEPs, define the interaction pattern a protocol uses to communicate between two participants. There are two basic MEP types: **request-response** and
one-way. TCP, for example, uses the former, whereas UDP uses the latter. Because
remote service calls are ultimately sent via a protocol, the SCA authors wanted to be
precise in their terminology.

How does an SCA runtime implement non-blocking behavior? This
depends in part on whether the client and service provider are co-
located or hosted in different processes. For a local call (that is,
between a co-located client and provider), the runtime will execute
the invocation on a different thread. If the call is remote, the runtime will ensure that the underlying communications infrastructure
uses asynchronous (one-way) delivery. This can be trivial with some
communications mechanisms such as JMS, which are inherently
asynchronous. However, it may be more involved with others that

are synchronous, such as RMI/IIOP. In these cases, the runtime may need to take extra steps (such as using a different thread) to ensure that the calls are sent in a non-blocking manner.

Reliability

One issue that often comes up with non-blocking invocations is reliability. Namely, given that the invocation is performed asynchronously and there is no return value, how does a client know if the target service successfully received the invocation? Reliable delivery is often achieved via the underlying communications channel. For example, an SCA runtime could use JMS or messaging middleware to send an invocation to a target service. As we cover at length in Chapter 7, "Wires," a client can place requirements such as reliable delivery on its communications with other services through the use of policy.

Exception Handling

Because one-way invocations return immediately without waiting for the service provider to complete processing an invocation, exceptions cannot be thrown and returned to the client. Instead, exceptions should be passed back to a client via a callback, the subject of the next section. After we have covered callbacks, we will return to a discussion on how to use them for error handling with non-blocking invocations.

Callbacks

In the previous example, we modified the `CreditService.checkCredit()` to be non-blocking. This poses a seeming problem: Because SCA requires non-blocking operations to have a `void` return type, how does the `checkCredit` operation return the credit score to a client? After all, the `CreditService` would be fairly useless if it did not return a credit rating.

SCA allows services with non-blocking operations to return responses to clients through a callback. A callback is essentially a proxy to the client given to the service provider when an invocation is made. This proxy can be used to invoke operations on the client—for example, to provide status updates or return a result. In

SCA allows services with non-blocking operations to return responses to clients through a callback.

Service providers that callback their clients are said to offer **bidirectional services**.

SCA, service providers that callback their clients are said to offer **bidirectional services**. That's because the service provider communicates with its client through a callback service. Callback services are just like regular service contracts. The only restriction SCA places on bidirectional services is that both the forward and callback service must either be remotable or local; it is not possible to mix service types.

When a client component wired to a component offering a bidirectional service is deployed, the runtime establishes two communications channels: one for the forward service and one for the callback (see Figure 3.8).

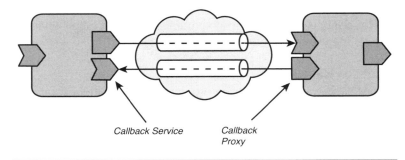

Callback Service   Callback
                          Proxy

Figure 3.8   Two communication channels are established for the forward service and a callback.

Callbacks are useful for implementing potentially long-running interactions in an efficient and scalable manner.

A callback is initiated by the service provider when it has finished processing a request or wants to update the client at a certain point in time. Callbacks are useful for implementing potentially long-running interactions in an efficient and scalable manner. A callback can be made in response to an invocation after a period of months. When used in conjunction with non-blocking operations, this allows a runtime to hold a network connection only for the time it takes to marshal the forward and callback invocations as opposed to the time spent processing.

To use a callback in Java, the service contract declares a callback interface that must be provided by the client. This is done via the `@Callback` annotation. Listing 3.8 lists the `CreditService` modified to specify a callback interface, `CreditCallback`.

Listing 3.8   *Specifying a Callback Interface*

```
import org.osoa.sca.annotations.OneWay;
import org.osoa.sca.annotations.Callback;

@Remotable
@Callback(CreditCallback.class)
public interface CreditService {

        @OneWay
        void checkCredit(String id);
}
```

The `CreditCallback` interface is defined in Listing 3.9.

Listing 3.9   *The Callback Interface*

```
@Remotable
public interface CreditCallback {

        @OneWay
        void onCreditResult(CreditScore score);
}
```

Using a callback in a component implementation is straightforward. The component uses the `@Callback` annotation to instruct the runtime to inject a proxy to the callback service. This is shown in Listing 3.10.

Listing 3.10   *Injecting and Invoking a Callback Proxy*

```
public class CreditComponent implements CreditService {

        private CreditCallback callback;

        @Callback
        public void setCallback(CreditCallback callback){
                this.callback = callback;
        }

        public void checkCredit(String id){
                // calculate credit rating and invoke the callback
                CreditResult result = //..
                callback.onCreditResult(result);
        }
}
```

Callback injection follows the same rules as reference and property injection: Public setter methods and fields, protected fields, and constructor parameters may be marked with the `@Callback` annotation.

In the composite, the `LoanComponent` and `CreditComponent` are wired as before. In other words, there is no special wiring information required for the callback. Listing 3.11 lists the composite.

Listing 3.11   *No Special Wiring Information Is Needed in a Composite for Bidirectional Services*

```
<composite …>
   <component name ="LoanComponent   ">
      <implementation.java class="com.bigbank.LoanComponent   "/>
      <reference name="creditService" target="CreditComponent "/>
   <component>

   <component name =" CreditComponent ">
      <implementation.java class="com.bigbank.CreditComponent "/>
   <component>
</composite>
```

The SCA runtime will be able to figure out from the annotations on the interface contracts that forward and callback communications channels need to be established between the `LoanComponent` and `CreditComponent`.

In the previous example, the callback interface specified only one operation, which returned the credit rating result. In many cases, a client and service provider will have a series of interactions. For example, a service provider may want to provide status updates to a client. Or the service provider may notify a client of different results for different forward operations. To do so, the callback interface may define multiple operations. For example, the `CreditCallback` could define a callback operation for status updates. As with regular services, callback services can be invoked multiple times.

When to Use @AllowsPassByReference

Previously, we introduced the @AllowsByReference annotation, which is used to have the runtime avoid copying parameters for co-located service calls. As a rule of thumb when implementing remotable services, @AllowsByReference should be used if parameters do not need to be modified. This will generally result in performance gains when the client and service implementation are co-located.

However, you should *not* use @AllowsPassByReference on one-way methods (that is, those marked with @OneWay), because the client might modify the input objects before the service has begun processing at them. This is because control is returned immediately to the client after it has invoked a one-way operation, regardless of whether the service provider has begun to process the request. @AllowsByReference should also not be used with callbacks, because the client may modify input objects when the callback is made.

Exception Handling, Non-Blocking Operations, and Callbacks

When we discussed non-blocking operations, we mentioned that exceptions encountered by a service provider cannot be thrown back to the client because the original invocation will likely have returned prior to processing. Instead, callbacks should be used to report error conditions back to the client. This can be done by adding operations to the callback interface, as shown in Listing 3.12.

Listing 3.12   *Reporting Service Provider Errors Using a Callback*

```
@Remotable
public interface CreditCallback {

    @OneWay
    void onCreditResult(CreditScore score);

    @OneWay
    void onError(CreditScoreError error);

}
```

Instead of throwing an error, the service provider invokes the call-back, passing an error object containing information detailing the nature of the exception.

Designing Local Services

Simple SCA applications may have just a few remotable services implemented by isolated classes. However, applications of any complexity will have remotable services implemented by components that rely on multiple classes to perform their task. One implementation strategy is for a component to directly instantiate the classes it needs. With this approach, each component is responsible for configuring the classes it needs.

The SCA authors believed that requiring individual components to manually assemble local objects would lead to brittle, difficult-to-maintain applications. As an application increases in complexity, having components instantiate classes directly makes configuration more difficult and inhibits sharing between components. Why not apply the same assembly techniques to local objects, making them components as well?

Local services are used to assemble finer-grained components hosted in the same process.

Local services are used to assemble finer-grained components hosted in the same process. These components interact to process a request made via a remotable service, as displayed in Figure 3.9.

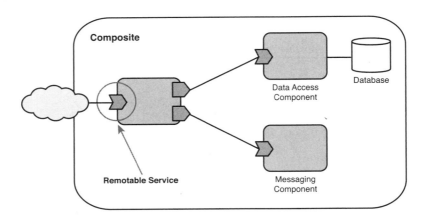

Figure 3.9   Local service assembly

Why are local services important in distributed applications? The simple answer is they enable developers to avoid having to make all services in an application remotable if they want to use the assembly capabilities of SCA.

Local services are much more performant than remotable services because they avoid network calls and having to pass parameters by value, which involves the expense of copying. (We explained pass-by-value in Chapter 2.) Local services also reduce application complexity, as clients do not need to account for service interruptions and latency when they are invoked. Perhaps most important, local services provide application-level encapsulation by enabling developers to restrict access to services that should not be exposed remote clients. Returning to our API analogy for remotable services, local services enable developers to provide cleaner interfaces by restricting access to parts of an application.

Local services should be designed using object-oriented principals instead of service-based principals. Because local services are co-located, they do not need to account for network latency or unreliability. Further, because all calls to local services are in-process, parameters are passed by-reference as opposed to by-value. (That is, no copy is made.) By dispensing with the degree of loose-coupling demanded by remotable services, application code can be greatly simplified. At the outset of the chapter, we stated SCA rejected the notion that object-oriented techniques should be applied to distributed components. In this context, it is also true that SCA rejects the notion that service-based techniques should be applied to local components.

Local services should be designed using object-oriented principals instead of service-based principals.

In contrast to remotable services, local service contracts should be fine-grained and perform very specific tasks. Finer-grained operations are generally easier for clients to use and provide more flexibility because processing can be broken down into a series of invocations. Finer-grained service contracts also tend to make applications more maintainable because components that implement them perform specific tasks. This allows applications to be organized better as discrete units. This has the added benefit of making testing easier.

In contrast to remotable services, local service contracts should be fine-grained and perform very specific tasks.

Implementing a component that offers a local service is straightforward. The implementation can be a plain Java class with no other requirements. It may have properties and references like any other component. Although not strictly required, the class should implement an interface that defines the service contract. Listing 3.13 illustrates a basic component implementation with one local service.

Listing 3.13   *A Local Service Implementation*

```
public class DataAccessComponent implements LocalDataService {

    public LoanRecord find(String id) throws DataAccessException {
        LoanRecord record = // find the record in the database
        return record;
    }

    public void save(LoanRecord record) throws DataAccessException {
        // save the LoanRecord to the database
        ...
    }

    public void delete(LoanRecord record) throws DataAccessException {
        // remove the LoanRecord from the database
        ...
    }

}
```

In a complete implementation, the class in Listing 3.13 would use a persistence technology such as JDBC or Java Persistence Architecture (JPA) to access the database. Chapter 11, "Persistence," covers persistence in detail, in particular using JDBC and JPA with SCA.

Component Scopes

Up to this point, we have discussed component life cycle only briefly. Although some applications may be composed entirely of stateless components, it is often the case that components need to preserve state across a number of requests. Components can maintain state manually—for example, by persisting it to a database. However, using a database is a fairly heavyweight solution. There are also cases where component initialization is expensive and it is appropriate to have one instance of a component handle multiple requests. To accommodate these cases, the SCA programming model allows component implementations to specify their life cycle, or **scope**. A scope defines the life cycle contract a component implementation has with the SCA runtime.

A scope defines the lifecycle contract a component implementation has with the SCA runtime.

Component Implementation Instances

In order to understand scopes, it is necessary to briefly explain how an SCA runtime dispatches a request to a component implemented in Java. Figure 3.10 illustrates how an SCA runtime forwards a request to a component.

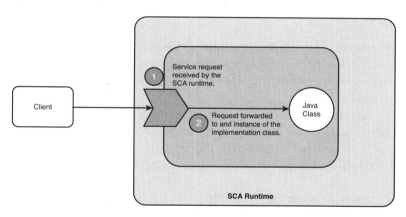

Figure 3.10   Dispatching to a component implementation instance

When a request is received, the runtime forwards the request to an instance of the component implementation.

Because an SCA runtime commonly handles multiple simultaneous requests, many instances of the component implementation class may be active at any given time. The SCA runtime is responsible for dispatching those requests to individual instances, as depicted in Figure 3.11.

Because an SCA runtime commonly handles multiple simultaneous requests, many instances of the component implementation class may be active at any given time.

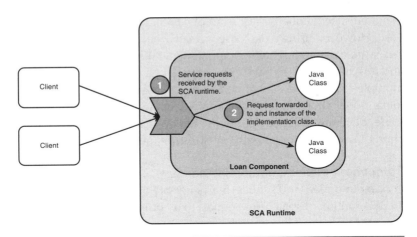

Figure 3.11   Dispatching to multiple component implementation instances

SCA defines three scopes: stateless, composite, and conversation.

Scopes are used by component implementations to instruct the SCA runtime how to dispatch requests to implementation instances. Scopes are specified using the @Scope annotation on the implementation class. Because scopes determine how requests are dispatched, they control the visibility of an implementation instance to clients. SCA defines three scopes: stateless, composite, and conversation. In this chapter, we cover the first two; conversation scope is the subject of Chapter 4, "Conversational Interactions Using Java."

Stateless-Scoped Components

For stateless components, the SCA runtime guarantees that requests are not dispatched simultaneously to the same implementation instance.

By default, components are stateless. For stateless components, the SCA runtime guarantees that requests are not dispatched simultaneously to the same implementation instance. This means that an instance will process only one request at a time. To handle simultaneous requests, an SCA runtime will instantiate a number of instances to process the requests concurrently. Further, if a client makes a series of requests to a stateless implementation, there is no guarantee that the requests will be dispatched to the same instance. (They likely will not.) Typically, a runtime will either create a new instance for every request or pull an instance from a pool.

Note that a component with a stateless scope is not necessarily devoid of state. The stateless scope means that only the SCA infrastructure will not maintain any state on the component's behalf.

The component may manage state manually through a database or some other storage mechanism, such as a cache.

Composite-Scoped Components

For components that are thread-safe and take a long time to initialize, having multiple implementation instances may result in unnecessary overhead. Sometimes only one implementation instance for a component should be active in a domain. In these cases, SCA allows implementations to be declared as composite-scoped by using the @Scope("COMPOSITE") annotation, as demonstrated in Listing 3.14.

Listing 3.14   *A Composite-Scoped Component Implementation*

```
import org.osoa.sca.annotations.Scope;

@Scope("COMPOSITE")
public class LoanComponent implements LoanService {
    // ....
    public LoanResult apply(LoanRequest request) {
        //…
    }
}
```

Composite-scoped implementations are similar to servlets: One instance in a domain concurrently handles all requests. Consequently, like servlets, composite-scoped implementations must be thread-safe. However, unlike servlets, the component implementation may store state in its fields and expect that every use of the component will have access to that state.

Composite-scoped implementations are similar to servlets: One instance in a domain concurrently handles all requests.

Officially, the lifetime of a composite-scoped instance is defined as extending from the time of its first use (that is, when the first request arrives or the component is initialized—more on this later) to the time its parent composite expires. During this period, the SCA runtime will create only one instance and route all requests to it. Note that some SCA runtimes may provide fault tolerance for composite-scoped components. In these cases, if the process hosting a composite-scoped component crashes, the runtime will guarantee that failover occurs to another process without losing data associated with the component.

Using Stateless Components

By default, components are stateless. Every invocation to a service offered by a stateless component may be dispatched by the SCA runtime to a different instance of the implementation class. In a distributed environment, stateless instances afford the domain flexibility in scaling an application. This is because state does not need to be maintained by the runtime between requests. Consequently, when a stateless component is deployed, it can be hosted in multiple runtime instances.

To understand how a component's scope affects scaling, consider the case where two components are clients to a service offered by a third component. If the two clients are deployed to separate processes, copies of the stateless service provider component may be co-located with the clients (see Figure 3.12).

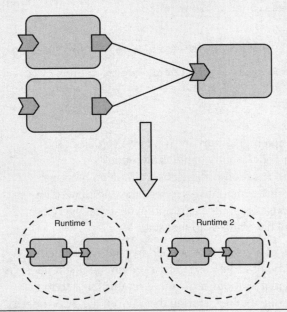

Figure 3.12 Co-locating three stateless components

Co-locating copies of the service provider component can be done because state is not managed by the runtime, allowing it to be replicated throughout the domain. This has the effect of improving application performance because requests from the two clients are not sent over the network. It also provides better fault tolerance because a failure affecting one runtime will affect only a single client.

Conversation-Scoped Components

SCA provides the ability to have the runtime manage state between a client and a component over a series of interactions known as a "conversation" by using conversation-scoped implementations. We provide an in-depth discussion of conversational services and conversation-scoped components in Chapter 4.

Initialization and Destruction Notifications

Component implementations can receive life cycle notifications by annotating public, zero-argument methods with the @Init and @Destroy annotations. A method annotated with @Init will be called by the SCA runtime when the implementation instance is created. Similarly, a method annotated with @Destroy will be called as the implementation scope expires and the component instance is released. Initialization and destruction callbacks can be used by implementations to set up and clean up resources. The following demonstrates initialization and destruction methods on a composite-scoped implementation. The initializer method will be called when the implementation instance is first created and all of its dependencies have been injected. If the class uses any setter-based or field-based injection, the constructor of the class isn't a very useful place to put initialization logic, so a method that is marked with @Init should be used. If only constructor injection is used, the constructor may also be used as the initializer.

Component implementations can receive lifecycle notifications by annotating public, zero-argument methods with the @Init and @Destroy annotations.

The component's destructor will be invoked when the parent composite is removed from the runtime, causing the component to expire (see Listing 3.15).

Listing 3.15   *Using @Init and @Destroy*

```
import org.osoa.sca.annotations.Scope;
import org.osoa.sca.annotations.Init;
import org.osoa.sca.annotations.Destroy;

@Scope("COMPOSITE")
public class CreditComponent implements CreditService {

    @Init
    public void init(){
        // perform initialization
    }
```

```
@Destroy
public void destroy(){
        // perform cleanup
    }

    // ...
}
```

Composite-scoped implementations can be set to eagerly initialize through use of the `@EagerInit` annotation.

Eager Initialization

By default, composite-scoped implementations are lazily instantiated by the SCA runtime—that is, they are instantiated as the first service request is received. In some cases, particularly when initialization is time-consuming, it is useful to perform instantiation upfront as the composite is activated in the domain. Composite-scoped implementations can be set to eagerly initialize through use of the `@EagerInit` annotation, as shown in Listing 3.16.

Listing 3.16   *An Implementation Marked to Eagerly Initialize*

```
import org.osoa.sca.annotations.Scope;
import org.osoa.sca.annotations.EagerInit;
import org.osoa.sca.annotations.Init;
import org.osoa.sca.annotations.Destroy;

@Scope("COMPOSITE")
@EagerInit
public class CreditComponent implements CreditService {

    @Init
    public void init(){
            // perform initialization
    }


    @Destroy
    public void destroy(){
            // perform cleanup
    }

    // ...
}
```

The preceding implementation will be instantiated as soon as the component is activated in the domain, prior to receiving requests. As part of the instantiation process, the `init` method will also be invoked by the SCA runtime. (The implementation could have omitted an initializer if it were not required.)

Testing Components

We conclude this chapter with a note on testing. A common question that arises when writing SCA components is how best to test them. In recent years, a wide range of testing methodologies has emerged, some of which have engendered a great deal of controversy. Choosing the right methodology, whether it is Test Driven Development (TDD) or a more traditional code-first approach, is a personal choice and depends on the requirements of a particular project. However, whatever approach to testing is adopted, SCA's reliance on inversion of control makes this process much easier.

How a programming model facilitates testing is of critical importance given the impact it has on project costs. As was learned with EJB, programming models that require complex test setup can be one of the primary impediments to developer productivity. Tests that are unnecessarily time-consuming to set up take away from development time and hinder the code-test-refactor process that is key to producing good software.

Moreover, complex setup often leads to poor test coverage, resulting in higher costs later in a project's life cycle. If tests are too complex to write and set up, developers will either avoid doing so or not be able to create ones that are fine-grained enough to exercise all parts of an application. Poor test coverage will inevitably result in more expensive bug fixing after an application has gone into production.

As an application enters maintenance mode, poor tests will continue to incur significant costs. Changes and upgrades will be difficult to verify and take longer to verify—all of which is to say that contrary to being relegated to an afterthought, testing strategy should be at the forefront of project planning. Further, the extent to which a programming model facilitates or hinders testing will have a direct impact on how successful it is in fostering productivity and cost savings.

A comprehensive and cost-effective testing strategy will include unit, integration, and functional testing. To broadly categorize, unit testing involves verifying small "units" of code, in isolation or with a few collaborating objects. In object-oriented languages, a unit of code is commonly a class, which may rely on a few other classes (collaborating objects). Unit tests are run on a developer's machine and periodically on dedicated testing servers. Integration testing involves verifying the interaction of various application "subsystems" and is therefore conducted at a coarser-grained level. Integration tests are typically run on dedicated testing servers and not part of the developer build. Functional testing entails an even broader scope, verifying application behavior based on end-user scenarios. Like integration tests, functional tests are typically run on separate testing servers.

In the days of CORBA and EJB 2.0, even unit testing typically required deploying and running the components in a container, often with complex harnesses for setting up required infrastructure. This quickly proved to be unwieldy as time-consuming testing hindered fast, iterative development. The difficulty of conducting efficient testing became one of the major drags on developer productivity with these earlier frameworks and a hidden source of significant project cost.

Having learned from this, SCA follows in the footsteps of other IoC frameworks, most notably Spring, in its approach to unit testing. By avoiding the use of APIs in all but exceptional circumstances, unit testing SCA components is trivial: Pick your favorite test harness, such as JUnit or TestNG, and instantiate them. In other words, verifying behavior is as simple as:

```
1  CreditService creditService = new
CreditComponent();
2  int result = creditService.scoreApplicant(applicantID);
3  // verify the result…
```

Unit testing becomes slightly more involved when collaborating objects are required. Take the LoanComponent from the example presented in this chapter: It requires a CreditService. One solution would be to simply instantiate a CreditComponent, as shown previously, and pass it to the LoanComponent. This, however, can quickly become unmanageable if the CreditComponent requires other services, which themselves depend on additional services, and so on.

A better solution is to introduce a "mock" for the `CreditService`. Mock objects, as they are referred to, mimic specific behavior of real objects and generally have trivial implementations. A mock `CreditService` implementation, for example, would always return a good or bad score. Mocks are manually set on component implementations by the unit test. Components then call mocks as if they were reference proxies to real service providers.

Mock Objects and EasyMock

Writing mock objects by hand can be tedious, particularly if only one method is required for a particular test case. Several mock object generation frameworks have emerged that automate much of this process. We recommend EasyMock (http://www.easymock.org) for testing SCA components. The following example demonstrates testing the `LoanComponent` using a mock `CreditService`:

```
1   CreditScoreService creditService =
    EasyMock.createMock(CreditService.class);
2   EasyMock.expect(creditService.scoreApplicant
    (EasyMock.isA(String.class))).andReturn(700);
3   EasyMock.replay(creditService);
4   LoanService loanService = new LoanComponent(creditService);
5   // test the loanService…
```

EasyMock works by first creating a mock, recording behavior (that is, the methods that will be called on it, including parameter and return values), and setting the mock into replay state before using it. In the previous example:

```
CreditService creditService = EasyMock.createMock
➡(CreditService.class);
```

creates the mock service. The expected behavior, a call to the `CreditService.scoreApplicant()` with a return value of `700`, is then recorded:

```
EasyMock.expect(creditService.scoreApplicant
➡(EasyMock.isA(String.class))).andReturn(700);
```

Finally, the mock service is placed in replay state:

```
EasyMock.replay(creditService);
```

after which it can be passed to the `LoanComponent` and invoked like the actual `CreditService` implementation. At the end of the test run, the unit test can verify that the mock service has been properly called by through the `verify` operation:

```
EasyMock.verify(creditService);
```

The efficiencies of using mocks with SCA are most evident when dealing with remotable services. When deployed to production, the `LoanComponent` and `CreditComponent` could be hosted on separate JVMs, where the SCA runtime would handle setting up the appropriate remote communications infrastructure (for example, web services). In a unit test environment, on a developer machine, deploying these components to separate containers and setting up remote communications is cumbersome. It is also unnecessary: The goal of unit testing the `LoanComponent` should be to ensure that it functions properly according to business requirements, not that it can communicate over a remote protocol to the `CreditService`. (The latter would be a goal of integration testing, which verifies that parts of a system work together.)

Investing upfront in a good testing strategy reduces overall project costs. Building on the lessons learned with CORBA and EJB, SCA was designed to facilitate efficient testing, particularly at the unit test level. When unit testing SCA components, keep three things in mind. First, don't use a container; instantiate component implementation directly in the test case. Second, use mocks to test component implementations in isolation. And if you cannot do one and two easily, refactor your component implementation because it is generally a sign of bad design.

Summary

This chapter covered the basics of developing loosely coupled services using the SCA Java programming model. These included service contract design, asynchronous communications, and component life cycle. Many of these features—particularly asynchronous communications—have their antecedents in integration and messaging software. The SCA Java programming model provides an arguably more unified and simpler approach to distributed applications than its predecessors. In the next chapter, we extend this discussion to creating conversational services using the Java programming model.

4

Conversational Interactions Using Java

The last two chapters covered service-based development using the SCA Java programming model. Putting this into practice in Chapter 3, "Service-Based Development Using Java," we refactored the BigBank loan application to reflect SCA best practices by taking advantage of loose coupling and asynchronous interactions. In this chapter, we continue our coverage of the Java programming model, focusing on building conversational services.

Conversational Interactions

Services in distributed applications are often designed to be stateless. In stateless architectures, the runtime does not maintain state on behalf of a client between operations. Rather, contextual information needed by the service to process a request is passed as part of the invocation parameters. This information may be used by the service to access additional information required to process a request in a database or backend system. In the previous chapters, the BigBank application was designed with stateless services: `LoanService` or `CreditService` use a loan ID as a key to manually store and retrieve loan application data for processing.

There are, however, many distributed applications that are designed around stateful services or could benefit from stateful services, as they are easier to write and require less code than stateless designs. Perhaps the most common example of such a distributed stateful application is a Java EE-based web application that enables users to log in and perform operations. The operations—such as filling a shopping cart and making a purchase—involve a client and server code (typically servlets and JSPs) sharing contextual information via an HTTP session. If a web application had to manage state manually, as opposed to relying on the session facilities provided by the servlet container, the amount of code and associated complexity would increase.

SCA provides a number of facilities for creating stateful application archi-tectures.

SCA provides a number of facilities for creating stateful application architectures. In this chapter, we explore how the SCA Java programming model can be used to have the runtime manage and correlate state so that service implementations do not need to do so in code. Chapter 10, "Service-Based Development Using BPEL" covers how to write conversational services using BPEL.

▪ Perspective: Conversations and OASIS

The conversational capabilities discussed in this chapter and throughout the book were defined when SCA was part of the OSOA collaboration and incorporated in the OASIS 1.0 SCA specifications. While working on the OASIS 1.1 SCA specifications, several vendors objected to conversations, claiming they were overly complex and difficult to implement. We, and others, countered on grounds that conversational capabilities were a powerful feature and being used extensively in a number of large-scale systems.

Unfortunately, these arguments failed to persuade the vendors who objected. As a result, conversational capabilities were deferred from the 1.1 OASIS version of the SCA specifications to a subsequent version.

Fabric3, and possibly other runtimes, will continue to support conversations. However, as they are not yet part of the latest OASIS standard, there is a risk that conversations will remain a proprietary feature of specific SCA runtimes.

Hopefully, popular support will influence a future version of the OASIS SCA specifications to accept conversations as an official feature. Until that time, as with all such proprietary features, there is a trade-off that must be assessed between ease-of-use and power versus potentially being locked into a specific runtime.

A Conversation

In SCA, a conversation is defined as a shared context between a client and service. For example, the interactions between `LoanComponent` and `CreditService` could be modeled as conversational, as shown in Figure 4.1.

In SCA, a conversation is defined as a shared context between a client and service.

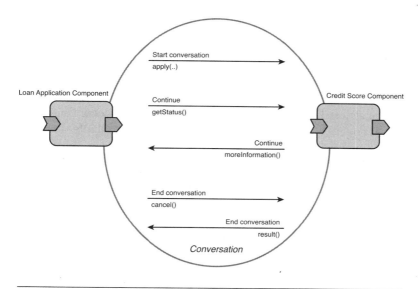

Figure 4.1   A conversational interaction

The conversation shown in Figure 4.1 has a start operation (`LoanComponent` requests a credit check), a series of continuing operations (get status and request for more information), and two end operations (cancel or result).

Conversations in SCA have a number of unique characteristics. First, in line with loosely coupled interactions, conversations may last for a brief period of time (for example, milliseconds) or for a long duration (for example, months). A second characteristic is that conversations involve shared state between two parties: a client and a service. In the previous example, the shared context is the loan applicant information.

The main difference between conversational and stateless interactions is that the latter automatically generate and pass contextual information for the conversation as part of the messages sent between the client and service (typically as message headers). With conversational interactions, the client does not need to generate the context information, and neither the client nor the service needs to "remember" or track this information and send it with each operation invocation. Runtimes support this by passing a *conversation ID*, which is used to correlate contextual information such as the loan applicant information. This is similar to a session ID in Java EE web applications, which is passed between a browser and a servlet container to correlate session information.

An application may be composed of multiple conversational services. How is conversational context shared between clients and service providers? Before delving into the details of implementing conversational services, we first need to consider how conversational contexts are created and propagated among multiple services.

In Figure 4.2, Component A acts as a client to the conversational service offered by Component B, creating a shared conversation context. As long as the conversation is active, for each invocation A makes to the service offered by B, a single conversational context is in effect.

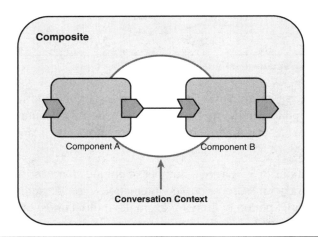

Figure 4.2   A conversation visualized

Because a conversation is between a client and a single service, if Component A invokes a conversational service offered by a third component, C, a separate conversational context is created, as shown in Figure 4.3.

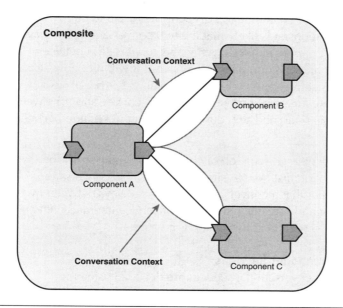

Figure 4.3   Multiple conversations

It is important to note that conversational context is not propagated across multiple invocations. If Component A invoked a conversational service on B, which in turn invoked another conversational service on C, two conversations would be created, as shown in Figure 4.4.

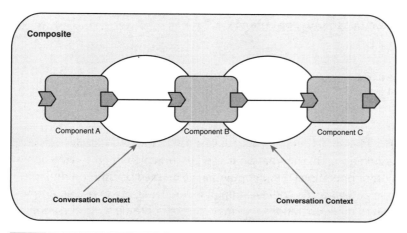

Figure 4.4   Conversations are not propagated across multiple invocations.

In this situation, although SCA considers there to be two different conversations, it is likely that the two conversations will have closely coupled lifetimes. When the conversation between Components B and C is complete, Component B will probably also complete its conversation with A. However, this is not always the case, and there are situations where multiple conversations between B and C will start and stop during a single conversation between A and B.

A simple way to grasp conversations is to remember that a conversation in SCA is always between two parties (a client and service).

The preceding discussion of conversations may seem somewhat complex on first read. A simple way to grasp conversations is to remember that a conversation in SCA is always between two parties (a client and service). If the client or service interacts with another service, a second conversation is created.

Conversational Services

In Java, conversational services are declared using the `@Conversational` on an interface, as shown in Listing 4.1.

Listing 4.1   *A Conversational Service*

```
import org.osoa.sca.annotations.Remotable;
import org.osoa.sca.annotations.EndsConversation;
import org.osoa.sca.annotations.Conversational;


@Remotable
@Conversational
public interface CreditService   {
      void apply(LoanApplicant applicant);

      int getStatus();

      @EndsConversation
      void cancel();

}
```

The preceding interface also makes use of the `@EndsConversation` annotation. This annotation is used to indicate which service operation or operations (`@EndsConversation` may be used on multiple operations) end a conversation. It is not necessary to use an annotation to mark operations that may start or continue a conversation, because any operation on a conversational interface will continue an existing conversation, if one is underway, or start a conversation if one is not.

In the previous listing, `CreditService.apply(..)` is intended to be used for initiating a conversation, whereas `CreditService.getStatus()` and `CreditService.cancel()` are intended to be used for already existing conversations (applications in process). The `cancel()` will also end the conversation. After an operation marked with `@EndsConversation` is invoked and completes processing, conversational resources such as the shared context may be cleaned up and removed. A subsequent invocation of another operation will result in a new conversation being started.

The fact that the `getStatus()` and `cancel()` operations have to be used only for existing conversations is not captured by an annotation, so it should be noted in the documentation on those methods. It is up to the application code for those operations to generate an exception if they are used to start a conversation.

SCA doesn't define annotations for starting or continuing conversations because they are really just a special case for more complex rules regarding which operations should be called before which other operations. For example, if the loan application service were more complicated and it included an operation for locking in an interest rate, that operation would only be legal during certain phases of the application process. This kind of error needs to be checked by the application code. SCA only includes the `@EndsConversation` annotation because the infrastructure itself needs to know when the conversation has ended, so that it can free up the resources that were associated with the conversation.

Implementing Conversational Services

Having covered the key aspects of defining a conversational service, we now turn to implementing one. When writing a conversational service implementation, the first decision that needs to be made is how conversational state is maintained. In SCA, developers have two options: They can use the state management features provided as part of SCA, or they can write custom code as part of the implementation.

Conversation-Scoped Implementations

Developers can have the SCA runtime manage conversational state by declaring an implementation as conversation-scoped. This works the same way as other scopes—that is, via the use of the `@Scope("CONVERSATION")` annotation, as in the extract shown in Listing 4.2.

Listing 4.2   *A Conversation-Scoped Implementation*

```
import org.osoa.sca.annotations.Scope;
@Scope("CONVERSATION")
public class CreditComponent implements CreditService {
    //…
}
```

Because conversations exist over multiple service invocations, the runtime will dispatch to the same instance as long as the conversation remains active.

Conversation-scoped implementations work just like other scopes. As discussed in Chapter 3, the SCA runtime is responsible for dispatching to the correct instance based on the client making the request. Because conversations exist over multiple service invocations, the runtime will dispatch to the same instance as long as the conversation remains active. If multiple clients invoke a conversational service, the requests will be dispatched to multiple implementation instances, as illustrated in Figure 4.5.

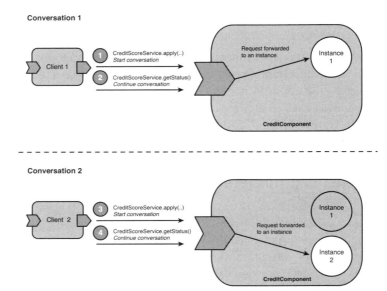

Figure 4.5   Runtime dispatching to conversation-scoped instances

Note that by default, a component implementation is considered conversation-scoped if it implements a conversational interface. That is, if a service contract is annotated with @Conversational, the component implementation class does not need to specify @Scope("CONVERSATION").

Because the runtime handles dispatching to the correct implementation instance are based on the current conversation, conversation state can be stored in member variables on the component implementation. This allows service contracts to avoid having to pass contextual data as part of the operation parameters. A modified version of CreditComponent demonstrates the use of conversational state (see Listing 4.3).

Listing 4.3   *Storing Conversational State in Instance Variables*

```
import org.osoa.sca.annotations.Scope;
@Scope("CONVERSATION")
public class CreditComponent implements CreditService {

    private LoanApplicant applicant;
    private int status;

     public void apply(LoanApplicant applicant){
          this.applicant = applicant;
     }

     int getStatus() {
          return status;
     }

    void cancel() {
          String id = applicant.getId();
          // cancel the request based on the applicant id for the
    ➥conversation ….
     }

}
```

In this implementation of CreditComponent, the applicant and status variables are associated with the current conversation and will be available as long as the conversation remains active.

In loosely coupled systems, interactions between clients and conversational services may occur over longer periods of time, perhaps months. Although SCA says nothing about how conversational instances are maintained, some SCA runtimes may choose to persist instances to disk or some other form of storage (for example, a database). Persistence may be done to free memory and, more importantly, provide reliability for conversational services; information stored in memory may be lost if a hardware failure occurs. Some runtimes may also allow conversational persistence to be configured—for example, disabling it when reliability is not required. As demonstrated in the previous example, however, how conversational state is stored is transparent from the perspective of application code. The developer needs to be aware that only Java serialization and deserialization may occur between operations of the component.

■ Practical Considerations for Conversation-Scoped Components

When planning to use conversational services, be sure to give special consideration to the performance and application migration implications these services entail. Reliable persistence of conversational state may introduce a significant performance penalty, as state changes must be recorded—for example, to the file system or a database. Does a particular conversational service really need to be reliable? Is the potential for occasional data loss tolerable? If so, you might be able to configure your SCA runtime to use less reliable—and more performant—means for storing conversational state (for example, in memory).

A second factor to consider is migration. Storing state means that you will need to handle migration issues in future versions of an application. If the type of state changes, existing stored state will need to be converted. Otherwise, a strategy for maintaining two versions of a service until the older state expires will need to be devised. Maintaining coexisting services is not a trivial task. Therefore, it is wise to plan for future migration and versioning upfront when using conversational services.

Custom State Management

In some situations, implementations may elect to manage state as opposed to relying on the SCA runtime. This is often done for performance reasons or because the conversational state must be persisted in a particular way. Implementations that manage their own state must correlate the current conversation ID with any conversation state. This will usually involve obtaining the conversation ID and performing a lookup of the conversational state based on that ID.

In this scenario, the conversation ID is still system-generated, and it is passed in a message header rather than as a parameter (using whatever approach to headers is appropriate for the binding being used). Because of this, the interface is still considered to be conversational. The fact that the conversational state is explicitly retrieved through application logic, rather than automatically maintained by the infrastructure, is an implementation detail that does not need to be visible to the client of the service. The fact that it is conversational, however, is still visible, because the client needs to know that a sequence of operations will be correlated to each other without being based on any information from the messages.

The current conversation ID can be obtained through injection via the @ConversationID annotation. The following version of the CreditComponent uses the conversation ID to manually store state using a special ConversationalStorageService. The latter could store the information in memory using a simple map or persistently using a database (see Listing 4.4).

Listing 4.4   *Manually Maintaining Conversational State*

```
import org.osoa.sca.annotations.Scope;
public class CreditComponent implements CreditService {
    private ConversationalStorageService storageService;
    private String conversationID;

    public CreditComponent(@Reference (name="storageService")
service){
        this.storageService = storageService;
    }

    @ConversationID
    public void setConversationID(String id){
        this.conversationID = id;
    }

    public void apply(LoanApplicant applicant){
        storageService.storeApplicant(conversationID, applicant);
    }

    int getStatus() {
```

```
            return storageService.getStatus(conversationID);
    }

    void cancel() {
    storageService.removeApplicant(conversationID);
    }

}
```

Similar to other injectable SCA-related information, the
@ConversationID annotation may be used on public and protected fields or setter methods.

Expiring Conversations

In loosely coupled systems, conversational services cannot rely on
clients to be well behaved and call an operation marked with
@EndsConversation to signal that conversational resources can be
released. Clients can fail or a network interruption could block an
invocation from reaching its target service. To handle these scenarios, SCA provides mechanisms for expiring a conversation using
the @ConversationAttributes annotation. @Conversation
Attributes is placed on a Java class and can be used to specify a
maximum idle time and maximum age of a conversation. The
maxIdleTime of a conversation defines the maximum time that can
pass between operation invocations within a single conversation.
The maxAge of a conversation denotes the maximum time a conversation can remain active. If the container is managing conversational state, it may free resources, including removing
implementation instances, associated with an expired conversation.
In the example shown in Listing 4.5, the maxIdleTime between
invocations in the same conversation is set to 30 days.

Listing 4.5   *Setting Conversation Expiration Based on Idle Time*

```
import org.osoa.sca.annotations.ConversationAttributes;

@ConversationAttributes(maxIdleTime="30 days")

public class CreditComponent implements CreditService {
    //....

}
```

Similarly, the example in Listing 4.6 demonstrates setting the `maxAge` of a conversation to 30 days.

Listing 4.6   *Setting Conversation Expiration Based on Duration*

```
import org.osoa.sca.annotations.ConversationAttributes;

@ConversationAttributes(maxAge="30 days")

public class CreditComponent implements CreditService {
    //....

}
```

The `@ConversationAttributes` annotation allows `maxAge` and `maxIdleTime` to be specified in seconds, minutes, hours, days, or years. The value of the attribute is an integer followed by the scale, as in "15 minutes."

Conversational Services and Asynchronous Interactions

Conversational services can be used in conjunction with non-blocking operations and callbacks to create loosely coupled interactions that share state between the client and service provider.

Non-Blocking Invocations

Operations can be made non-blocking on a conversational service using the `@OneWay` annotation discussed in Chapter 3 (see Listing 4.7).

Conversational services can be used in conjunction with non-blocking operations and callbacks to create loosely coupled interactions that share state between the client and service provider.

Listing 4.7   *Using Conversations with Non-Blocking Operations*

```
import org.osoa.sca.annotations.Remotable;
import org.osoa.sca.annotations.EndsConversation;
import org.osoa.sca.annotations.Conversational;
import org.osoa.sca.annotations.OneWay;


@Remotable
@Conversational
public interface CreditService  {

    @OneWay
    void apply(LoanApplicant applicant);
```

```
    int getStatus();

    @OneWay
    @EndsConversation
    void cancel();

}
```

Without the @OneWay annotation, the client developer knows if the operation returns without throwing an exception.

The preceding example makes the `CreditService.apply(..)` and `CreditService.cancel()` operations non-blocking, where control is returned immediately to the client, even before the operation request has been sent to the service provider. This is different from just having the operation return void without having been marked with the `@OneWay` annotation. Without the `@OneWay` annotation, the client doesn't regain control until the operation completes, so the client developer knows that if the operation returns without throwing an exception, the operation has successfully completed.

By contrast, a `@OneWay` operation may not be started until well after the client program has moved well beyond the place where the operation had been called. This means that the client cannot assume that the operation has successfully completed, or even that the operation request has been able to reach the service provider. Often, in this scenario, it will be advisable to require reliable delivery of the message so that the request is not lost merely because the client or the service provider crashes at an inopportune time. Reliable delivery can be guaranteed by using SCA's policy intent mechanism. In this case, the annotation would be `@Requires` `("ExactlyOnce")`. This will constrain the deployer to configure the runtime to use some form of reliable delivery. Policy intents are described in more detail in Chapter 6, "Policy."

Using reliable delivery will not, however, help with the fact that the client code can't see exceptions that are raised by the `@OneWay` operation. When developing these operations, if an error is discovered in the way the client has invoked the service (an invalid parameter, for example), the error must be sent back to the client through the callback interface, which is described in the next section.

Note that the `CreditComponent` implementation does not need to change; if the implementation is conversation-scoped, the SCA runtime will continue to manage state, even if the invocation is made in an asynchronous manner.

Callbacks

In addition to non-blocking operations, conversational services may also be used in conjunction with callbacks. Like operations on `CreditService`, callback operations can be annotated with `@EndsConversation`. Invoking a callback method marked with `@EndsConversation` will end the current conversation started by the client. Listing 4.8 shows the `CreditServiceCallback` interface.

In addition to non-blocking operations, conversational services may also be used in conjunction with callbacks.

Listing 4.8   *Using Conversations with Callbacks*

```
import org.osoa.sca.annotations.Remotable;
import org.osoa.sca.annotations.EndsConversation;
import org.osoa.sca.annotations.Conversational;
import org.osoa.sca.annotations.OneWay;


@Remotable
@Conversational
public interface CreditServiceCallback  {

    EmploymentHistory requestMoreInformation();

    @OneWay
    @EndsConversation
    void creditResult(CreditResult result);


}
```

Accessing the callback from the `CreditComponent` is no different than accessing it from a stateless implementation (see Listing 4.9).

Listing 4.9   *Accessing a Callback During a Conversation*

```
import org.osoa.sca.annotations.Scope;
@Scope("CONVERSATION")
public class CreditComponent implements CreditService {
    //...
    private CreditServiceCallback callback;

    @Callback
```

```
public setCallback(CreditServiceCallback callback) {
    this.callback = callback;
}

void apply(LoanApplicant applicant) {
    // do some processing…
    CreditResult result = //....
    callback.creditResult(result);
}

}
```

Callbacks to Conversational and Stateless Clients

Perhaps the most common conversational interaction pattern involving callbacks is when both the client and service provider are conversation-scoped.

Perhaps the most common conversational interaction pattern involving callbacks is when both the client and service provider are conversation-scoped. In this case, callbacks from the service provider will be dispatched to the originating client instance. This allows clients and service providers to avoid passing context information as service parameters. The `CreditComponent` in the previous listing was written with the assumption that the client is conversational. When `CreditServiceCallback` is called, only the credit score result is passed back and not the entire loan application. Because the `LoanComponent` is conversation-scoped, it can maintain a pointer to the loan application in an instance variable prior to making the original credit score request and access it when the callback is received.

It is possible to have a stateless client and conversational service provider.

Although conversation-scoped clients and service providers are likely to be the norm when callbacks are used in conversational interactions, it is possible to have a stateless client and conversational service provider. We conclude this section with a brief discussion of this scenario.

In Figure 4.6, if the original `LoanComponent` client were stateless, the callback invocation would most likely be dispatched by the runtime to a different instance. Figure 4.6 illustrates how callbacks are dispatched when the client is stateless.

The advantage to using stateless clients is that the runtime can perform a callback optimization.

The advantage to using stateless clients is that the runtime can perform a callback optimization. Because a callback to a stateless client does not have to be dispatched to the same client `instance` that originated the forward invocation, the runtime can route the callback to an instance co-located with the service provider. Figure 4.7 depicts how this optimization is performed.

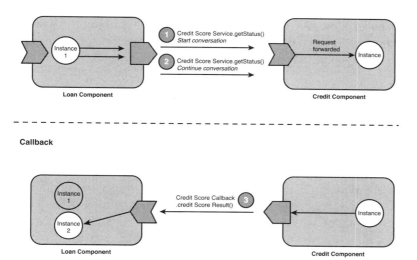

Forward Invocation

Callback

Figure 4.6   Callback dispatching to a stateless client

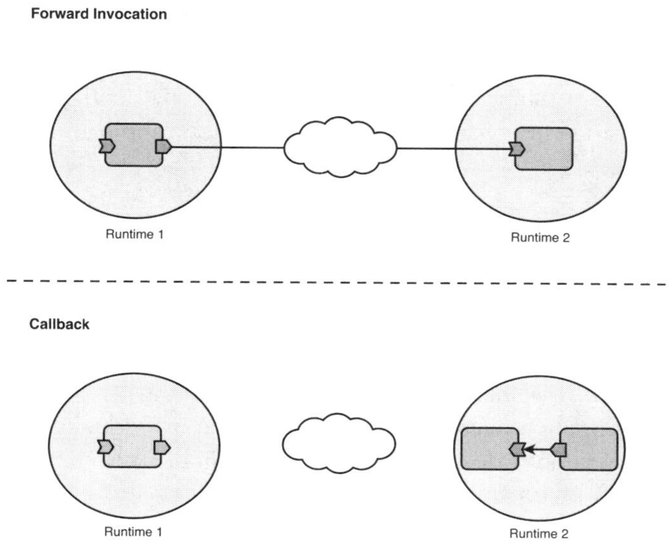

Forward Invocation

Runtime 1

Runtime 2

Callback

Runtime 1

Runtime 2

Figure 4.7   Routing a callback to a co-located stateless client

Conversation Propagation

*Fabric3 provides the capability to **propagate** transactions to other services.*

In SCA, conversations are between two parties: a client and service provider. However, there are situations where it is useful to allow other services to participate in a conversation. Fabric3 provides the capability to **propagate** transactions to other services.

▦ Conversation Propagation and SCA

Although not officially standardized as part of the SCA specifications, the Fabric3 developers felt it important to add conversation propagation as a proprietary feature. The feature was originally based on a user requirement to share context information across multiple services. With the standard SCA conversation mechanisms, the only way to share context information was either to pass it explicitly to other services or have a single service that performed multiple tasks. The first option was ruled out due to the complexity placed on application code. The second would violate the principle of separation of concerns, where services should be designed to perform a single, specific task.

Conversation propagation provided a solution to this problem and was raised as an enhancement request to the SCA specification working group. Unfortunately, it was rejected as "too complicated." Whether the feature is too complicated for end users or vendors to implement in their runtimes, we will leave open for judgment. The upshot is that if you plan on using conversation propagation in your application, be aware that it is specific to Fabric3.

Figure 4.8 shows a conversation initiated by an interaction between Components A and B propagated to C.

When the conversation is propagated, all requests from A to B and B to C will be dispatched to the same component instances. Conversational propagation can be enabled on individual components (for example, on Components A and B in the preceding example) or on an entire composite. For simplicity, it is recommended that conversation propagation be enabled on a per-composite basis. This is done using the `requires` attribute in a composite file (see Listing 4.10).

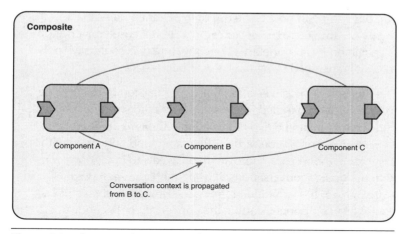

Figure 4.8   Conversation propagation

Listing 4.10 *Setting Conversation Propagation for a Composite*

```
<composite xmlns="http://www.osoa.org/xmlns/sca/1.0"
           xmlns:f3="http://fabric3.org/xmlns/
sca/1.0"
           name="ConversationPropagationComposite"
           requires="f3:propagatesConversation">

    <component name="A">
          <!-- … -->
    </component>

    <component name="B">
          <!-- … -->
    </component>

    <component name="C">
          <!-- … -->
    </component>

</composite>
```

We haven't yet discussed what the `requires` attribute is, and it may seem a bit strange that it is used instead of setting an attribute named `propagatesConversation` to true. In SCA, the `requires` attribute is the way to declare a policy—in this case, for a composite. We will cover policy in Chapter 6, but for now think of the `requires` tag as a way to declare that for all components in the composite, conversation propagation is required to be in effect.

The other thing to note is the use of the Fabric3 namespace, `http://fabric3.org/xmlns/sca/1.0`. Because conversation propagation is a proprietary Fabric3 feature (we could say "policy"), it is specified using the Fabric3 namespace.

@EndsConversation should generally only be used on services initiating a conversation.

The lifecycle of a conversation that is propagated to multiple participant services is handled in the same way as a two-party conversation. That is, it can be expired using the `@Conversation Attributes` annotation or by calling a method annotated with `@EndsConversation`. There are two caveats to note, however, with multiparty conversations. If using the `@Conversation Attributes`, the expiration time is determined by the values set on the first component starting the conversation. Second, `@EndsConversation` should be used only on services initiating a conversation. In our A-B-C example, `@EndsConversation` should be specified on the service contract for A, or a callback interface implemented by A. Otherwise, if a conversation is ended on B or C and there is a callback to A, a conversation expiration error will be raised.

To conclude our discussion of conversation propagation, it is worth briefly taking into account the diamond problem. The diamond problem is when interactions among four or more components form a "diamond." For example, Figure 4.9 illustrates A invoking B and C, which in turn invoke D.

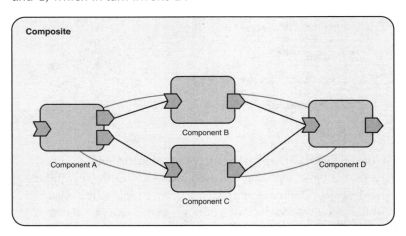

Figure 4.9   The diamond problem

As shown in Figure 4.9, if conversation propagation is enabled for the composite, when B and C invoke D, they will dispatch to the same instance of D. Similarly, if D invoked callbacks to B and C, which in turn invoked a callback to A, the same instance of A would be called. Finally, if the callback from C to A ended the conversation, conversational resources held by the runtime for A, B, C, and D would be cleaned up.

Summary

In this chapter, we covered designing and implementing conversational services. The conversational capabilities provided by SCA simplify application code by removing the need to pass context information as service operation parameters and manually manage state in component implementations. Having concluded the majority of our discussion of the SCA Java programming model, in Chapter 5, "Composition," we return to assembling composites and in particular deal with how to architect application modularity through the SCA concept of "composition."

5

Composition

The last two chapters focused on the SCA programming model; in this chapter, we take a closer look at how applications are assembled using composites. Here we introduce another key concept, *composition*. In short, composition is the capability to build larger components and services from a series of smaller ones. The power of composition is that it provides a mechanism for more easily maintaining and evolving applications over time by making them more modular. With composition, sets of services encompassing various functional areas of an application can be more easily reused, upgraded, replaced, and changed. After working through this chapter, you will have a solid foundation in how composites are used to achieve a modular application design.

Composition is the capability to build larger components and services from a series of smaller ones.

Composition

Most modern programming languages and models support some form of encapsulation. That is, they have constructs for breaking down parts and isolating them from one another. Modern programming languages and models also have mechanisms for reuse. Object-oriented languages are often designed around interfaces and classes, which serve both functions. SCA has services and components.

Up to this point, we have discussed how services and components provide reuse and encapsulation in several ways. First, services provide a way for multiple clients to address and invoke a unit of code contained in a component. Services also provide encapsulation as they hide implementation details from clients. Component implementations may be reused multiple times, potentially with different property values and wiring.

For many applications, this level of reuse and encapsulation is sufficient. However, as an application becomes more complex and the number of components grows, the need may arise to encapsulate sets of components that expose a few services. A credit appraisal process may be composed of multiple components but needs to expose only one service to its clients. Here, the fact that the credit appraisal process is handled by multiple components is an implementation detail; in the future, these "internal" components and their wiring may change.

In addition, as system complexity grows, the need may arise to reuse not just single components, but sets of components. Perhaps a group of components together perform an operation such as validating and persisting an employee record to a database. It would be beneficial to reuse this set of components as a single unit across a number of disparate applications, hiding the details of the components from clients. It would also be useful if there were facilities for making slight configuration changes to the components as a whole, rather than modifying the individual components.

To handle these cases—encapsulation and reuse of multiple, related components—SCA supports composition, or the capability to assemble larger components from smaller ones. SCA does this in a very simple but powerful way. Consider the visual representation of encapsulation shown in Figure 5.1.

The composite contains four components, three of which interact to provide a service to the fourth. A component that performs credit scoring may use data validation and auditing components. These details should be hidden from clients using the credit-scoring service. A solution to this problem would be to allow components to be composed from other components like building blocks. We can modify the previous diagram to include this "composite" component, as illustrated in Figure 5.2.

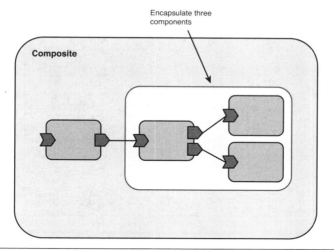

Figure 5.1   Encapsulating three components

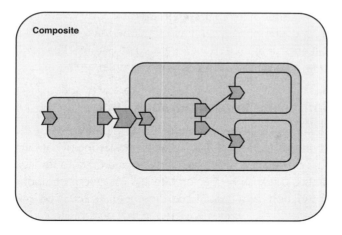

Figure 5.2 A composite component

The composite component encapsulates the three components and their wires by exposing a single service to clients. SCA takes this a step further and makes the composite itself a type of component. In other words, composites are a component implementation type just like Java, BPEL, or C++. Our earlier diagram can now be represented as a series of nested components (see Figure 5.3).

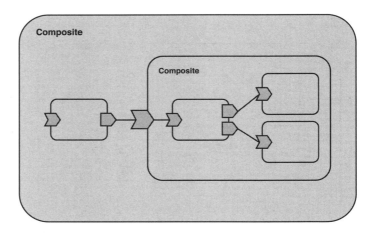

Figure 5.3 Nested composite components

Because composites are just a particular type of component, they can also be reused like other components. As we explain in the next sections, composites can have services, references, and properties that are configured in their parent composite. We now look at how to use a composite as a component implementation.

The Composite Implementation Type

Suppose the previous credit-scoring function performed by the loan application involved a multistep process consisting of data validation, score calculation, and producing an audit record for legal compliance. This may best be architected using four components: one that functions as a central coordinator (the `CreditComponent`) and delegates to the other services; one that performs data validation (the `ValidationComponent`); one that serves as a scoring engine (the `ScoringComponent`); and one that writes audit messages to a log (the `AuditingComponent`). `CreditService Composite`, shown in Listing 5.1, assembles these four components.

Because composites are just a particular type of component, they can also be reused like other components. Composites can have services, references, and properties that are configured in their parent composite.

Listing 5.1   The `Credit Service Composite`

```
<composite xmlns="http://www.osoa.org/xmlns/sca/1.0"
   targetNamespace="http://www.bigbank.com/xmlns/ loanApplication/1.0"
   name=" CreditServiceComposite">

   <component name ="CreditComponent">
      <implementation.java class="com.bigbank.CreditComponent"/>
      <reference name="validationService"
target="ValidationComponent"/>
      <reference name="scoringService" target="ScoringComponent"/>

      <reference name="auditService" target="AuditingComponent"/>
   <component>

   <component name ="ValidationComponent">
      <implementation.java class="com.bigbank.ValidationComponent"/>
   <component>

   <component name ="ScoringComponent">
      <implementation.java class="com.bigbank.ScoringComponent"/>
   <component>

   <component name ="AuditingComponent">
      <implementation.java class="com.bigbank.AuditingComponent"/>
   <component>

</composite>
```

We could have chosen to include these four components in the original `LoanApplication` composite. However, as the application grows, that strategy will likely result in a brittle and difficult-to-maintain system. In the future, all or part of the credit-scoring components may need to be changed. In addition, configuring all components in one composite is likely to result in a very unstructured application that is difficult to decipher (not to mention developers stepping on one another as they modify parts of the single composite).

Instead, good design suggests that we encapsulate the credit-scoring function in a composite, which is then used as a component by the `LoanApplication` composite. Figure 5.4 depicts this visually.

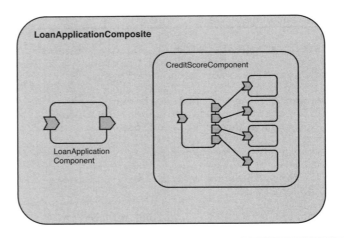

Figure 5.4   Encapsulating the credit-scoring process

The SCDL in Listing 5.2 configures `LoanComponent` and
`CreditComponent`.

Listing 5.2   *The Credit Score Composite SCDL*

```
<composite … name="LoanApplication">
   <component name ="LoanComponent">
      <implementation.java class="com.bigbank.LoanComponent"/>
   <component>

   <component name ="CreditComponent">
      <implementation.composite name="loan:CreditServiceComposite"/>
   <component>

</composite>
```

The key part of the preceding SCDL is the use of the
`<implementation.composite>` element. This instructs the
SCA runtime to use a composite as the component implementation,
just as if we had specified `<implementation.java>` or
`<implementation.bpel>`. However, instead of referencing the
class name, we refer to the fully qualified name of the composite
using the "name" attribute. The fully qualified name, or QName,
consists of the target namespace and name of the composite. This
is equivalent to specifying the package and class name for Java
implementation types.

Composite Qualified Names

It is worth highlighting one of the subtleties associated with using composite qualified names for `<implementation.composite>`. Namely, the QName does not need to correspond to a particular file location or composite filename. The QName is only a logical name. The `CreditComposite` could be defined in a file named `CreditComposite.composite` located in the `META-INF` directory of a jar contribution. (Recalling from Chapter 2, "Assembling and Deploying a Composite," composites are packaged into contribution archives for deployment.) Or the composite could be located in some other directory or defined in a file named `credit.composite`.

Regardless of the filename or location, the SCA runtime is responsible for mapping the QName specified in `<implementation.composite>` to the actual composite SCDL. This makes assembly less susceptible to breaking during refactoring. The filename or location could change, and the assembly would continue to work. All that is required is that the QName must uniquely identify one composite within the contribution.

In addition, as we mentioned in Chapter 2 and will discuss in more detail in Chapter 9, "The Domain," composites may be reused from other contributions. By referring to composites using their QName, the client or importing contribution need not be aware of the internal structure of the contribution providing or exporting the composite.

Service Promotion

The next step in encapsulating the credit-scoring process is to expose the `CreditService` from the `CreditComposite`. Exposing— or as SCA terms it, promoting—a service in a composite serves two purposes. It allows other references from outside the composite to be wired to it. It also provides a mechanism for the service to be configured by the composite using it as an implementation. We discuss each of these in turn.

Services are promoted using the `<service>` element in the composite, as demonstrated in the SCDL fragment in Listing 5.3.

Exposing—or as SCA terms it, promoting—a service in a composite serves two purposes. It allows other references from outside the composite to be wired to it. It also provides a mechanism for the service to be configured by the composite using it as an implementation.

Listing 5.3   *Service Promotion*

```
<composite … name=" CreditServiceComposite">

   <service name="CreditService"
promote="CreditComponent/CreditService">
   </service>

   <component name ="CreditComponent">
            …
   <component>

…

</composite>
```

The `<service>` element configures a composite service by setting its name and identifying a service to promote via the `promote` attribute. In the example, the `CreditService` provided by the `CreditComponent` is promoted. Because the `CreditComponent` implements only one service, we could have omitted explicitly identifying the `CreditService` and written `promote="CreditComponent"`.

Wiring to the `CreditService` provided by the composite is done like wiring to any other service (see Figure 5.5).

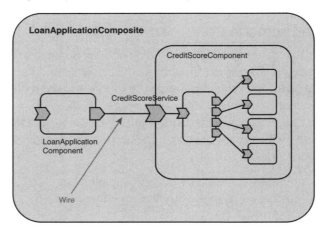

Figure 5.5   Wiring to a promoted service

In SCDL, wiring is done as shown in Listing 5.4.

Listing 5.4   *The SCDL for Wiring a Promoted Reference*

```
<composite … name="LoanApplication">

   <component name ="LoanComponent">
      <implementation.java class="com.bigbank.LoanComponent"/>
      <reference name="creditService" target="CreditComponent"/>
   <component>

   <component name ="CreditComponent">
      <implementation.composite name="loan:CreditServiceComposite"/>
   <component>

</composite>
```

The wire defined in the previous SCDL connects the
`creditService` reference of `LoanComponent` just like any other
component, thereby hiding internal implementation details.

The Performance Implications of Composition

In the primary example for this chapter, we have been demonstrating how to encapsulate the credit-scoring function of the BigBank loan application as a composite. By creating a separate credit-scoring composite and using it as a component, we are better able to hide the implementation details of the credit-scoring service. Composition—the process of creating components from composites that in turn assemble smaller components—leads to more robust application architectures and makes applications easier to maintain.

You may be wondering about the runtime performance implications of composition. Specifically, does wiring to a composite service, which promotes a service on a contained component, introduce an extra invocation hop when servicing a request? For example, when the `LoanComponent` invokes the `CreditService`, does the call flow first to the promoted service on the composite and then to the service on the contained component (as depicted in Figure 5.6)?

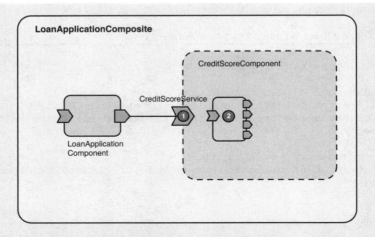

Figure 5.6   Do promoted services require two hops?

The short answer is that, in a good runtime implementation, there should be absolutely no negative performance impact. This is because the runtime can optimize away the composite service and connect the two components directly. For example, Fabric3 will flow a call directly to the target service, as shown in Figure 5.7.

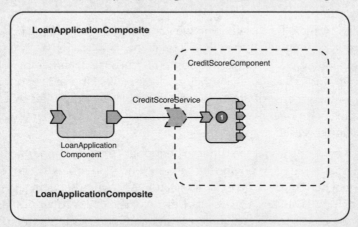

Figure 5.7   Optimizing the promoted service hop away

Because composite services are optimized away by the SCA runtime, composition can be used without fear of negatively impacting runtime performance with extra invocation hops.

Service Bindings

Composite services have all the characteristics of a component service, including the capability to be bound to a particular remote communications transport. In Chapter 2, we described how to expose the `LoanService` as a web service via the SCA web services binding (see Listing 5.5).

Composite services have all the characteristics of a component service, including the ability to be bound to a particular remote communications transport.

Listing 5.5   *Binding a Service as a Web Service Endpoint*

```
<component name="LoanComponent">
   <implementation.java class="com.bigbank.LoanComponent"/>
   <service name="LoanService ">
      <binding.ws/>
   </service>
</component>
```

Binding the `LoanService` using `<binding.ws>` instructs the runtime to make the service available as a web service endpoint for external clients.

If BigBank also wanted to expose the `CreditService` as a web service endpoint, the corresponding SCDL for the composite component would look the same (see Listing 5.6).

Listing 5.6   *Binding a Composite Service as a Web Service Endpoint*

```
<component name="CreditComponent">
      <implementation.composite name="loan:CreditServiceComposite"/>
   <service name="CreditService">
      <binding.ws/>
   </service>
</component>
```

Recalling that the `CreditComposite` promoted the `CreditService` from the `CreditComponent`, look at Listing 5.7.

Listing 5.7   *The Promoted Service*

```
<composite … name=" CreditServiceComposite">

   <service name="CreditService"
promote="CreditComponent/CreditService">
   </service>

   <component name ="CreditComponent">
```

```
   ...
   <component>
...

</composite>
```

The SCDL in Listing 5.8 instructs the SCA runtime to bind the CreditService provided by the CreditComponent as a web services endpoint.

SCA also allows bindings to be specified on a promoted service inside a composite.

SCA also allows bindings to be specified on a promoted service inside a composite. Instead of specifying <binding.ws> on the composite component, the prior example could be recast as that shown in Listing 5.8.

Listing 5.8   *Specifying a Binding on a Promoted Service Inside a Composite*

```
<composite ... name="CreditServiceComposite"
targetNamespace="http://www.bigbank.com/xmlns/loanApplication/1.0">

   <service name="CreditService"
promote="CreditComponent/CreditService">
      <binding.ws/>
   </service>

   <component name ="CreditComponent">
      ...
   <component>
...

</composite>
```

The component that uses the composite could be recast, as shown in Listing 5.9.

Listing 5.9   *The Binding Information Is Not Set When Using the Composite from Listing 5.8*

```
<component name="CreditComponent"    xmlns:loan="
http://www.bigbank.com/xmlns/loanApplication/1.0">
      <implementation.composite name="loan:CreditServiceComposite"/>
</component>
```

The SCDL in Listing 5.8 also instructs the SCA runtime to make the `CreditService` available as a web service endpoint. However, it is subtly different than the previous example. Specifying the binding on a composite service will apply to all uses of the composite. In contrast, specifying the binding in the component configuration will only apply to the specific component. For example, if the `CreditComposite` were reused several times, multiple `CreditService` endpoints would be activated.

Specifying the binding on a composite service will apply to all uses of the composite. In contrast, specifying the binding in the component configuration will only apply to the specific component.

Reference Promotion

Components implemented by composites can also have references that are wired to services. Similar to a composite service, a composite reference is created by promoting the reference of a contained component. The earlier version of the credit score component contained an auditing component. It is likely that this auditing capability will be needed by other components and is therefore a good candidate to be refactored into a generalized service used by the various loan application composites. Refactoring the auditing component can be done by moving it to the parent `LoanApplication` composite, as shown in Figure 5.8.

Components implemented by composites can also have references that are wired to services.

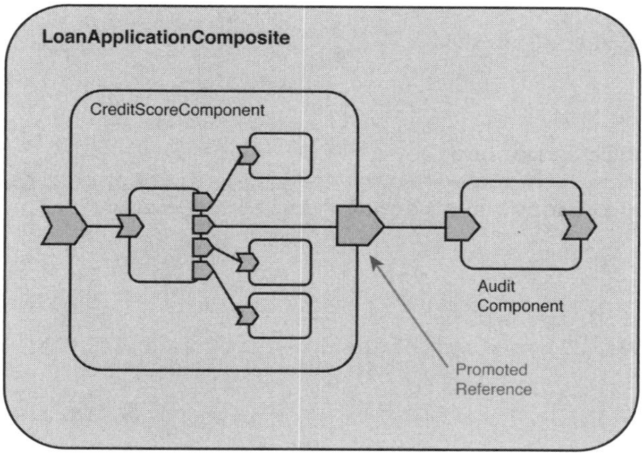

Figure 5.8   A wired composite reference

Figure 5.8 also demonstrates how reference promotion is used to wire from a component contained in the credit score component to the auditing service. In SCDL, reference promotion is done using the `<reference>` element (see Listing 5.10).

Listing 5.10   *Reference Promotion*

```
<composite ... name="CreditServiceComposite"
    targetNamespace="http://www.bigbank.com/xmlns/loanApplication/1.0">

    <component name ="CreditComponent">
        <implementation.java class="com.bigbank.CreditComponent"/>
        <reference name="validationService"
target="ValidationComponent"/>
        <reference name="scoringService" target="ScoringComponent"/>
    <component>

    ...
    <reference name="auditService"
promote="CreditComponent/auditService"/>

</composite>
```

The <reference> entry creates a composite reference that pro-motes the auditService reference on the CreditComponent. When the CreditComposite is used as a component implementation, this reference must be wired to a service as done in the SCDL in Listing 5.11.

Listing 5.11   *Wiring a Promoted Reference*

```
<composite ... name="LoanApplication">

    ...

    <component name ="CreditComponent">
        <implementation.composite name="loan:CreditServiceComposite"/>
        <reference name="auditService" target="AuditComponent"/>

    <component>

    <component name ="AuditComponent">
        <implementation.java class="com.bigbank.AuditComponent"/>
    <component>

</composite>
```

In a slightly more complex scenario, a promoted reference may be wired to a promoted service. This is shown in Figure 5.9, which changes the AuditComponent to be implemented by a composite containing two components.

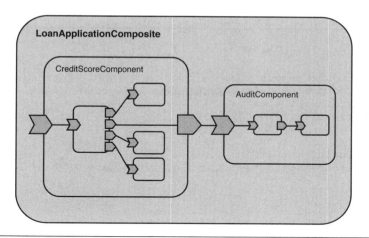

Figure 5.9   Wiring from a promoted reference to a promoted service

Take the audit composite SCDL shown in Listing 5.12.

Listing 5.12   *The* AuditComposite

```
<composite … name="AuditComposite">

    <service name="AuditService"
promote="AuditComponent/AuditService"/>

    <component name ="AuditComponent">
        <implementation.java class="com.bigbank.AuditComponent"/>
        <reference name="logComponent" target="LogComponent"/>
    <component>

    <component name ="LogComponent">
        <implementation.java class="com.bigbank.LogComponent"/>
    <component>

</composite>
```

The wiring to the audit service would remain the same as in
Listing 5.11. The only difference would be the substitution of
<implementation.composite> for <implementation.java>
(see Listing 5.13).

Listing 5.13   *The Revised* `LoanApplication` *Composite*

```
<composite … name="LoanApplication">
   …
   <component name ="CreditComponent">
      <implementation.composite name=" loan:CreditServiceComposite"/>
      <reference name="auditService"
target="AuditComponent/AuditService"/>
   <component>

   <component name ="AuditComponent">
      <implementation.composite name=" loan:AuditComposite"/>
   <component>

</composite>
```

More on Runtime Performance Optimizations

We have already mentioned that wiring to a promoted service should not result in a negative impact on performance. This is because runtimes can optimize composite services away and connect references directly to services provided by components contained in the composite.

The same optimization can be performed when wiring a promoted reference to a promoted service. The current example where we wire from the promoted `auditService` reference to the promoted `AuditService` service can be reduced to a single connection by an SCA runtime. Fabric3, for instance, will create the connection shown in Figure 5.10.

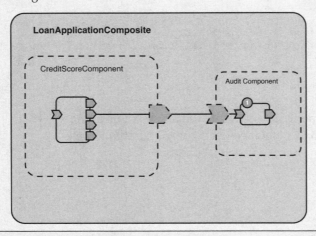

Figure 5.10   Optimizing the wire from a promoted reference to a promoted service

As we see in the diagram, an efficient SCA runtime replaces the series of wires defined in SCDL with a single wire that flows a call directly to the service provider.

Reference Bindings

In Chapter 1, "Introducing SCA," we discussed how references can be bound to a particular communication protocol. This is typically done when a component requires a service that is external to the SCA domain. (Perhaps it is a web service not written using SCA.) For example, a component may be dependent on an external web service that provides interest rates, as shown in Listing 5.14.

Listing 5.14   *Binding a Reference*

```
<component name="RateComponent">
     <implementation.java class="com.bigbank.RateComponent"/>
     <reference name="rateService">
          <binding.ws uri="http://www.bigbank.com/rateService"/>
     </reference>
</component>
```

The `<binding.ws>` element configures the reference to connect to the web service endpoint located at http://www.bigbank.com/ rateService. Invocations from the component will be dispatched via web services to the endpoint by the SCA runtime.

Because composite references are like any other component reference, they may also be bound. And, as with composite services, the binding may be configured either in the composite SCDL or as part of the composite component configuration. We look at both examples in turn.

Because composite references are like any other component reference, they may also be bound.

Listing 5.15 demonstrates binding the `rateService` reference using promotion—it is almost identical to the previous example.

Listing 5.15   _Binding a Promoted Reference_

```
<composite … name="RateComposite">
   <component name="RateComponent">
      <implementation.java class="com.bigbank.RateComponent"/>
   </component>
   <reference name="rateService" promote="RateComponent/rateService">
      <binding.ws uri="http://www.bigbank.com/rateService"/>
   </reference>

</composite>
```

Alternatively, if we wanted to configure the binding as part of the composite component configuration, we would first remove the binding from the promoted the reference, as shown in Listing 5.16.

Listing 5.16   _The Promoted Reference_

```
<composite … name="RateComposite">
   <component name="RateComponent">
      <implementation.java class="com.bigbank.RateComponent"/>
   </component>
   <reference name="rateService" promote="RateComponent/rateService">
   </reference>
</composite>
```

Then we'd configure the composite component reference, as shown in Listing 5.17.

Listing 5.17   _Binding a Composite Reference as Part of the Composite Component Configuration_

```
<composite … name="LoanApplication">
   <component name="RateComponent">
   <implementation.composite name=" loan:RateComposite"/>
      <reference name="rateService">
         <binding.ws uri="http://www.bigbank.com/rateService"/>
      </reference>
   </component>
</composite>
```

It is important to bear in mind that binding a promoted reference (as represented by Listing 5.15) and binding the reference as part of the composite component configuration (Listing 5.16 and Listing 5.17) are *not* the same. The SCDL in Listing 5.15 will bind the reference for every use of the composite as a component implementation. In contrast, the SCDL in Listing 5.16 leaves the binding open. In other words, the binding may be changed each time the composite is used as a component.

It is important to bear in mind that binding a promoted reference and binding the reference as part of the composite component configuration are not *the same.*

Perspective: Use Bindings Only at the Domain Level

SCA provides several ways to configure bindings. At times, it may not always be apparent which alternative is best. In most cases, a simple rule can be applied: Even though bindings may be specified on references of encapsulated components—*don't do it.* Specify bindings only on references of the components in the top-level composite (that is, the composite being deployed into the SCA domain) and avoid doing so on components of nested composites.

It is okay to specify bindings on the composite-level references of nested composites, but they should be considered to be just hints, because they can be overridden.

Specifying component reference bindings only at the top-level composite brings several advantages. First, it allows bindings to be changed as late as deployment. Second, it places all endpoints provided by the SCA domain and dependencies on services outside the SCA domain at the same level, so they are easier to visualize and manage.

Figure 5.11 demonstrates using promotion to bind two services and two references in top-level composites.

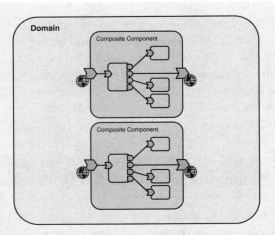

Figure 5.11   Binding two services and references in the top-level composite

A complaint that could be raised against this approach is that promotion is more verbose than simply inlining the binding configuration directly in the component definition. In this case, it is important to remember that binding a service or reference without promoting it is essentially "hardcoding" an endpoint. As with code, hardcoding can save time initially but be costly when a change is needed after an application has gone into production.

Consider the preceding example. If the services or references were directly bound in the two inner components and they were not promoted, there would be no way to change them without changing the two composite SCDLs. This would involve a modification to the application and redeployment.

In contrast, if the bindings are set in the top-level composites, they can be modified without altering the inner composite SCDLs. In fact, some SCA runtimes may allow these modifications to be done without requiring a redeployment.

Composite Properties

*Composite compo-
nents may also
have properties.*

Given that composite components may have services and references, it should come as no surprise that they may also have properties. The composite in Listing 5.18 declares two integer type properties.

Listing 5.18   *Composite Property Declarations*

```
<composite … name="CreditServiceComposite"
    xmlns:xs="http://www.w3.org/2001/XMLSchema">

    <property name="min" type="xs:integer">200</property>

    <property name="max" type="xs:integer">700</property>

    <component name ="CreditComponent">
      …
    <component>

  …
</composite>
```

The example provides default values of 200 and 700, respectively.

The properties can be set when the composite is used as a component implementation, as shown in Listing 5.19.

Listing 5.19   *Composite Property Configuration*

```
<component name="CreditServiceComponent">
    <implementation.composite name=" loan:CreditServiceComposite"/>

    <property name="min">100</property>

    <property name="max">800</property>

</component>
```

The preceding example sets the min and max properties to 100 and 800, respectively, overriding the default values.

Note that in Listing 5.18, we declared the property type to be integer as defined by XML Schema (the use of the "xs" prefix). SCA defines the range of valid property types to include those defined by XML Schema—for example, string, integer—and user-defined complex types (more on that later).

More on XML Schema

A lot has been written on XML Schema. To learn more, you can consult the specifications at http://www.w3.org/XML/Schema. As the specifications are quite dense, we recommend *XML Schema* by Eric van der Vlist (O'Reilly, 2002), which provides a thorough overview of the technology.

Composite properties are optional by default—that is, they do not need to be configured when the composite is used as a component implementation. If a property is not configured and a default value is provided, the property will be set to that value. If the `Credit Component` in Listing 5.19 had not specified `min` and `max` property values, the SCA runtime would have substituted the default values of `200` and `700`.

A property configuration can be made mandatory by setting the `mustSupply` *attribute on the property declaration in the composite to* `true`.

A property configuration can be made mandatory by setting the `mustSupply` attribute on the property declaration in the composite to `true` (by default, it is set to `false`). This is shown in Listing 5.20.

Listing 5.20   *Optional Composite Property Declarations*

```
<composite … name="CreditServiceComposite"
    xmlns:xs="http://www.w3.org/2001/XMLSchema">

    <property name="min" mustSupply="true" type="xs:integer"/>

    <property name="max" mustSupply="true" type="xs:integer"/>

    <component name ="CreditComponent">
        …
    <component>

    …
</composite>
```

When `@mustSupply` is set to `true`, a property must be configured when the composite is used as a component implementation.

Configuring Composite Properties

Composite properties would not be very useful unless they could
be accessed by contained components. The SCDL in Listing 5.21
demonstrates how to do this.

Listing 5.21   *Referencing a Composite Property*

```
<composite … name="CreditServiceComposite"
    xmlns:xs="http://www.w3.org/2001/XMLSchema">

    <property name="min" type="xs:integer">200</property>

    <property name="max" type="xs:integer">700</property>

    <component name ="CreditComponent">
        …
        <property name="min" source="$min"/>
        <property name="max" source="$max"/>
    <component>

    …
</composite>
```

The @source attribute of the <property> element instructs the
SCA runtime to set the value of the property to the given composite
property value. The source attribute value is an XPath expression.
We discuss XPath in more detail later in the chapter, but if you are
not familiar with it, XPath is essentially a technology for addressing
parts of an XML document. Because SCDL is XML, SCA uses XPath
to refer to XML values. In the example, the $ character is an XPath
operator that instructs the SCA runtime to select the min and max
properties.

Why did the SCA authors choose XPath as the expression language
for referencing composite properties as opposed to something
simpler, such as just referring to the property name? As we show in
the next sidebar, basic XPath is relatively easy to write. Also, there
are times when only part of a composite property or subelement
needs to be selected, such as when the property is a complex type
containing several data parts. (We cover complex types in a later
section.) XPath is a widely accepted standard for doing this, and
inventing a technology would likely lead to more complexity as
people would need to master a new approach.

Fortunately, most applications are likely to make much more use of simple property types, such as string and integer, than complex ones. In the cases where simple types are used, the only XPath you need to remember is the $ character preceding the composite property name being referenced.

Multivalued Properties

Property values may contain multiple values, such as a collection of strings or integers.

Property values may contain multiple values, such as a collection of strings or integers. Multivalued properties are declared by setting the @many attribute to true (the default is false), as shown in Listing 5.22.

Listing 5.22   *Declaring a Multivalued Property*

```
<composite … name="CreditServiceComposite"
   xmlns:xs="http://www.w3.org/2001/XMLSchema">

   <property name="validStates" many="true" type="xs:NMToken">
      CA
      MA
      NY
      ..
   </property>

   <component name ="CreditComponent">
      …
   <component>

   …
</composite>
```

The property declaration in Listing 5.22 provides multiple default values. When the composite is used as a component, values can be set for property by creating multiple <property> entries (see Listing 5.23).

Listing 5.23   *Configuring a Composite Property Using a Complex Type*

```
<composite name="CreditComposite"
   xmlns:bb="http://bigbank.com">

   <component name="CreditServiceComponent">
      <implementation.composite name=" loan:CreditServiceComposite"/>

      <property name="validStates">CA</property>
      <property name="validStates">MA</property>
```

```
    </component>

</composite>
```

At runtime, any component that accesses the `validStates` composite property will be given a collection containing the strings `CA` and `MA`. If no value were set for the property, the default values as defined in Listing 5.23 would be provided: namely `CA`, `MA`, and `NY`.

Using Complex Property Types

Sometimes configuration consists of information that is best represented using a data structure as opposed to a simple type. Consider the case where the BigBank loan application contains a number of components that validate data at various stages in the approval process. The credit data validator ensures that all required information is present and in the correct format. The validation rules are name-value pairs, where the name corresponds to a data element name and the value is a regular expression defining the formatting rules for the field.

Instead of hardcoding the formatting rules in the component implementation, BigBank has decided to use a composite property. BigBank could have used a database to store this configuration but opted not to do so for two reasons. First, validation information is static and does not change. Requiring an additional database table will make the application more difficult to configure than is necessary. Second, more practically, storing the configuration information in a database table would require changes to the corporate database, which is often subject to a lengthy review processes.

Listing 5.24 is the property declaration for the validation rules using a complex type, `validationRules`.

Listing 5.24   *Declaring a Property Using a Complex Type*

```
<composite … name="CreditServiceComposite"
    xmlns:bb="http://bigbank.com"
    xmlns:xsd="http://www.w3.org/2001/XMLSchema">

    <property name="validationRules" type="bb:validationRules"/>

    …
</composite>
```

As shown in this example, where the @type attribute is set to bb:validationRules, complex property types are defined in SCA using XML Schema.

XML Schema can be somewhat complex and verbose, but it is the most widely accepted way to specify the set of rules to which an XML document must conform (also known as a "schema language"). Other alternative schema languages exist, such as DTDs, RELAX NG, and Schematron, but SCA chose XML Schema largely due to its ubiquity and existing software support. The XML Schema for validationRules is listed in Listing 5.25.

Listing 5.25   *The validationRules XML Schema*

```
<xs:schema xmlns="http://www.w3.org/2001/XMLSchema"
    targetNamespace="http://bigbank.com/">
<xs:element name="validationRules">
   <xs:complexType>
     <xs:sequence>
       <xs:element name="rule" minOccurs="0"
           maxOccurs="unbounded">
         <xs:complexType>
           <xs:sequence>
             <xs:element name="name" minOccurs="0"
                 type="xs:string"/>
             <xs:element name="format" minOccurs="0"
                 type="xs:string"/>
           </xs:sequence>
         </xs:complexType>
         <xs:attribute name="name" type="xs:string" use="required"/>
       </xs:element>
     </xs:sequence>
   </xs:complexType>
</xs:element>
</xs:schema>
```

When the loan application is deployed, the XML Schema file would typically be packaged as part of the contribution containing the CreditComposite.

The SCDL in Listing 5.26 sets the validationRules property on the CreditComponent.

Listing 5.26   *Configuring a Composite Property Using a Complex Type*

```
<composite name="CreditComposite"
   xmlns:bb="http://bigbank.com">

   <component name=" CreditServiceComponent">
      <implementation.composite name=" loan:CreditServiceComposite"/>

      <property name="validationRules">
         <bb:validationRules>
            <bb:rule name="ssn">
               <bb:field>ssn</b:field>
               <bb:format>^\d{3}-\d{2}-\d{4}$</bb:format>
            </bb:rule>
            <bb:rule name="zip">
               <bb:field>zipCode</bb:field>
               <bb:format>^\d{5}$|^\d{5}-\d{4}$</bb:format>
            </bb:rule>
            …
         </bb:validationRules>
      </property>

   </component>

</composite>
```

This approach of including the value of a complex property within a composite file is awkward, because the application developer is likely going to want to manage the contents of this configuration as part of a separate file. In this example, it would be most natural to have a `validationRules.xml` configuration file. That way, the configuration rules can be modified without modifying the composite that uses it.

It is possible to specify the value of any property by referring to the contents of a separate file. The file is specified using a relative URI—in this case, relative to the location of the composite file. So, if the `validationRules.xml` file is kept in the same directory as the composite, the new composite would look like Listing 5.27.

It is possible to specify the value of any property by referring to the contents of a separate file. The file is specified using a relative URI—in this case, relative to the location of the composite file.

Listing 5.27 *Configuring a Composite Property Using a File*

```
<composite name="CreditComposite"
   xmlns:bb="http://bigbank.com">

   <component name=" CreditServiceComponent">
      <implementation.composite name=" loan:CreditServiceComposite"/>

      <property name="validationRules" file="validationRules.xml"/>

   </component>

</composite>
```

The `validationRules.xml` document contents can then be a little simpler, because it can use the bigbank.com namespace as the default namespace (see Listing 5.28). It also is easier for tools to validate it against its schema.

Listing 5.28 *File Contents Used for the Composite Property*

```
<validationRules xmlns="http://bigbank.com">
   <rule name="ssn">
      <field>ssn</b:field>
      <format>^\d{3}-\d{2}-\d{4}$</format>
   </rule>
   <rule name="zip">
      <field>zipCode</field>
      <format>^\d{5}$|^\d{5}-\d{4}$</format>
   </rule>
   ...
</validationRules>
```

Having walked through the configuration of complex property types, is the complexity and time required to define an XML Schema worth it? Most applications can likely make do with simple types. However, considering that an XML Schema only needs to be written once, the benefits it affords (most notably validation of property values) are well worth it.

Binding XML Schema Types

In our property examples, we did not discuss how property values are set on component instances. This will vary by implementation type and runtime. For example, a BPEL component gets an infoset representation of the XML value used for the property.

In contrast, a Java implementation must have XML used for property types translated into Java types (that is, primitives or types defined by the JDK, such as `java.util.Integer` or `java.util.List`) or user-defined classes. How the property type is mapped to Java types will vary by runtime. Some SCA runtimes may support a data-binding technology such as JAXB, which defines standard mappings from XML to Java. In a JAXB-enabled runtime, the validation rules example would bind to a `java.util.Map`.

At the time of this writing, Fabric3 supports binding XML Schema built-in types to their Java type equivalent as defined by the JAXB specification. However, Fabric3 does not currently support binding complex or user-defined data types.

Given these differences, it is wise to check the particular runtime documentation before using complex property types.

Referencing Complex Property Values

Previously, we mentioned that it is possible for a component property to reference part of a composite property via an XPath expression. Suppose a component needs access to only one validation rule, such as the correct format for Social Security numbers. This can be referenced using the "source" attribute with the XPath shown in Listing 5.29.

Listing 5.29   *Using XPath to Access Parts of a Complex Property*

```
<composite name="CreditComposite"
    xmlns:bb="http://bigbank.com">

    ...

    <property name="validationRules" type="bb:validationRules"/>

    <component name="ValidationComponent">
    ...
        <property name="ssnPattern"
source="$validationRules//rule[@name='ssn']"/>
    </component>

</composite>
```

The XPath expression, `$validationRules//rule`
`[@name='ssn']`, instructs the SCA runtime to select the rule whose
name is `ssn` (remember that the actual rule values are set when the
composite is used as a component; refer to Listing 5.25). As you
can see, even nontrivial XPath expressions are easy to read. At the
same time, they are a powerful tool, as evidenced by our example
of selecting a specific validation rule.

More on XPath

In addition to properties, SCA uses XPath to configure policy. We briefly touched
upon policies in the first chapter and will provide in-depth coverage in Chapter 6,
"Policy."

For the majority of application use cases, simple XPath expressions are likely to suf-
fice. However, for more advanced scenarios, a deeper understanding will be required. As XPath is beyond the scope of this book, we recommend the following
sources for more information:

- *XPath and XPointer* by John E. Simpson (O'Reilly, 2002)
- The XPath Specification at http://www.w3.org/TR/xpath

Overrides

In some situations, it is necessary to override a service, reference, or
property configuration at a higher level of composition. In this section, we look at several of the more common override scenarios.

Services and References

Overriding a binding is done by promoting the service or reference.

One of the most common cases where a service or reference configuration needs to be overridden involves changing a binding.
Overriding a binding is done by promoting the service or reference.
Suppose the `RateComposite` bound the `rateService` using the
web services binding in the following manner:

```
<composite … name="RateComposite">
   <component name="RateComponent">
      <implementation.java class="com.bigbank.RateComponent"/>
   </component>
   <reference name="rateService" promote="RateComponent/rateService">
      <binding.ws uri="http://www.bigbank.com/rateService"/>
   </reference>

</composite>
```

Now suppose that after the rate composite has been packaged, installed, and activated in a domain, BigBank offers a new loan type to small businesses, which requires a different rating service from its consumer division. Fortunately, the rate composite can be reused by having the `rateService` reference use a different service. To do this, the reference binding can be overridden when the composite is used as a component implementation. The SCDL in Listing 5.30 shows how to do this.

Listing 5.30   *Overriding a Reference Binding*

```
<composite … name="LoanApplication">
   <component name="RateComponent">
   <implementation.composite name=" loan:RateComposite"/>
      <reference name="rateService">
         <binding.ws
uri="http://www.bigbank.com/smallBusiness/rateService"/>
      </reference>
   </component>
</composite>
```

In the preceding SCDL, reconfiguring the binding in the component definition overrides the binding information in the composite implementation. In addition to overriding binding settings, reference and service bindings can be changed entirely at outer levels of a composition. When overriding the rate service binding, JMS could have been substituted for web services. The basic rule for bindings is that the outer level always replaces inner levels of composition. (For other service and reference configuration, such as policies, the rules are different—we deal with these in later chapters.)

When Are Binding Overrides Useful?

The previous rate service example demonstrates another reason why it is best practice to avoid specifying bindings except in top-level composites that are deployed to a domain (see the earlier sidebar entitled "Perspective: Use Bindings Only at the Domain Level"). Binding overrides tend to make reading and understanding SCDL difficult.

However, binding overrides are useful for integration and predeployment testing. In the rate service example, BigBank may have a QA and staging environment for testing applications prior to placing them in production. This environment may have slightly different configurations, such as a specific rate service for testing located at a different endpoint address. Overrides provide a mechanism to accommodate environmental differences as an application is tested before it is moved into production.

The SCA Binding

Sometimes it is necessary to "unbind" a reference. Again, take the example we used previously where the reference to the rate service was bound to a web service endpoint:

```
<composite … name="RateComposite">
   <component name="RateComponent">
      <implementation.java class="com.bigbank.RateComponent"/>
   </component>
   <reference name="rateService" promote="RateComponent/rateService">
      <binding.ws uri="http://www.bigbank.com/rateService"/>
   </reference>

</composite>
```

Suppose the new rate service for commercial loans was not a web service but rather provided by another SCA component deployed in the domain. The reference binding needs to be overridden and the reference wired to the target service instead.

SCA defines a binding called the "SCA binding," or binding.sca. This binding can be used to override a binding set in a composite and instruct the SCA runtime to create a wire to a target service.

In order to accomplish this, SCA defines a binding called the "SCA binding," or binding.sca. This binding can be used to override a binding set in a composite and instruct the SCA runtime to create a wire to a target service. Listing 5.31 details how the SCA binding is used.

Listing 5.31   *The SCA Binding*

```
<composite … name="LoanApplication">
   <component name="RateComponent">
      <implementation.composite name="loan:RateComposite"/>
      <reference name="rateService" target="RateService">
         <binding.sca/>
      </reference>
   </component>
</composite>
```

The configuration overrides the web services binding set in the composite SCDL and replaces it with a wire to a target service provided by another component in the domain.

Properties

In SCA, properties are not, strictly speaking, overridden. Rather, a combination of using the default value and the `@source` attribute on the `<property>` element can be used to expose a property for configuration higher up in the composition hierarchy. Taking the earlier `min` and `max` properties:

```
<composite … name="CreditServiceComposite" ..>

   <property name="min" type="xs:integer">200</property>

   <property name="max" type="xs:integer">700</property>

   …
</composite>
```

To make the `min` and `max` properties optionally configurable when the loan application composite is used, declare the `RateComponent` properties to be set by two properties in the `LoanApplication` composite using the `@source` attribute (see Listing 5.32).

Listing 5.32   *Configuring Properties*

```
<composite … name="LoanApplication">

   <property name="min"/>
   <property name="max"/>

   <component name="RateComponent">
```

```
    <implementation.composite name="loan:RateComposite"/>
        <property name="min" source="$min"/>
        <property name="max" source="$max"/>
    </component>
</composite>
```

The SCDL in Listing 5.32 effectively allows the default property values defined in the `CreditServiceComposite` to be overridden outside the loan application composite.

Inclusion

Often, different developers may be responsible for component implementations that reside within a composite. This can create difficulties, as multiple people need to modify a composite file during development. One solution to this problem is to use composition to break the composite into multiple composites, which are then contained in a common parent composite.

Using composition in this manner can be somewhat tedious, particularly if components in different composites need to be wired together. Because composites provide encapsulation, components in different composites cannot be wired directly. Instead, the source reference and target service would each need to be promoted in their respective composites. Then, the promoted reference would need to be wired to the promoted service in the parent composite. With multiple wires, this can result in a lot of extra configuration that will be difficult to maintain.

In cases where encapsulation is not required but it is helpful to separate a composite into multiple files, SCA supports the ability to include a composite in another.

In cases where encapsulation is not required but it is helpful to separate a composite into multiple files, SCA supports the ability to include a composite in another. Specifically, inclusion inlines a composite in another. For those familiar with C, inclusion is similar to `#include`: including a composite within another merges its contents. Inclusion is done using the `<include>` element and setting the `@name` attribute to the qualified name of the included composite. Unlike C's `#include`, composite inclusion is not a textual include, because XML concepts like namespace prefix declarations don't apply across an include (see Listing 5.33).

Listing 5.33   *Two Included Composites*

```
<composite … name="ParentComposite"
xmlns:bb="loan:CreditServiceComposite ">

    <include name="bb:CompositeA"/>

    <include name="bb:CompositeB"/>

    …
</composite>
```

In the preceding, two composites are inlined into the
ParentComposite. When inlining a composite, its contained components become children of the parent composite. This means that
encapsulation is not enforced between two composites included in
a common parent. Consequently, it is possible to wire between
them without requiring promotion. For example, given
CompositeB:

```
<composite … name="CompositeB"
targetNamespace="http://www.bigbank.com/xmlns/ loanApplication/1.0">

    <component name="ComponentB">
        …
    </component>
    …
</composite>
```

It is possible to wire to ComponentB directly from a component
contained in CompositeA:

```
<composite … name="CompositeA"
targetNamespace="http://www.bigbank.com/xmlns/ loanApplication/1.0">

    <component name="ComponentA">
        . . .
        <reference name="serviceB" target="ComponentB"/>
    </component>
    …
</composite>
```

*Because inclusion
inlines components
directly in the parent,
the same rules and
conventions apply as
if the components
were all defined in a
single composite.*

It is important to note that because inclusion inlines components directly in the parent, the same rules and conventions apply as if the components were all defined in a single composite. In particular, care should be taken to avoid component name clashes.

Inclusion Versus Composition

A common question people raise is when to use inclusion versus when to instead use composition. One way of answering this is to say that composition should be used as part of the architectural design, whereas inclusion should be done for expediency. In other words, when you want to make a set of components within a composite replaceable as a unit or hide their wiring details, use composition. When you need an easy way to allow more than one person to work on a composite without clashing, break out the contained components into multiple included composites.

Summary

This chapter illustrated how composition is used to achieve application modularity in SCA. Composition allows services to be built from composites that contain more fine-grained components. Composition fosters modularity in two ways. First, it provides encapsulation by allowing composites to be treated as single components that provide services to clients. Additionally, composition fosters reuse by allowing composites to be configured as component implementations multiple times, potentially using different property values or wiring. With composition in hand, you will be able to create applications that are easier to manage, maintain, and evolve.

6

Policy

The term "policy" can mean many things. When some people talk about policy, they are referring to governance rules that mandate steps and procedures that must be followed in order to develop, deploy, or modify an application. This is not what is meant by "policy" in SCA.

In SCA, a **policy** is a statement that controls or constrains some capability that is provided by the infrastructure.

*In SCA, a **policy** is a statement that controls or constrains some capability that is provided by the infrastructure.*

Policy Examples

Examples of infrastructure capabilities that can be managed using SCA's policy framework include the following:

- Authentication
- Confidentiality (encryption)
- Integrity (signing)
- One-way message reliability
- Transaction propagation

These are not just arbitrary examples. They are the set of policies that were in the minds of the designers of SCA's policy mechanism, so they should work fairly well. For other things that might be described as policies, the more they differ from the preceding examples, the less likely they are to be well-suited to SCA's policy framework. Service level agreements (SLAs), such as promises about the average latency that will be provided by a service, are near the edge of this distinction. We do not know of any reason why they should not be well-suited to SCA's policy framework, but there is also very little experience with the framework.

When we say that policies are capabilities provided by the infrastructure, we are differentiating them from the capabilities that are part of the code of components. Application code should not deal with the numerous transport and protocol issues that surround the sending and receiving of messages. Developers should be able to just concentrate on the application logic.

Nonetheless, it is sometimes necessary for *someone* to provide details about how certain infrastructure capabilities will be provided. For example, what encryption standard will be used to achieve confidentiality? In SCA, the person who makes those decisions and configures the associated details is the **policy administrator**.

SCA Policy in Brief

Before going into more detail on features of the policy framework, it is useful to get an overview of the policy mechanism by looking at how encryption would be specified by the various roles involved in application development.

The developer specifies an `@Confidentiality` annotation next to the `@Reference` annotation that designates a reference. This turns into a reference declaration in the component type that includes the following:

```
<reference requires="sca:confidentiality" …>
```

That `@requires` attribute holds a list of **intents**. This means that the developer requires that some mechanism must be used to ensure confidentiality on calls through this reference.

It is the job of the policy administrator to make sure that the "confidentiality" intent lines up with a `policySet`. The policy set definition contains policy assertions (usually in the form of WS-Policy), the intent that is guaranteed by that policy set, and the circumstances in which it applies. The circumstances are in the form of an XPath expression run on the binding where the policy will be used, although in many cases, the XPath expression can just be the name of the binding type (for example, `@appliesTo="binding.ws"`).

Policy administrators install these policies by including them in definitions.xml files that are installed into the domain using the contribution mechanism, which will be described in Chapter 9, "The Domain."

Intents

An intent specifies a capability without identifying how it will be provided. The definition of an intent is specified in a definition.xml file that may be installed into a domain using a contribution. However, runtimes usually have a number of intents preinstalled, such as the intents that are specified by the SCA standard itself.

Listing 6.1 provides the definition of SCA's confidentiality intent.

Listing 6.1   *Confidentiality Intent Definition*

```
<intent name="confidentiality" constrains="sca:binding">
      <description>
          Communication through this binding must prevent
          unauthorized users from reading the messages.
      </description>
</intent>
```

The intent can be specified in implementation files, interface files, component types, and composites. In component types and composites, the intents are specified as a space-separated list in an `@requires` attribute. The attribute can be put on any element. For binding and implementation elements, the attribute directly affects the element.

For any other element, the effect is indirect. The required intents are added to any binding or implementation element that is a descendent of the element that defines it (using the XML hierarchy). This enables you to specify confidentiality on every binding within a composite by specifying @requires="sca:confidentiality" on the composite element itself. In some cases, compositewide intents might be overridden by intents on lower-level elements.

PropagatesTransaction—An Example of a Required Intent

Transaction policy is an example of a situation where the component developer needs to be able to declare that it needs something from the infrastructure. Only the developer of a component knows if an atomicity **guarantee** is required for a component. If atomicity is required, the component must be developed in a way that guarantees any operation will either complete in its entirety, or the system will be put back into the same state it was in before the operation began.

One way to achieve this guarantee is for both client and service providers to create appropriate **compensation logic**, which undoes any completed steps if there is a failure before the entire logical transaction completes. Creating such compensation logic is a pain but is necessary if transactions can't be used. This can happen if a component has references to services that can't enlist in the same transaction as the component.

If transactions can be used, guaranteeing atomicity is much simpler. In order to include a service call in the transaction of the caller, SCA defines an intent called propagatesTransaction. If this intent is present on a reference, the reference *must* be wired to a service that can enlist in the transaction. This frees the developer from creating compensation logic. However, it also constrains the deployer, because the reference can only be wired to services that can join the transaction. The propagatesTransaction intent places this constraint.

In the example from the previous chapter, the credit component might mark its references to the scoring system and the audit system as needing to enlist in the transaction, so the scoring result is recorded in the audit log, no matter what. Figure 6.1 shows the references that require propagatesTransaction in white.

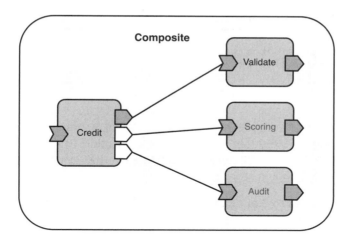

Figure 6.1 Credit components require some references to propagate transactions.

policySets

`policySet`s are defined by policy administrators, and they state the details of how a particular intent should be accomplished under various circumstances. `policySet` definitions are found in definition.xml files, which can be installed in a domain via a contribution.

`policySet` definitions hold collections of **policy assertions** that accomplish some intent (or set of intents) under curtain circumstances. The policy assertions are typically WS-Policy expressions, although other policy languages are allowed. The intents that the `policySet` accomplishes are listed in the definition of the policy set in a `@provides` attribute. The circumstances where the `policySet` applies are represented as an XPath expression inside an `@appliesTo` attribute.

For example, the `propagatesTransaction` intent listed previously would be provided by the following `policySet` (see Listing 6.2).

policySets are defined by policy administrators, and they state the details of how a particular intent should be accomplished under various circumstances.

Listing 6.2   A Composite Scoped Component Implementation

```
<policySet provides="sca:propagatesTransaction"
           appliesTo="sca:binding.ws">
   <wsat:ATAssertion/>
</policySet>
```

The contents of this `policySet` is a WS-Policy assertion that was defined in the WS-AtomicTransaction specification. The `@provides` attribute lists the `sca:propagatesTransaction` intent as the only intent that is provided by the `policySet`.

The `@appliesTo` attribute is actually a relative XPath expression, although in this case, as in many cases, it is simply a QName.

How `@appliesTo` Is Used

The processing rule for the `@appliesTo` XPath expression is that it runs against the parent element of every binding or implementation element in the document. If the relative XPath expression returns the binding or implementation element that you are checking, this `policySet` applies to this binding; if not, it doesn't.

The result of this processing rule is that the most common thing that determines the applicability of a `policySet`, the binding type, is specified with an XPath expression that is just the QName of the binding, such as `"sca:binding.ws"`. That XPath expression run on the parent element of some binding.ws element will return all bindings with a QName of `sca:binding.ws`. Because the binding being checked is in this set, the `policySet` applies.

If you only wanted a `policySet` to apply if the `@uri` attribute on the binding starts with the "https" scheme, you would write the `appliesTo` attribute as follows:

```
appliesTo="sca:binding.ws[starts-with(@uri, "https:")]"
```

You can also apply bindings only when they are used in specific contexts. For example, you could write a `policySet` that is used on services or references that use the `CreditService` WSDL interface, by using an `appliesTo` of the following:

```
sca:binding.ws[../interface.wsdl/@interface="bb:CreditService"]
```

The conditional part traverses to the parent element (the "`..`"), which will be either a service or a reference element. Either of these can specify their interface using interface.wsdl, so this finds the ones whose interface.wsdl has a `@name` attribute with the QName of `"bb:CreditService"`.

Finding the Right Policy Set

The SCA Policy Framework specification has a detailed algorithm that describes how to propagate intents down the XML hierarchy and how to find a matching policy set. The algorithm works on a composite, and the result of the algorithm should be that all intents are discovered to be satisfied in some way—either by finding an appropriate policy set or because of the built-in capabilities of bindings or implementations.

Some of the basic steps in the algorithm are the following:

1. Copy intents from each component type (that is, from the implementation) into the components that use those component types.
2. Copy in the intents from the interfaces used by any service or reference.
3. Propagate intents down the XML tree.
4. For each binding or implementation in the composite, find the smallest set of policy sets that provide all the intents listed for that binding or implementation and where the `@appliesTo` matches.

If there are any bindings or implementations where no set of `policySets` can be found that achieve that set of intents, there is an error. If more than one set can be found that achieve it, the deployer has to choose.

■ Perspective: Declarative Policy Versus API

SCA's separation of policy details from application logic is not new. Transaction monitors, database systems, message-oriented middleware (MOM), and other infrastructure software products have always made it possible to offload the implementation of these capabilities from the average developer. However, in the past, these systems have been made available through APIs. This means that calls to control these infrastructure capabilities have been intermixed with application logic. Often it is the case that the amount of code devoted to calling infrastructure APIs dwarfs application logic. For example, the following is an example of reliably sending a message to a JMS queue:

```
Context ctx = new InitialContext();
QueueConnectionFactory qconFactory =
  (QueueConnectionFactory) ctx.lookup(JMS_FACTORY);
QueueConnection qcon =
    qconFactory.createQueueConnection();
QueueSession qsession =
    qcon.createQueueSession(false,
    Session.AUTO_ACKNOWLEDGE);
Queue queue = (Queue) ctx.lookup("myQueue");
QueueSender qsender = qsession.createSender(queue);
TextMessage msg = qsession.createTextMessage();

qcon.start();
qsender.send(msg, DeliveryMode.PERSISTENT, 0, 0);
qsender.close();
qsession.close();
qcon.close();
```

The concepts of the queue connection, queue session, and queue sender are all needed so that there are places to put the APIs for configuring the numerous capabilities of JMS.

This approach has the following disadvantages:

- The application logic is hard to follow by looking at the code. If application conditions change, it is hard to find the corresponding logic that needs to change.

- Organizations have to hire developers who know both the subtleties of the options available through the infrastructure APIs, as well as the potentially complex control flows and business rules that are critical to the business.

- If, after deployment, it is discovered that some different infrastructure option would be better-suited for some component or some communication path, the code has to be rewritten.

SCA does not assume that all the complexities associated with the myriad of capabilities provided by infrastructure software will suddenly disappear. Rather, it assumes that those complexities will continue to exist but they will be separated from application code. The component developer will specify as little as possible in order to guarantee the correct execution of the component. The infrastructure choices will then be specified declaratively, using either binding configuration or through policy.

The "little as possible" mentioned previously has to do with the fact that sometimes the writer of the business logic knows that certain capabilities from the container must be provided in order for the component to operate correctly.

Now consider what it looks like in SCA to send the previous JMS message persistently:

```
@Requires(EXACTLY_ONCE)
protected GreetingReceiver target;
...

void f()
{
    target.sendGreeting("hi");
}
```

Some of the differences have nothing to do with policy. JMS is loosely typed, so it uses a general-purpose `send()` method. SCA requires a more specific operation signature for each asynchronous method.

The policy aspect of this is the top line, which requires the `exactlyOnce` intent. This is saying that the one-way method invocation should be delivered using whatever infrastructure configuration is necessary in order to get the message there exactly one time (no duplicates and no dropped messages). The details of how the system is going to achieve this, including the timeout values that should be used, the persistent mechanism to be used, and other such details, are left to the policy administrator.

Wire Validity

When policy sets are found for each binding, SCA has to make sure the resulting wires are valid from a policy perspective. SCA does not define how it accomplishes this for anything other than WS-Policy.

For WS-Policy, SCA uses the policy intersection algorithm that was defined in WS-Policy. The policy expressions on the bindings on each side of a wire have to line up (intersect) in order for the wire to be valid.

With our `PropagatesTransaction` example, the WS-Policy assertion is `<wsat:ATAssertion>`. In order for there to be a match, both sides of the wire need to have that assertion. If both sides don't specify it, there is no match and the wire is invalid.

The fact that the WS-Policy matching algorithm would fail when the reference has the `ATAssertion` and the service does not is appropriate in this scenario. In essence, the reference is saying: "I must be wired to a service that knows how to undo its work if I ever roll back, because I don't have any compensation handling logic." If the service doesn't declare that it can join the transaction, as far as SCA can tell, it will not be able to, and the requirement made by the reference is not met.

WS-Policy

The preceding scenario used a trivial WS-Policy expression. It had a single policy assertion, `<wsat:ATAssertion>`, which had to exist on both sides of the wire. In general, WS-Policy matching is a bit more complicated than this, because each side of the wire can include arbitrarily complex expressions that involve optional policy assertions or alternative assertions. WS-Policy does not define any specific policies; it just describes an expression language for combining them. The concepts defined by WS-Policy are the following:

- **Policy assertion**—Policy assertions are the atoms from which larger policy expressions can be built. A policy assertion is simply an XML element. It can come from any namespace. Two policy assertions definitely match if they have the same element QName, the same attribute values, and the same subelements (if any). If they differ, the policy assertions may or may not match—it depends on the definition of the policy assertion (what a pain!).

- **ExactlyOne E1, E2, ...**—This says that E1, E2, and so on are policy choices. Exactly one of those policy expressions must be used when using the service.

- **All E1, E2, ...**—This says that expressions E1, E2, and so on are policy expressions that must be enforced together.

- **Optional policy assertions**—A policy assertion may be marked with an attribute of `wsp:optional="true"`. This means that the policy is available if the other side of the wire asks for it, but it isn't required by this side. It is defined as a macro expansion of an ExactlyOne with two subexpressions—one with the assertion, and one without it.

- **Ignorable policy assertions**—A policy assertion may be marked with an attribute of `wsp:ignorable="true"`. This is used to declare characteristics of a service that don't require cooperation from both sides—such as audit logging. One side of the wire is declaring that it is going to do something (for example, log messages). This way, if the other side of the wire requires that it should only be wired to services that do such logging, the assertion is there to cover it. If the other side doesn't care, the wire will work anyway (and the logging will happen anyway).

Looking at the preceding concepts, you can see that they are basically the XOR and AND operators from predicate logic. It is notable that they do not have the inclusive OR operator or the NOT operator. The lack of a NOT operator means that it is not possible for a reference, for example, to say that it must not be wired to a service that does audit logging.

The lack of an inclusive OR means that if a service can do A, B, or A and B, instead of just being able to say:

```
</Or><A/><B/></Or>
```

it must say:

```
<ExactlyOne>
  <A/>
  <B/>
  <All><A/><B/></All>
</ExactlyOne>
```

So, inclusive OR is possible; it is just ugly.

Because WS-Policy doesn't define any policy assertions, it must leave those to other specifications. Some of the specifications that define standard policy assertions include WS-AT, WS-SecurityPolicy, or WS-ReliabilityPolicy.

There is one final important concept that WS-Policy defines, as follows:

- **Policy intersection**—This is used for determining if two policies are "compatible." The two policies are set side-by-side, and any place one side has an `exactlyOne`, the other side has to have a policy expression that matches one of the alternatives (possibly also within an `exactlyOne`). The intersection continues in a predictable manner given the concepts defined previously. One thing that is noteworthy about WS-Policy intersection is that it is symmetric. The service provider and the service client both specify policy expressions, and the two sides are treated the same. This may seem odd at first, because service providers seem like the more natural place to declare requirements on any client of that service. (After all, WSDL is only defined for the provider side, not for clients.) But, in fact, clients may sometimes have requirements of their own, which need to be communicated to whatever human or system is going to be finding a matching service.

Returning to our example, consider the one wire between the `Credit` and the `Scoring` components (see Figure 6.2).

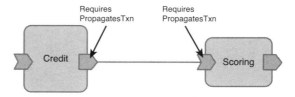

Figure 6.2   Required intents on the two ends of a wire

Each of these intents will resolve to the same `policySet`—namely, the `policySet` mentioned previously:

```
<policySet provides="propagatesTransaction" appliesTo="binding.ws">
   <wsat:ATAssertion/>
</policySet>
```

The policy infrastructure requires the intersection of the policies on each end of the wire in order to determine the policy actually used.

In this case, this becomes the intersection of a `policySet` with itself, so the intersection is the same as the original `policySet`.

Because the `<wsat:ATAssertion/>` policy assertion is present on the wire, the transaction will be propagated.

Policies for One-Way Messaging

SCA also defines a few intents related to the reliability of one-way messaging.

Let's return to the application presented in Chapter 5, "Composition," but this time after it ended up looking like what is shown in Figure 6.3.

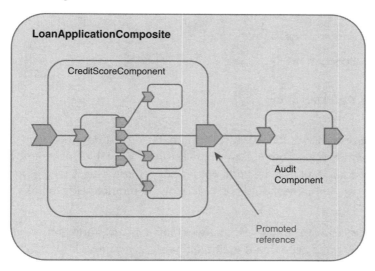

Figure 6.3   Big Bank's top-level composite

The outermost composite in this picture is shown in Listing 6.3.

Listing 6.3   *Wiring to the Audit Component*

```
<composite … name="LoanApplicationComposite">

    …

    <component name ="CreditComponent">
        <implementation.composite name="loan: CreditServiceComposite"/>
        <reference name="auditService" target="AuditComponent"/>
```

```
<component>

<component name ="AuditComponent">
   <implementation.java class="com.bigbank.AuditComponent"/>
<component>

</composite>
```

We haven't previously looked at the interface for the `AuditComponent`, so let's do that now. `AuditComponent` will have a single `@OneWay` operation called `auditEntry`, which takes as a parameter a string representation of the auditable step that needs to be recorded (see Listing 6.4).

Listing 6.4   *Interface for the AuditComponent*

```
import org.osoa.sca.annotations.OneWay;
@Remotable
public interface AuditComponent {

      @OneWay
      void auditEntry(String entry);
}
```

The operation is a one-way operation, because it does not want to slow down the normal flow of the business logic. However, it is also important that the audit entries not get lost! This is where policy can help. We should add the following requirements to this wire:

- **exactlyOnce**—So that we don't lose any audit entries, and none get entered multiple times
- **authentication**—So that no one forges an audit entry
- **integrity**—So that the entries are signed, preventing third-party modification of the audit entry

To add these requirements to `LoanApplicationComposite`, all that is necessary is to add an entry for each of these requirements into a `@requires` attribute of the reference (see Listing 6.5).

Listing 6.5   *Wiring to the AuditComponent*

```
<composite … name="LoanApplicationComposite">

   …

   <component name ="CreditComponent">
      <implementation.composite name="loan:CreditServiceComposite"/>
      <reference name="auditService" target="AuditComponent"
       requires="exactlyOnce authentication integrity"/>

   <component>

   <component name ="AuditComponent">
      <implementation.java class="com.bigbank.AuditComponent"/>
   <component>

</composite>
```

Qualified Intents

There are times when a developer might want to specify more about *how* a generic capability is going to be provided than is possible with simple intents. **Qualified intents** are intents that provide this additional detail beyond some existing simple intent.

Consider the confidentiality intent that was introduced at the beginning of this chapter. Confidentiality is typically accomplished through encryption, although different mechanisms exist. Some handle encryption on a point-to-point basis. This is typically called **transport-level encryption**. Other techniques exist to encrypt a message in such a way that intermediaries can process and route the message without decrypting the body of the message. This is called **message-level encryption**.

If a developer specifies that she requires `sca:Confidentiality` on a reference, this does not constrain the kind of encryption technique that is used. However, some developers may know enough about the data and the way it is supposed to be protected to know that message-level encryption is required. In this case, it should be possible to require message-level encryption, but still to do it at the level of intents, rather than having to dive down into the details of a specific binding.

> **Qualified intents** *are intents that provide this additional detail beyond some existing simple intent.*

In SCA, an intent may be **qualified** *by extending it with a "." and the name of some valid qualifier for that intent.*

In SCA, an intent may be **qualified** by extending it with a "." and the name of some valid qualifier for that intent. In the case of confidentiality, there are two qualifiers, which are written as `sca:Confidentiality.Message` and `sca:Confidentiality.Transport`.

Qualified intents are not independent intents from intents that they qualify. The most important relationship between them is the fact that anything that satisfies a qualified intent also implicitly satisfies the intent that it qualifies. This is especially useful between the various roles involved in application development. If a developer requires a specific intent, an assembler or deployer may *further refine* that requirement by requiring a qualified version of the intent.

Even within a single role, it is sometimes valuable to specify a more general intent that applies broadly, perhaps to everything within a composite, and then to refine that general intent down to a specific intent for some specific service. For example, the confidentiality intent might be specified on the composite, but some of its services might specify `Confidentiality.Message`.

Profile Intents

A profile intent is a single intent that expands into other intents.

There are times when a collection of intents are so frequently used together that it makes sense to have a single intent that expands into other intents. A **profile intent** is such an intent. The definition of a profile intent includes a `@requires` attribute that lists the intents that it should expand into.

Among the set of standard SCA intents, the reliability intent of `sca:ExactlyOnce` is a profile intent that expands to `sca:AtLeastOnce` and `sca:AtMostOnce`. As is always the case with an `@requires` attribute, the semantics of the list is AND—all the intents must be satisfied.

Listing 6.6 presents the definition of the `sca:ExactlyOnce` profile intent.

Listing 6.6   *ExactlyOnce Intent Definition*

```
<intent name="ExactlyOnce" constrains="sca:binding"
      requires="sca:AtLeastOnce sca:AtMostOnce">
    <description>
    The binding implementation guarantees that a
    message sent by a service consumer is delivered
    to the service implementation. Also, the binding
    implementation guarantees that the message is not
    delivered more than once to the service
    implementation.
    </description>
</intent>
```

Standard Intents

A variety of the standardized intents have been referenced in the previous section. The following is an exhaustive list of the intents that have been standardized as of SCA 1.0. All these intents are in the SCA namespace.

Security Intents

The security intents include the following:

- **Authentication**—The identity of the requestor of the service must be verified.

- **Confidentiality**—Some mechanism (such as encryption) must be used to prevent a message from being read by anyone other than the intended recipient of the message.

- **Integrity**—A message must be protected from being surreptitiously modified after it has been created (such as by attaching an electronic signature).

Each of the three preceding intents have the following two qualifiers:

- **Transport**—The guarantee need only be guaranteed at the transport level (that is, for a single hop).

- **Message**—The guarantee should be at the message level. It should provide an end-to-end guarantee.

Delivery Intents

The delivery intents include the following:

- **AtLeastOnce**—At least one copy of the message must be delivered (duplicates allowed).

- **AtMostOnce**—At most, one copy of the message must be delivered (no duplicates; dropped messages allowed).

- **ExactlyOnce**—The message must be delivered once and only once.

- **Ordered**—Messages from the same client must be delivered in the same order that they were sent.

Transaction Intents

Transaction intents include the following:

- **PropagatesTransaction**—The intent requires that the other side of the wire must be able to be in the same transaction. If the intent is on a reference, it means that the service provider must be able to join the transaction. If it is on a service, it means that the client must be able to provide a transaction to join. This must be used with ManagedTransaction.global on the implementation.

- **SuspendTransaction**—This intent goes on service and references and prevents any transaction that might be active from being shared across that wire.

- **ManagedTransaction**—This intent goes on implementations and means that the components must be run within some kind of transactional environment, although it may not be global. Usually this means that it has to be able to use a database to do the work of a method as one atomic unit (without having to specify explicitly transaction boundaries), but doesn't need to share its transaction with its clients or its downstream services.

- **ManagedTransaction.Global**—This is a qualified intent that extends ManagedTransaction to say that the transaction must be one that can enlist upstream or downstream components.

- **`ManagedTransaction.Local`**—This qualifier clarifies that a local transaction, rather than a global transaction, should be used. This provides better performance, but introduces the possibility that a system crash could cause the changes to one resource to be lost even while changes made from the same transaction to a different resource are committed.

- **`NoManagedTransaction`**—No managed transaction should be used.

Miscellaneous Intents

Miscellaneous intents include the following:

- **`SOAP`**—The SOAP messaging model should be used. Note that this does not constrain the transport that might be used to send the SOAP message. If it is unqualified, any version of the SOAP standard may be used.

- **`SOAP.1_1`**—The SOAP v.1.1 standard message model must be used.

- **`SOAP.1_2`**—The SOAP v.1.2 standard message model must be used.

- **`JMS`**—This application uses the JMS API, so the binding must support this API.

- **`NoListener`**—The binding must be able to handle any incoming traffic through the back channel of an outbound request. There is no listener for inbound traffic. For asynchronous responses, the binding may need to use polling.

■ Differences from Java EE Transactions

Java EE also provides transactional component behavior through declarative configuration. In Java EE, this capability is called **container-managed transactions**. In J2EE version 2.1 and earlier, the deployment descriptor would mark the session beans with a `<transaction-type>` element with a value of `Container`. There is then a separate section that describes which Java EE transaction mode each of these beans requires. A small example in SCA would be represented as the following:

```
<component name="myAppBean"
requires="ManagedTransaction">
     <implementation.java
class="examples.MyAppImpl"/>
</component>
```

The same component might be represented in a deployment descriptor, as follows:

```
<ejb-jar>
 <enterprise-beans>
<session>
    <ejb-name>myAppBean</ejb-name>
    <home>examples.MyAppHome</home>
    <remote>examples.MyApp</remote>
    <ejb-class>examples.MayAppImpl</ejb-class>
    <session-type>Stateful</session-type>
    <transaction-type>Container</transaction-type>
</session>
<assembly-descriptor>
    <container-transaction>
      <method>
       <ejb-name>MyAppBean</ejb-name>
       <method-intf>Remote</method-intf>
       <method-name>*</method-name>
      </method>
      <trans-attribute>Required</trans-attribute>
</container-transaction>
  </assembly-descriptor>
</ejb-jar>
```

This declares that the MyAppBean will require the existence of a transaction, which should be guaranteed by the container. In this case, the ManagedTransaction intent basically maps to the Required Java EE transaction attribute. The values for that attribute are: NotSupported, Supports, Required, RequiresNew, Mandatory, and Never.

One of the problems with the Java EE transaction attributes is that they confuse two concepts, as follows:

- Should the component be run in a transaction?
- Should the transaction be the one propagated from the client?

For example, the "Mandatory" Java EE attribute says that the component should run in a transaction, and the client must propagate a transaction for it to join.

In SCA, the preceding two questions are represented by separate intents. The ManagedTransaction intent says that the component should be run in a transaction. This is an implementation intent, so it is not seen by clients. However, clients can see a separate interaction intent called `PropagatesTransaction`. This intent says that the clients must send a transaction that the component can join. If the interaction intent had been `SuspendsTransaction`, the client could know that any transaction associated with the client would *not* be used by the component.

In general, it is not really part of the component contract if the component uses a transaction but does join in the transaction of the client. The client doesn't need to know whether it uses transactions in that case.

Summary

This chapter has covered using SCA policy to declaratively configure such things as transactions, security, and reliability. One of the key goals of SCA policy is to abstract the complexity associated with specifying security, reliability, and other qualities of service from application code. SCA achieves this policy abstraction by providing policy intents that are used by developers to signal the need for an abstract quality of service, and then are turned into concrete policies by policy administrators.

7

Wires

This chapter picks up more advanced topics associated with wiring components. In particular, it covers wiring to multiple providers of a service, autowire, and wire reinjection after a component has been deployed to a domain.

Wiring to Multiple Service Providers

In distributed systems, there is often a need for clients to make the same request to a number of services. A common scenario where this arises is when a request-for-quote is issued: A client will make the same request to multiple service providers, as illustrated in Figure 7.1.

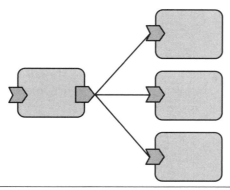

Figure 7.1   Wiring to multiple service providers

In Figure 7.1, the client contains a collection of references that it iterates through and invokes with the same request. If BigBank wanted to expand its credit check procedures, it could use multiple credit score components that produced ratings based on different criteria. Let's see how this is done.

A reference can be wired to multiple targets by specifying more than one component name in the @target attribute of the <reference> element.

A reference can be wired to multiple targets by specifying more than one component name in the @target attribute of the <reference> element. Component names are separated by a space. Listing 7.1 shows the same composite with the LoanComponent reference wired to multiple CreditComponents.

Listing 7.1   *Wiring to Multiple Targets*

```
<composite xmlns="http://www.osoa.org/xmlns/sca/1.0"
      targetNamespace="http://www.bigbank.com/xmlns/loanApplication/
name="LoanApplicationComposite">
   <component name ="LoanComponent">
      <implementation.java class="com.acme.LoanComponent"/>
      <reference name="creditService"
      target="CreditComponent1 CreditComponent2"/>
   <component>

   <component name ="CreditComponent1">
      <implementation.java class="com.acme.CreditComponent1"/>
   <component>

   <component name ="CreditComponent2">
      <implementation.java class="com.acme.CreditComponent2"/>
   <component>
</composite>
```

A reference with multiple wires is injected into a component implementation instance as a collection.

A reference with multiple wires is injected into a component implementation instance as a collection. In Java, the component implementation could choose to have the reference injected as a java.util.List, as shown in Listing 7.2.

Listing 7.2   *Multiple Wire Injection*

```
public class LoanComponent implements LoanService {
   private List<CreditService> services;


   public void LoanComponent (@Reference List<CreditService> services){
      this.services = services;
   }

   //…
}
```

When handling a request, the component iterates and invokes the various services individually, as shown in the excerpt in Listing 7.3.

Listing 7.3   *Invoking Multiple Wires*

```
public class LoanComponent implements LoanService {
      private List<CreditService> services;


      public void LoanComponent (@Reference List<CreditService>
⮕services){
            this.services = services;
      }
public LoanResult apply(LoanRequest request) {
   String id = request.getCustomerId();
   List<CreditScore> scores = new ArrayList<CreditScore>();
         for(CreditService service : services) {
            CreditScore score = service.checkCredit(id);
            Scores.add(score);
         }
         // process the credit scores …
      }

}
```

When a reference is configured with multiple wires, it is said to have a multiplicity greater than one. Multiplicity defines the number of wires a reference may have. Recalling that references may be required or optional (in Java, setting the "required" attribute on the @Reference annotation to true or false), references may have the following multiplicities:

- **0..1**—Denotes an optional reference. In Java, the reference is specified using `@Reference(required = false)`.

- **1..1**—Denotes a required reference. In Java, the reference is specified using `@Reference(required = true)` or simply `@Reference`.

- **0..n**—Denotes an optional reference that may be configured with multiple wires. In Java, the reference type must be a `java.util.Collection` and is specified using `@Reference(required = false)`.

- **1..n**—Denotes a required reference that may be configured with multiple wires. In Java, the reference type must be a `java.util.Collection` and is specified using `@Reference(required = true)` or `@Reference`.

Those familiar with modeling languages may recognize that the 0..1, 1..1, 0..n, and 1..n notation used by SCA to express multiplicity derives from Unified Modeling Language (UML).

Perspective: Why SCA Did Not Use UML

With its concepts of services, components, and wires, SCA lends itself naturally to modeling an application and representing it visually. Unified Modeling Language (UML) is the industry-recognized standard for modeling applications. Given this, why did SCA not adopt UML as its starting point?

Although UML is a powerful modeling tool, the SCA authors didn't want its complexity. A key goal of SCA is to create a simplified programming model. At the same time, SCA's modeling requirements were modest in comparison to UML's scope. It was felt that requiring people to learn UML would have resulted in the need to master more concepts than strictly required.

The `<wire>` Element

Having to specify target names using a space-delimited list in the `@target` attribute of the `<reference>` element can be difficult to read by humans. Going back to the multiplicity example we used previously, it may not be immediately apparent that the `LoanComponent.creditService` reference is wired to multiple services (see Listing 7.4).

Listing 7.4   *Wiring Multiple Targets for the LoanComponent*

```
<composite …>
   <component name ="LoanComponent">
      <implementation.java class="com.acme.LoanComponent"/>
      <reference name="creditService"
      target="CreditComponent1 CreditComponent2"/>
   <component>


</composite>
```

To make configuration more readable (and for those who prefer to separate wiring from component definitions), SCDL also supports a <wire> element, which may be used to define multiple wires for a reference (see Listing 7.5).

SCDL provides the <wire> element as a way to specify multiple wires for a reference.

Listing 7.5   *Using the <wire> Element*

```
<composite …>
   <component name ="LoanComponent">
      <implementation.java class="com.acme.LoanComponent"/>

   <component>

   <!--define wires separately -->

   <wire source="LoanComponent/creditService"
   target=" CreditComponent1"/>
   <wire source="LoanComponent/creditService"
   target=" CreditComponent2"/>


</composite>
```

The <wire> element has source and target attributes. The source attribute identifies the reference the wire configures and is specified using the component and reference names separated by a /. The target attribute identifies the target service the reference is wired to, which is done using the name of the component providing the service and the service name separated by a /. The preceding example omitted the service name because both CreditComponents have only one service (recalling from Chapter 2, "Assembling and Deploying a Composite," that if a component implements more than one service, the service name would have to be specified using the "component name/service name" SCDL syntax). Similarly, if the source component had only one reference, it does not need to be specified. If `LoanComponent` only had the "`creditService`" reference, the preceding SCDL could have specified the source as `source="LoanComponent"`.

Multiplicity and Callbacks

In the previous example, the interaction pattern used when wiring to multiple providers was blocking request-response—that is, the `LoanComponent` iterated through the collection of wires and waited for a response after each `CreditService` invocation. In situations where there are many providers or where a response may take some time, a callback may be more appropriate.

Using non-blocking operations and callbacks with references having multiple wires is not really different from references having a single wire. Recalling that the `CreditService` is defined using a Java interface, annotating the `checkCredit` operation with `@OneWay` will make it non-blocking. As the `LoanComponent` iterates through the collection of credit service wires, it will be able to invoke each without blocking, resulting in the client issuing multiple invocations without waiting for others to complete. This can greatly improve the overall performance of an application because a number of tasks can be processed at the same time.

To return a result from a non-blocking operation, a service provider uses a callback, which we discussed in Chapter 3, "Service-Based Development Using Java." To enable callbacks, the `Loan Component` implements the `CreditScoreCallback` interface, as shown in Listing 7.6.

Listing 7.6   *The CreditScoreCallback Interface*

```
@Remotable
public interface CreditScoreCallback {

     void onResult(CreditScore score);
}
```

When a credit `CreditComponent` is invoked (also written in Java), it is injected with a callback proxy, which it uses to return the credit score response. As each `CreditComponent` finishes processing the request, it invokes the `onResult` operation on the callback proxy.

This results in the `LoanComponent` receiving multiple callbacks. In this case, it is likely that the `LoanComponent` will want to correlate the credit score with the service provider that made the callback. This can be done by adding additional information to the `CreditScore` data, such as a provider ID.

What's Behind a Wire?

How are wires manifested in an SCA runtime? Although SCA runtimes may implement wires differently, the principles remain the same. A wire is a proxy that implements the service contract required by a reference and is responsible for flowing an invocation to a target, potentially a remote web service or service offered by another SCA component (see Figure 7.2).

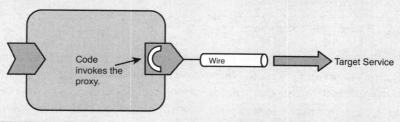

Figure 7.2   A wire is a proxy that dispatches an invocation to a target service.

A wire may be responsible for dispatching an invocation over a remote binding, such as web services or RMI. In this case, it would be responsible for serializing the invocation parameters, possibly in a SOAP message, and invoking a transport-specific API. In the case of synchronous invocations (that is, ones expecting a direct response), the wire would also deserialize the return value to the client or throw an exception if one occurred.

Wires may perform additional tasks related to an invocation, such as flowing transactional or security context. One common way of implementing this is through an interceptor. **Interceptors** are linked units of code that perform a specific action and pass on processing to the next interceptor in a chain. In Java, servlet filters are a common type of interceptor. Common tasks include passing (or "propagating") security credentials or transaction context.

When an invocation is made on the proxy, the wire is responsible for dispatching it down the appropriate interceptor chain. After the interceptor chain has finished processing, the invocation is then dispatched through a communications layer to the target service (see Figure 7.3).

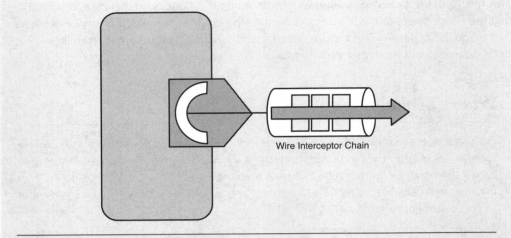

Wire Interceptor Chain

Figure 7.3   A wire interceptor chain

In Java-based runtimes, wires can be implemented using JDK proxies or through more exotic (and potentially more performant) means, such as bytecode generation. Fortunately, these details remain hidden from components, which interact with wires as if they were normal Java objects. From application code, dispatching over a wire appears as a standard method invocation.

Automated Wiring: Autowire

To help reduce excessive XML and make wiring easier, SCA allows references to be automatically wired, or "autowired," by the runtime.

XML-based configuration can become verbose and fragile, particularly as the number of components and wires in an application increases. To help reduce excessive XML and make wiring easier, SCA allows references to be automatically wired, or "autowired," by the runtime. When a reference is autowired, the runtime selects a suitable target service, as opposed to having it explicitly specified in the target attribute of a `<reference>` or `<wire>` element. When autowiring a reference, the runtime will attempt to select a matching service from all services provided by components in the same composite. The runtime will perform the selection by comparing the required service contract of the reference with the service contract of the target service to see if they are compatible (for more information on compatibility, see the following sidebar). If more than one suitable target is found, the runtime will select one in an implementation-specific manner. This may be as simple as selecting one at random, or more complex, such as preferring a collocated service for performance reasons.

Service Compatibility

When wiring references to services, SCA requires their service contracts to be compatible. Be careful not to confuse this with equality. In other words, the service contract required by a reference does not have to be the *same* as the target service. For example, the required contract for a client component written in Java may be determined by the Java interface used by the reference. When autowiring, a target service could be selected that is provided by a BPEL-based component, whose interface would be defined by WSDL. In this case, the runtime would check compatibility between the Java interface and WSDL definition.

What constitutes compatibility? SCA defines a series of rules for determining compatibility, as follows:

- The operations defined by the target service contract must be the same or be a superset of those defined by the source.
- Operation matching is determined by the following criteria. The operation name, parameter types, and return types must be the same. The order of operation parameters and return values (for languages that support multiple return values) must be the same. Finally, the set of faults and exceptions declared by the source and target contracts must be the same.
- Callback service contracts, if present, must match.
- The source and target contracts must either both be local or remotable.
- Other specified attributes must also be the same. For example, if a source service contract is conversational, the target contract must be as well.

For cases where both source and target contracts are the same (that is, Java-to-Java or WSDL-to-WSDL), matching is straightforward. Where things get interesting is when the contracts are not the same. For example, it is possible in SCA to wire a reference to a service that uses different Java interfaces to define their service contracts. As long as they are compatible, the runtime is responsible for establishing the connection. This may involve some form of mediation as a request is flowed from the source to the target service.

Fortunately, the complexity associated with matching source and target service contracts is hidden from applications. However, it is useful to understand how matching is performed and to not assume that it rests on both sides of a wire being the same.

The composite shown in Listing 7.7 demonstrates the use of autowire.

Listing 7.7   *A Composite Using Autowire*

```
<composite xmlns="http://www.osoa.org/xmlns/sca/1.0"
     targetNamespace="
http://www.bigbank.com/xmlns/loanApplication/1.0:LoanApplicationComposite"
     name="LoanApplicationComposite"
     autowire="true">
   <component name ="LoanComponent">
      <implementation.java class="com.acme.LoanComponent"/>
   <component>

   <component name ="CreditComponent">
      <implementation.java class="com.acme.CreditComponent"/>
   <component>

</composite>
```

By default, autowire is disabled. Unless explicitly enabled, the runtime will not attempt to wire unconfigured references. The SCDL in Listing 7.7 enables autowire for the entire composite by setting the "autowire" attribute on the composite definition to true. As a result, component references not explicitly wired to a target will be wired by the runtime. Because `LoanComponent#creditService` is not configured (that is, there is no corresponding `<reference>` entry in the SCDL), the runtime will automatically wire it to a suitable matching target—in this case, the `CreditService` provided by the `CreditComponent`.

SCA allows autowire to be enabled for a composite, a component, or a reference. If we had wanted to autowire just the `LoanComponent` references, we would have set the autowire attribute to true on its `<component>` element (see Listing 7.8).

Listing 7.8   *Using the Autowire Attribute on a Component*

```
<component name ="LoanComponent" autowire="true">
      <implementation.java class="com.acme.LoanComponent"/>
</component>
```

Similarly, we could have restricted autowire to the individual reference (see Listing 7.9).

Listing 7.9 ***Using the Autowire Attribute on a Reference***

```
<component name ="LoanComponent>
   <implementation.java class="com.acme.LoanComponent"/>
   <reference name="creditService" autowire="true"/>
</component>
```

Autowire can also be disabled for specific components or references. For example, if autowire is enabled for a composite, it may be turned off for specific components and references by setting their autowire attribute to false.

Autowire can also be used to wire references with a multiplicity greater than one. In these situations, the runtime will inject wires for *all* matching services in the composite. So, if the `LoanComponent` was a multiplicity, as shown in Listing 7.10, and autowire was enabled as in the previous SCDL examples, the component implementation would be injected with all matching `CreditServices`.

Listing 7.10 ***Autowire and Multiplicity References***

```
public class LoanComponent implements LoanService {
      private List<CreditService> services;

      public void LoanComponent (@Reference List<CreditService>
➥services){
            this.services = services;
      }

//...
}
```

Perspective: When to Use Autowire

Autowire is a somewhat controversial feature. We prefer autowire because it reduces the amount of "manual" assembly required for applications. Moreover, it makes the resulting composite configuration less susceptible to breaking during refactoring. If a component name changes, or a service is moved to a different component, autowired references will automatically be adjusted by the runtime. Explicitly targeted references will need to be manually updated.

Some (rightfully) point out that autowire makes wiring less apparent when looking at the composite XML. Although graphical tooling can help visualize how references will be autowired, it can't help with avoiding unintended consequences, such as the runtime selecting the "wrong" service. This can happen if two services implement the same interface contract and the runtime is unable to select among them. In these cases, the best option is explicit wiring because it will guarantee that the correct target service is chosen.

Autowire and Composition

Autowire has specific rules for composition—namely, if not specified for a composite, the autowire setting is inherited from the composition hierarchy. To understand how this works, consider the case where the `LoanApplicationComposite` contains a component whose implementation is provided by the `CreditScore Composite`. If the `CreditScoreComposite` does not specify an autowire value and the `LoanApplicationComposite` does, autowire will be inherited from the latter, as shown in Figure 7.4.

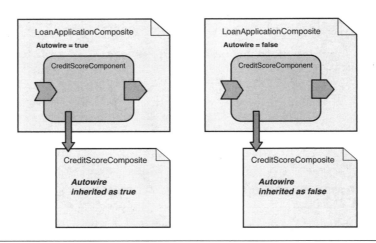

Figure 7.4   Inheriting autowire settings

In contrast, when autowire is explicitly set in the `CreditScore Composite`, this value takes precedence over settings in the `LoanApplicationComposite` (see Figure 7.5).

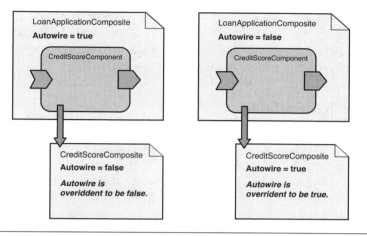

**Figure 7.5   Explicitly setting autowire in the
`CreditScoreComposite`**

Now consider a slightly different case where the `CreditScore Composite` inherits its autowire setting (that is, it does not specify autowire), but the `CreditComponent`, which uses the composite as its implementation, explicitly declares an autowire setting. In this case, the inherited value will be determined from the `CreditComponent` setting (see Figure 7.6).

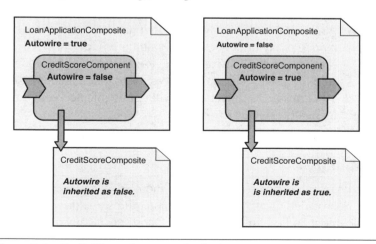

Figure 7.6   Explicitly setting autowire in the `CreditComponent`

If autowire values are not set, inheritance will be calculated by examining the composition hierarchy for an autowire declaration until the top-level domain composite is reached. If no setting is found, autowire will be false, because it is the default.

Wire Reinjection

SCA is often misinterpreted as being based on a static wiring model—that is, once a component is deployed, the services to which its references are wired cannot be changed. In fact, SCA allows for wires to be changed dynamically at runtime in certain circumstances. How rewiring is done (for example, through a management tool, command-line utility, or other means) is runtime-specific. SCA defines the following rules for how reinjection occurs:

- The component must be composite or conversation scoped. Rewiring stateless components would not make much sense and could have potentially damaging results as the target of a reference could change in the middle of a request being processed. For conversation-scoped components, a wire can only be changed if a conversation is not active. (If the change occurred during a conversation, the runtime would apply the change after the conversation has ended.)

- When a reference is rewired, the runtime injects a new service proxy or collection containing service proxies in the case of a multiplicity reference. Reinjection will be done for field- and setter-based references. Note that if a component uses constructor injection, it will not be injected with a new service proxy (or proxies).

Summary

This chapter has covered some of the more advanced wiring capabilities provided by SCA. The next chapter turns to a discussion of deployment and runtime management, and specifically in-depth coverage of SCA domains.

8

Bindings

Applications rarely exist in isolation. External clients inside or beyond an organization's firewall may require access to services offered by an application. Likewise, an application may need to access services hosted by other applications.

Within an SCA domain, wires are used to integrate services that may be co-located or hosted on different machines. However, it is often the case that a service may need access to another service that is not hosted in the same domain or is not an SCA service at all. In SCA, bindings provide the means to communicate outside the domain. **Bindings** are used to expose services to external clients via a network protocol such as web services. In addition, bindings connect references to external services hosted outside the domain using a network protocol.

In SCA, bindings provide the means to communicate outside the domain.

In previous chapters, we introduced the basics of using bindings to expose SCA services as web service endpoints. In this chapter, we cover the web service binding in more detail and connecting services to enterprise message buses. By the end of this chapter, you will have a thorough understanding of how to use bindings to integrate SCA services with applications and services hosted outside a domain, whether they are web services or message-based.

Interoperable Communications Outside the Domain: The Web Service Binding

In SCA, bindings establish communications outside the domain. Bindings are used to expose a service as an endpoint over a remote transport. Bindings also are used to connect references to an external service via a remote transport.

When SCA was created, it was envisaged that there would be many different types of bindings corresponding to the range of remote protocols used by distributed applications today. When performance is a concern, a binary-based binding such as RMI/IIOP could be used. In cases where interoperability is required—for example, when a service needs to be available to clients written in other languages, such as one of the .NET languages—the web service binding is the logical choice. In this section, we look at the details of working with the web service binding.

Making a service available as a web service endpoint or accessing a web service using SCA is fairly simple. The composite presented in Listing 8.1 promotes a service and reference using the web service binding.

Listing 8.1   *Using the Web Service Binding*

```
<composite ….>
   <service name="LoanService" promote=" LoanComponent">
      <binding.ws uri="http://bigbank.com/services/LoanService">
   </service>

   <component name="LoanComponent">
   …
   </composite>

   <reference name="rateService" promote="LoanComponent/rateService">
      <binding.ws uri="http://somecompany.com/rateService"/>
   <reference>
</component>
```

In this example, the LoanService is made available as a web service endpoint at the following address: http://bigbank.com/services/LoanService. The LoanComponent#rateService reference is bound to the web service endpoint located at http://somecompany.com/rateService.

It's valuable to briefly describe the steps performed by the runtime to make this happen. First, when activating the `LoanService` endpoint, the runtime needs to generate a WSDL document for the service (remember from Chapter 2, "Assembling and Deploying a Composite," WSDL is the language used by web services for describing services and their operations). Because the service is implemented using Java, the WSDL will be generated from a Java interface. After the WSDL is generated, the runtime needs to provision the endpoint at the address specified in the `@uri` attribute of the `<binding.ws>` element. At this point, the service will be ready to accept and process incoming requests.

On the reference side, the runtime needs to create a remote communications channel from the component to the remote endpoint. In the case of Java, this channel will be similar to one created for a wire (see the "What's Behind a Wire" sidebar in Chapter 7, "Wires"). If the component is implemented in Java, a proxy will be created that dispatches an invocation on the reference over web services. In order to dispatch an invocation correctly, the proxy needs to map from the invoked Java method to a web service operation. After it has mapped the invocation, it needs to encode the request as a SOAP message and dispatch it over the network to the address specified by the `@uri` attribute on the `<binding.ws>` element.

Having dealt with the basics of the web service binding (they are fairly trivial), we turn to some of the more common configuration options that may be needed by applications.

Using WSDL as the Interface Definition Language

In top-down development, service contracts are defined before implementations are written. This is often done to facilitate interoperability across different technology platforms. By defining services, operations, and their messages using a language-neutral format such as WSDL, top-down development can avoid using features specific to a particular platform.

WSDL is also essential when connecting systems managed by independent organizations. Because it is difficult for an organization to control or mandate the technology clients use to connect to a service, a language-independent mechanism for describing services such as WSDL is the best way to facilitate integration.

Given these scenarios, it may be necessary to use a predefined WSDL as opposed to having the runtime generate one when using the web service binding. To understand how this is done, we need to briefly review some key WSDL concepts.

In WSLD 1.1, a **port** is some unit of code that is reachable at a given network address over a particular protocol. This unit of code is often referred to as an endpoint. For example, an endpoint may be located at http://somecompany.com/rateService or at www.somecompany.com/rateService using the HTTP protocol. A port contains a set of operations that process messages in a given format. The `RateService` endpoint has a `#getRates` operation that takes several data, including the date to return rates for. When the endpoint is invoked, it receives a message containing this data via HTTP encoded in a specified format—for example, SOAP 1.1.

Ports are broken down into a number of separate elements. A `portType` defines the set of operations for an endpoint. It is roughly analogous to an interface in Java. A binding defines the message format (for example, SOAP 1.1) and protocol details for a `portType` (for example, HTTP). Finally, a port specifies an address where the endpoint can be contacted. WSDL separates out these elements so that they can be reused. Two ports may use the same `portType` but different bindings. Two different endpoints would be created that perhaps were available over different protocols but offered the same set of operations to clients.

WSDL 1.1 somewhat confusingly (at least from the perspective of SCA) also defines the concept of a "service," which is different than an SCA service. In WSDL 1.1, a service is a collection of related ports.

In response to limitations and complaints about the complexity of WSDL 1.1, WSDL 2.0 introduced several important changes. Although we will not document the changes here, there are two that you need to be aware of. First, WSDL 2.0 has renamed `portType` to `interface` and `port` to `endpoint`. Second, a `service` is now restricted to one interface (as opposed to WSDL 1.1, which allowed multiple `portType`s).

More on WSDL

In this book, we don't explain the details of WSDL. At some point, it is worth becoming more familiar with the technology. The WSDL 1.1 (http://www.w3.org/TR/wsdl) and WSDL 2.0 (http://www.w3.org/TR/wsdl20-primer, http://www.w3.org/TR/wsdl20, http://www.w3.org/TR/wsdl20-adjuncts, and http://www.w3.org/TR/wsdl20-bindings) specifications are options, although they can be tedious reading.

Having reviewed some of the key WSDL concepts, we now examine how to use WSDL with the web service binding. As Listing 8.2 illustrates, an existing WSDL document can be specified for the service and reference interface contracts using the `<interface.wsdl>` element.

Listing 8.2   *Using WSDL 1.1 to Define Service and Reference Contracts*

```
<composite ….>
    <service name="LoanService" promote=" LoanComponent">
        <interface.wsdl wsdlElement="http://www.bigbank.com/
➥loanapplication#wsdl.port(LoanService/LoanApplicationPort)
"/>
       <binding.ws/>
    </service>

    <component name="LoanComponent">
    …
    </composite>

    <reference name="rateService" promote="LoanComponent/rateService">
        <interface.wsdl wsdlElement="http://www.somecompany.com/rates#
➥wsdl.port(RateService/RatePort)
"/>
       <binding.ws/>
    <reference>
</component>
```

Listing 8.2 uses WSDL 1.1 to specify interface contracts via the @wsdlElement attribute. When using WSDL 1.1, the format for the @wsdlElement attribute is as follows:

```
<WSDL-namespace-URI>#wsdl.port(<service-name>/<port-name>)
```

In Listing 8.2, the service and reference interfaces are configured to use the portTypes defined by the LoanApplicationPort and RatePort, respectively. When this is done, the runtime will do two things. First, it will introspect the WSDL identified by the <service> entry to find the portType and map the portType operations to the promoted SCA service, LoanService, which is promoted from LoanComponent. The runtime will also introspect the WSDL specified by the <reference> configuration to find the portType so that it can map invocations to the correct endpoint operation.

The web service binding configuration in Listing 8.2 did not include an @uri attribute as it had when <interface.java> was used. This is because WSDL ports (or endpoints in WSDL 2.0) include an address. When <interface.wsdl> is used, the SCA runtime uses the address provided in WSDL.

Note that both the <service> and <reference> declarations in Listing 8.2 do not specify the physical location from which to retrieve the WSDL. How does the runtime know where to get the WSDL? If the WSDL is bundled as part of the same contribution archive as the composite file, the runtime will have access to it. If the WSDL is located elsewhere (for example, in another contribution archive), the WSDL will need to be imported. We briefly discussed contribution imports in Chapter 2 and provide a more detailed account in Chapter 9, "The Domain." Until then, we can assume the WSDL is packaged in the same contribution as the composite file.

Using WSDL 2.0 is slightly different from WSDL 1.1, and specifying interface contracts is one of those areas that involves those slight differences. Listing 8.3 modifies the previous example (refer to Listing 8.2) to show how this is done.

Listing 8.3   *Using WSDL 2.0 to Define Service and Reference Contracts*

```
<composite ….>
   <service name="LoanService" promote=" LoanComponent">
     <interface.wsdl wsdlElement="http://www.bigbank.com/
➥loanapplication# wsdl.endpoint(LoanService/LoanApplicationEndpoint)
"/>
     <binding.ws/>
   </service>
```

```
<component name="LoanComponent">
...
</composite>

<reference name="rateService" promote="LoanComponent/rateService">
        <interface.wsdl wsdlElement="http://www.somecompany.com/rates#
➥wsdl.endpoint(RateService/RateEndpoint)
"/>
      <binding.ws/>
   <reference>
</composite>
```

The difference between the WSDL 1.1 and WSDL 2.0 examples is the use of `wsdl.endpoint` in place of `wsdl.port`. The format for the `@wsdlElement` attribute when using WSDL 2.0 is as follows:

```
<WSDL-namespace-URI>#wsdl.port(<service-name>/<endpoint-name>)
```

Also note that we changed the name of `LoanApplicationPort` to `LoanApplicationEndpoint` and `RatePort` to `RateEndpoint` to reflect the new WSDL 2.0 terminology.

Perspective: Should WSDL Be Used When Specifying Service Contracts?

Although we have discussed `<interface.wsdl>` in conjunction with the web service binding, it can also be used in other contexts. Specifically, WSDL can be used as the interface definition language for any service or reference, whether it is explicitly bound or wired. WSDL can also be used to define the interface contracts on both sides of a wire, as the following illustrates:

```
<composite name="LoanApplicationComposite">
   <component name ="LoanComponent">
      ...
   <component>

   <reference promote="LoanComponent/creditScoreService">
        <interface.wsdl wsdlElement=" wsdlElement="http://
➥www.bigbank.com/loanapplication#wsdl.port(CreditScore/Credit
➥ScorePort)
"/>
   </reference>
```

```
</composite>

<composite name="CreditScoreComposite">
   <service promote="CreditScoreComponent/CreditScoreService">
      <interface.wsdl wsdlElement=" wsdlElement=
➥"http://www.bigbank.com/loanapplication#wsdl.port(CreditScore/
➥CreditScorePort)
"/>
   </service>

   <component name ="CreditScoreComponent">
      ...
   <component>

</composite>
```

Most applications probably don't need the added complexity of explicitly specifying WSDL except in special circumstances. For example, when wiring references to services, the runtime will establish a remote communications channel without requiring WSDL to be specified.

One case where the added complexity of using WSDL directly may be beneficial is binding a service or reference. In these situations, the WSDL may be created prior to the service implementation to facilitate interoperability between service clients and providers written in different languages. Using explicitly defined WSDL avoids the possibility that WSDL generated by the SCA runtime when a service or reference is bound will contain subtle differences.

Specifying WSDL may also beneficial when applications are assembled from components written in multiple languages. For these types of applications, it may be easier to write WSDL upfront and generate interfaces for clients in their respective languages. Similar to the previous case, explicitly declaring WSDL avoids the possibility that runtime-generated WSDL will contain subtle differences from that used during development.

Non-Blocking Interactions Using Web Services

After a non-blocking operation is invoked, control is returned immediately to the client so that it can continue processing.

The web service binding examples so far have used synchronous operations. When a client invokes a synchronous operation, it waits until a response is received. As we explained in Chapter 3, "Service-Based Development Using Java," in loosely coupled systems where network connections introduce latency, it is often better to use non-blocking operations. After a non-blocking operation is invoked, control is returned immediately to the client so that it can continue processing. Non-blocking operations do not return a response. Instead, if a response is needed, the service provider must make a callback.

Using non-blocking operations with the web service binding is straightforward. When creating the service interface, define its operations as one-way. In Java, recall that this is done using the `@OneWay` annotation for a service that records a loan approval event (see Listing 8.4).

Listing 8.4   *Non-Blocking Operations and Web Services*

```
public interface ApprovalService {

    @OneWay
    void approved(LoanApplication application);

}
```

Because the `approved` operation is marked as one-way, when a reference to the `ApprovalService` is bound using web services, the SCA runtime returns control immediately to the client component when the operation is invoked. The client will not block while the invocation is sent to the `ApprovalService`.

Callbacks and Conversations with Web Services

In theory, using callbacks and conversations with the web service binding is straightforward. For example, a service bound using web services and requiring a callback must simply annotate its Java interface with `@Callback`, specifying the callback interface. Similarly, a conversational service needs to mark only its Java interface with `@Conversational`. In both cases, when an invocation is made, the runtime needs to add additional information to the message it sends out over the network to the target service. In the case of callbacks, the runtime must send some form of endpoint address the target service can use to make a callback. Similarly, for conversations, an ID must be sent with the message so the target service can correlate multiple requests. Otherwise, the target service will not know which conversational a particular request is part of.

Because SCA does not specify the format for propagating callback and conversational information, vendors will likely implement such features using proprietary approaches, making interoperability more difficult.

In practice, at least at the present time, things are not likely to work as simply as this. If both a client and service provider communicating via web services are hosted by the same SCA runtime implementation, problems are not likely to occur. Rather, issues are likely to arise when the client and service provider are hosted either by different SCA vendor runtimes or one is not built using SCA at all (for example, it is a .NET service). Because SCA does not specify the format for propagating callback and conversational information, vendors will likely implement such features using proprietary approaches, making interoperability more difficult. At some point, SCA may standardize how callback and conversational information is propagated. However, until that happens, it is best to avoid using these features unless a client and service provider are deployed to the same SCA vendor implementation.

Accessing Messaging Infrastructure: The JMS Binding

The JMS binding allows references to flow invocations to a target service using JMS topics and queues. The binding also allows services to receive incoming requests from topics and queues.

Message-oriented middleware (MOM) is often a key part of enterprise architectures. MOM products typically function as a messaging backbone that integrates disparate corporate systems. SCA standardizes connecting to messaging infrastructure via the Java Message Service (JMS) binding. The JMS binding allows references to flow invocations to a target service using JMS topics and queues. The binding also allows services to receive incoming requests from topics and queues. In this section, we look at the details of working with the JMS binding.

One-Way Messaging with JMS

JMS is an asynchronous messaging API—that is, messages may be sent to a destination after control has returned to the client. Due to its asynchronous nature, JMS is a natural transport to use with non-blocking service operations.

Suppose BigBank already has a legacy auditing system in place. This system is used by all corporate applications to record credit rating results, lending statistics, and other information mandated by law. Further, the system is accessed through JMS.

BigBank has plans to convert the system to SCA as part of the second phase of their loan application build-out. To minimize the amount of work for the first phase, BigBank has decided to have the SCA loan application components access the legacy auditing system via JMS. In the second phase, the legacy system will be replaced by an SCA-based implementation similar to the auditing composite we introduced in Chapter 6, "Policy." Because existing, non-SCA systems will still require access to auditing via JMS, the replacement composite will expose the auditing service as a JMS endpoint.

Binding References to JMS

The first step in accessing the legacy auditing system from an SCA component is to define a service interface for auditing operations. Because the system was built using JMS, it has a message-based API, as opposed to a service-based API. An example of using the original message-based API is given in Listing 8.5.

Listing 8.5   Accessing the Auditing System Using JMS

```
//…
String auditData = … // the audit information to record
Connection connection = // obtain a JMS connection;
Destination destination = // obtain the audit destination
Session session = connection.createSession(true,
Session.AUTO_ACKNOWLEDGE);
MessageProducer producer = session.createProducer(destination);
TextMessage message = session.createTextMessage();
message.setText(auditData);
producer.send(message);

//… cleanup resources
```

In contrast, the service-based API is defined by the `AuditService` interface listed in Listing 8.6.

Listing 8.6   The Service-Based API for the Auditing System

```
public interface AuditService {

    @OneWay
    void record(String data);
}
```

Because the auditing operation will be performed asynchronously, we declare the `record` operation to be non-blocking by using the `@OneWay` annotation. Listing 8.7 illustrates how the service-based API is used instead of the message-based API shown previously in Listing 8.5.

Listing 8.7   *Using the Service-Based API*

```
public class CreditServiceComponent implements CreditScoreService {
   private AuditService auditService;

   @Reference
   void setAuditService(AuditService auditService) {
      this.auditService = auditService;
   }

   public void checkCredit(String id) {
      // …
      String data = //..
      auditService.record(data);
   }

}
```

In the preceding example, when the audit service reference is configured to use the JMS binding, the SCA runtime will flow service requests—calls to `CreditScoreService.checkCredit(..)`—as JMS messages. Let's see how that is done.

As Listing 8.8 demonstrates, binding a reference using JMS is simple.

Listing 8.8   *Using the JMS Binding*

```
<composite ….>
   <component name=" CreditScoreService">

   …
   </composite>

   <reference name="auditService" promote="CreditScoreService
/auditService">
      <binding.jms>
         <destination name="AuditQueue"/>
      </binding.jms>
   <reference>
</composite>
```

In the preceding example, the JMS binding configuration specifies the `AuditQueue` for flowing invocations to the `AuditService`, as depicted in Figure 8.1.

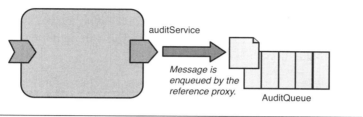

Figure 8.1   Enqueuing a reference invocation

When the audit service reference is invoked, the reference proxy converts the invocation to a JMS message and enqueue. At that point, the JMS provider delivers the message to its intended destination—in this case, a consumer attached to the `AuditQueue`.

Perspective: Why Not Use JMS Directly?

Would it be better to have a component implementation use the JMS API directly as opposed to binding a reference? This question could be raised about bindings in general: Wouldn't it be easier to use transport APIs directly? An argument can be made that dealing with an API is easier than having to create and maintain XML configuration.

Although it is hard to make sweeping generalizations and claim that using bindings for external communications is always the better approach, it does provide a couple of key advantages.

First, bindings decouple component implementations from the transports used to invoke dependent services. If BigBank decided to rewrite its audit service to use something other than JMS, client code would not have to be modified.

The second advantage bindings bring is that they externalize communications configuration. Some may say placing configuration in XML makes applications more difficult to maintain. However, the advantage in doing so is that it allows remote communications to be reconfigured without modifying code. For example, an SCA runtime could change the JMS queue used by a bound reference without requiring a code change. If the configuration is buried away in code, runtimes can't provide this type of dynamic behavior.

Binding Services with JMS

For the second phase of refactoring the auditing system, BigBank has decided to re-implement it as an SCA composite. Because existing non-SCA clients will still access auditing via JMS, the new composite must maintain backward compatibility with the old system by binding a service to the `AuditQueue`. This can be done using the configuration shown in Listing 8.9.

Listing 8.9   *Using the JMS Binding*

```
<composite ….>
   <service name="AuditService" promote="AuditComponent">
      <binding.jms>
         <destination name="AuditQueue"/>
      </binding.jms>
   </service>

   <component name="AuditComponent">
   …
   </composite>
</composite>
```

As the composite is deployed, the SCA runtime registers a listener on the `AuditQueue`. When an incoming message arrives on the queue, the listener dispatches the message to the service for processing, as depicted in Figure 8.2.

Existing clients can continue to send messages to the `AuditQueue`. The SCA runtime will be notified by the JMS provider when messages arrive and will forward them to the `AuditService`.

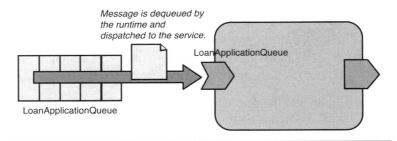

Figure 8.2   Dequeuing a message and dispatching it to a service

Operation Selection

The JMS messaging model differs from the SCA programming model in that it deals with messages and destinations (that is, queues and topics), as opposed to service operations and endpoints. This requires the JMS binding to perform two types of mapping. Incoming JMS messages must be mapped to service operations, and outgoing invocations must encode service operation information in the JMS message. In addition, input and output data for service invocations (that is, the operation parameters and return values) must be mapped to and from the JMS message. We refer to these processes of mapping operations and data as operation selection and message data binding, respectively. SCA defines default behavior and provides the ability for applications to specify custom behavior for operation selection and message data binding. We now look at how this is done. In the next section, we discuss message data binding in more detail.

The JMS binding was designed to map a single service to a destination (topic or queue). In other words, a JMS destination is always associated with one service. Although it is possible to bind a service multiple times to different destinations (using multiple `<binding.jms>` configurations), different services should be bound to individual destinations.

When dispatching to a target service for a destination, the SCA runtime must select the correct operation. To do this, SCA defines a set of rules for encoding operation information in a JMS message. These rules are straightforward. If the target service has only one operation, it is automatically selected. If the target service has more than one operation, the runtime looks for a user property on the JMS named `"scaOperationName"` and uses its value to map to the appropriate operation. If the user property is not found and the service has more than one operation, the runtime looks for an operation named `"onMessage"`.

When non-SCA external clients invoke a service bound to JMS, they may have to encode the operation information manually (assuming the service contains more than one operation and no `"onMessage"` operation). Going back to the `AuditService` example, because the service has only one operation—`record`—no encoding needs to be done because the SCA runtime will

automatically map incoming messages to it. However, if
`AuditService` had multiple operations, clients would need to
specify the operation in the JMS message. The example in Listing
8.10 modifies the code originally listed in Listing 8.5 to include the
addition of the operation information as a message property.

Listing 8.10   *Flowing Operation Information Manually Using the JMS API*

```
//…
String auditData = … // the audit information to record
Connection connection = // obtain a JMS connection;
Destination destination = // obtain the audit destination
Session session = connection.createSession(true,
Session.AUTO_ACKNOWLEDGE);
MessageProducer producer = session.createProducer(destination);
TextMessage message = session.createTextMessage();
message.setStringProperty("scaOperationName", "record");
message.setText(auditData);
producer.send(message);

//… cleanup resources
```

When the message is dequeued on the receiving end, the SCA runtime will dispatch to the `record` operation by reading the value of
the `"scaOperationName"` set on the JMS message.

Message Data Binding

In addition to encoding and decoding operations, the JMS binding
must also map parameter data to and from messages. If the invoked
service operation has one parameter, the data is serialized and sent
as XML. How the data is serialized to XML is determined in one of
two ways. If WSDL is used to specify the service interface (that is,
`<interface.wsdl>`), the SCA runtime will use it to determine how
to serialize the parameter data. For example, in Listing 8.11, the
interface for the `AuditService` is configured using WSDL.

Listing 8.11   *Using interface.wsdl with the JMS Binding*

```
<composite name="LoanApplicationComposite" ….>
   <service name="LoanService" promote=" LoanComponent">
     <interface.wsdl wsdlElement="http://www.bigbank.com/audit#
➥wsdl.port(AuditService/AuditPort)
"/>
     <binding.jms>
       <destination name="AuditQueue"/>
```

```
        </binding.jms>
    </service>

    ...
</composite>
```

The WSDL for the `AuditService` will contain definitions for its operations and the messages they receive and return. A message definition in WSDL is specified using XML Schema.

When a message is enqueued, the SCA runtime will serialize parameters as part of the JMS message. SCA mandates parameters be sent using JMS text messages. The format for parameter serialization is, however, left unspecified. The Fabric3 SCA runtime uses JAXB for complex types, and it is likely that other vendor implementations will support the data-binding technology. In addition, Fabric3 also supports sending JMS object messages (when parameter types implement `java.lang.Serializable`), JMS stream messages, and JMS bytes messages for primitive types (for example, int or long).

Request-Response Messaging with JMS

Message-based communication is often one-way. However, there are times when a response is needed. In SCA, there are two ways to propagate responses, either as a return value to an operation or through a callback. In this section, we discuss request-response operations using the JMS binding. In the next section, we cover callbacks.

One of the loan application requirements is that new mortgage applications be appraised for their value on the secondary market. After a loan is made, BigBank often sells the right to collect interest and principal payments to a third party. The appraisal is handled by a legacy system accessible via BigBank's JMS provider.

Like the auditing function, BigBank defines a service interface to the legacy appraisal system, which is listed in Listing 8.12.

Listing 8.12 *The Secondary Market Appraisal Legacy System*

```
public interface SecondaryAppraisalService {

    AppraisalResult appraise(LoanApplication application);
}
```

The `SecondaryAppraisalService` uses request-response style messaging: After the service has been invoked, the client blocks waiting for a response.

How does this interface map to JMS, given that messages are sent in a one-way, asynchronous fashion? Request-response messaging is commonly implemented in JMS using separate request and reply queues (see Figure 8.3).

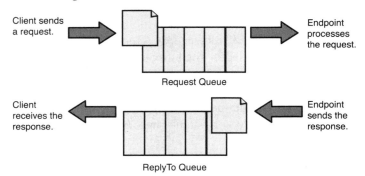

Figure 8.3   Request-response messaging with JMS

JMS has built-in support for request-response messaging with the `replyTo` message header. Using the JMS API directly, a client sets the `replyTo` header to the queue on which it receives responses. The message endpoint in turn uses the `replyTo` header for the queue to return a response. An example of setting the `replyTo` queue is given in Listing 8.13.

Listing 8.13   *Setting the JMS replyTo Header*

```
//…
 String loanApplication = … // the loan information in XML form
 Connection connection = // obtain a JMS connection;
 Destination destination = // obtain the audit destination
 Session session = connection.createSession(true,
Session.AUTO_ACKNOWLEDGE);
 MessageProducer producer = session.createProducer(destination);
 Message message = session.createMessage();
 message.setJMSReplyTo(replyDestination);
 message.setText(loanApplication);
 producer.send(message);

 //… cleanup resources
```

Similarly, the message endpoint accesses the `replyTo` queue by calling `Message.getJMSReplyTo()` on the received message.

One missing piece we have not yet discussed is how a client associates a response with the original request. Because JMS is asynchronous, a client may send multiple requests before it receives any responses. Consequently, it needs a way to correlate response messages with its original request. JMS provides built-in support for message correlation via the `correlationId` message header. The correlation ID is most commonly set to the message ID of the original request by the message endpoint. Listing 8.14 shows how an endpoint sets the correlation ID.

Listing 8.14   *Setting the JMS Correlation ID Header*

```
//…
Message requestMessage = // the request message

//… process the message and then send the reply

Connection connection = // obtain a JMS connection;
Destination destination = message.getJMSReplyTo()
Session session = connection.createSession(true,
Session.AUTO_ACKNOWLEDGE);
MessageProducer producer = session.createProducer(destination);
Message message = session.createMessage();
message.setJMSCorrelationID(requestMessage.getJMSNMessageID());
producer.send(message);

//… cleanup resources
```

When the client receives the response, it can use the correlation ID to match the message to the original request.

Setting up request and response queues and managing correlation can be tedious. An SCA runtime will handle this so that request-response invocations can be made without having to perform these tasks in application code. Listing 8.15 shows how to invoke the `SecondaryAppraisalService` and receive a response over JMS—it's no different than invoking any other reference.

Listing 8.15   *Invoking the LoanAppraisalService*

```
public interface LoanComponent implements LoanService {

    private SecondaryAppraisalService appraisalService;
```

```
@Reference
public void setAppraisalService(SecondaryAppraisalService service) {
    appraisalService = service;
}

public LoanResult apply(LoanRequest request) {
    //…
    LoanApplication application = //…
    // invoke the service and wait for a response
    AppraisalResult result = appraisalService.appraise(application);
    //…
}
}
```

Notice that in the example, the client invokes the service and waits for a response. When the invocation is made, the SCA runtime is responsible for enqueuing the message and having the client block until a response is received. This requires the runtime to manage message correlation transparent to the component implementation. When using the JMS binding, components don't need to deal with request and response queues or correlation IDs. Handling these transport specifics is the job of the SCA runtime.

Configuring a service or reference to use request-response style messaging with the JMS binding is only slightly more involved than one-way messaging. Listing 8.16 provides an example of how to bind a reference.

Listing 8.16   *Configuring Request-Response Messaging with the JMS Binding*

```
<composite name="LoanApplicationComposite" ….>
   <component name="LoanComponent">
      …
   </component>
   <reference name="SecondaryAppraisalService" promote="
LoanComponent/appraisalService">
      <binding.jms>
         <destination name="AppraisalQueue" />
         <response>
            <destination name="AppraisalResponseQueue" />
         </response>
      </binding.jms>
   </reference>
   …
</composite>
```

The preceding example configures the reference to send requests to the `AppraisalQueue` and receive responses from the `AppraisalResponseQueue`. Setting up the required message consumer and correlation infrastructure will be automatically done by the SCA runtime when the composite is deployed.

How Are Destinations Created?

The JMS binding supports a number of options for creating destinations (topics and queues). The default—which we have been using in the examples—is to have the SCA runtime create the destination if it does not exist. The options for creating destinations are specified using the `@create` attribute on the `destination` element:

```
<binding.jms>
    <destination create="ifnotexist"
    name="AppraisalQueue" />
</binding.jms>
```

Valid values are `"ifnotexist"` (the default), `"always"`, and `"never"`. If `"always"` is used and a destination already exists, the runtime will raise an error.

Performing Callbacks with JMS

In request-response messaging, clients block waiting for a response. In loosely coupled applications, this synchronous communication style may not be appropriate. For example, the secondary loan appraisal system may take some time to deliver a response. Or it may be down for maintenance during certain times of the day, in which case message delivery must be temporarily halted and done at a later time. Having component instances block in these situations will be inefficient and likely introduce bottlenecks.

As with wires, asynchronous two-way invocations over JMS are done using callbacks. Instead of blocking, clients make a service request and return immediately. After a period of time, they will be called back with a response. The `SecondaryAppraisalService` is modified in Listing 8.17 to use a callback.

Asynchronous two-way invocations over JMS are done using callbacks.

Listing 8.17   *Using Callbacks with the Secondary Appraisal Service*

```
@Callback(SecondaryAppraisalCallback.class)
public interface SecondaryAppraisalService {

    @OneWay
    void appraise(LoanApplication application);
}
```

The callback interface is listed in Listing 8.18.

Listing 8.18   *Using Callbacks with the Secondary Appraisal Service*

```
public interface SecondaryAppraisalCallback {

    appraisalResponse(AppraisalResult result);
}
```

When the `SecondaryAppraisalService` is invoked and a call-back made, the SCA runtime performs the sequence of steps depicted in Figure 8.4.

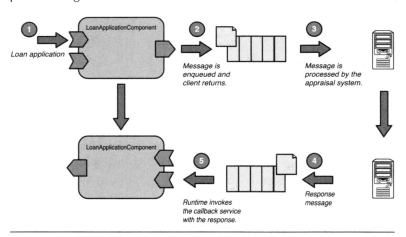

Figure 8.4   The callback sequence over JMS

In the preceding sequence, the `LoanComponent` invokes the appraisal service and returns immediately, enabling it to perform additional processing prior to the arrival of the response. At some later point in time, the component will be called back on its `SecondaryAppraisalCallback` interface. The `LoanComponent` implementation is presented in Listing 8.19.

Listing 8.19   *The LoanComponent Using a Callback*

```
public class LoanComponent implements LoanService,
SecondaryAppraisalCallback {
   private SecondaryAppraisalService appraisalService;

   @Reference
   public void setAppraisalService(SecondaryAppraisalService service) {
      appraisalService = service;
   }


// ….
   public LoanResult apply(LoanRequest request) {
      LoanApplication application = //…
      // invoke the service and return immediately
      appraisalService.appraise(application);
//… continue processing
   }

   public void appraisalResponse(AppraisalResult result) {
      // … process the result from the previous appraise operation
   }

}
```

Configuring the appraisal service reference to use a callback is done in exactly the same way as setting up a request-response interaction. We relist the composite used in the previous section in Listing 8.20.

Listing 8.20   *Configuring Callback Messaging with the JMS Binding*

```
<composite name="LoanApplicationComposite" ….>
   <component name="LoanComponent">
      …
   </component>
   <reference name="SecondaryAppraisalService" promote="
LoanComponent/appraisalService">
      <binding.jms>
         <destination name="AppraisalQueue" />
         <response>
            <destination name="AppraisalResponseQueue" />
         </response>
      </binding.jms>
   </reference>
   …
</composite>
```

The same binding configuration can be used because the SCA runtime knows from the reference service contract that a callback is required (remember, `SecondaryAppraisalService` was annotated with `@Callback` in Listing 8.17). Again, as with request-response operations, the SCA runtime will set up the appropriate JMS infrastructure—queues and message consumers—to flow request and callback invocations.

When a request is initiated, the SCA runtime will include the callback queue as part of the JMS message header in the `"scaCallbackQueue"` property. Message receivers that use the JMS API directly can use this information to return a response. When a response is sent to the callback queue, the SCA runtime will dequeue it and invoke the corresponding callback operation.

Optional JMS Binding Configuration

In our coverage of the JMS binding, we don't discuss all the possible configuration options. The JMS binding specification includes a variety of additional options, including setting alternative correlation schemes, message delivery modes, and message headers.

Most of these options will need to be used only for specific binding scenarios. For a listing and explanation, see the *JMS Binding Specification*, available from http://www.osoa.org.

Using Publish-Subscribe Messaging Patterns

So far, the JMS binding examples we have presented make use of queues. The JMS binding also supports publish-subscribe style messaging using topics. When binding a reference to a topic, from the component implementation perspective, things remain the same: The reference proxy is invoked like any other service.

There is, however, one important restriction when binding to a topic. Namely, service operations must be one-way—that is, they cannot be request-response operations. If a response is needed, a callback can be used.

To configure a topic, the binding makes use of the `@type` attribute on the destination element (see Listing 8.21).

Listing 8.21   *Publish-Subscribe Messaging with the JMS Binding*

```
<composite ….>
  <component name=" CreditScoreService">
  …
  </composite>

  <reference name="auditService" promote="CreditScoreService
/auditService">
     <binding.jms>
        <destination type="topic" name="AuditTopic"/>
     </binding.jms>
  <reference>
</composite>
```

In Listing 8.21, the binding configuration sets the audit service reference to publish to the `AuditTopic`. This results in the audit message being broadcast to topic subscribers instead of being delivered to a single receiver.

Conversational Interactions with JMS

If a JMS binding is used with a conversational interface, it is up to the provider of the JMS binding to make sure that a conversation ID is assigned to each conversation and passed in each message in the `scaConversationID` user property. The developer of the implementation does not create any code specific to JMS.

Proprietary Bindings

SCA runtimes are not restricted to the JMS and web service bindings. In fact, it was the intention of the SCA authors to enable runtimes to support a host of proprietary communications mechanisms. One of the advantages of SCA is that components can use these bindings without tying application code to proprietary APIs.

Using Bindings for Communicating Within a Domain

SCA allows bindings to be specified on services and references that are not promoted. In other words, SCA allows bindings to be specified on wires for services that will never be exposed outside the domain. This is a capability that we recommend that users not take advantage of. There really is no reason to specify a binding for services that are not exposed outside of the domain. If there are aspects of the implementation that imply that something about a binding is required, that requirement can be specified with an intent.

For example, if there is a strict requirement that the SOAP is used, it can be accomplished by requiring the "SOAP" intent. If there is a strict requirement that the binding be accessible through the JMS API, the "JMS" intent can be required. By using intents, it frees the runtime to pick any binding that can provide whatever guarantee is required by the intent, rather than being limited to using one specific intent.

Bindings Overrides

Having covered the web service and JMS bindings in detail, we now turn to the subject of binding overrides. Sometimes it is necessary to override a binding configuration in a higher-level composite. This may be for a variety of reasons. Perhaps the most common case where this comes up is when there is a need to deploy a composite in a testing and production domain. In the testing domain, bound references need to be configured to point to mock endpoints, whereas in the production domain, they need to point to the "live" services.

These two variations could be accommodated by not binding the references until deployment. This would require the deployer to specify the binding configuration when the composite is activated in the domain. Another, less error-prone option is to have the bindings for the production domain configured in the composite. This will avoid the need to specify bindings when the composite is deployed in production. When the composite is deployed to the test domain, the production configuration can be overridden.

Overriding a binding on a promoted reference is straightforward. To do so, add a new binding configuration to the component that uses the composite. Listing 8.22 shows how this is done.

Listing 8.22   *Overriding a Binding on a Promoted Reference*

```
<component name ="CreditScoreComponent">
  <implementation.composite name="bigbank:CreditScoreComposite"/>
  <reference name="auditService" target="AuditService">
```

```
      <binding.jms>
        <destination name="TestAuditQueue"/>
      </binding.jms>
   <reference>
</component>
```

The preceding example overrides binding configuration in the CreditScoreComposite and replaces it with the JMS binding set to use the TestAuditQueue. One additional thing to keep in mind is that binding overrides are complete—that is, they completely re-place any binding settings made at lower levels in the composition.

The SCA Binding

In addition to the web services and JMS bindings, the SCA specifications talk about the "SCA binding." This binding is not a transport protocol invented specifically for use with SCA applications. Rather, it refers to the remote communications protocol selected by the runtime to establish a wire. Because a runtime may select different protocols for different wires, the SCA binding may vary. In other words, a runtime may use more than one protocol for the SCA binding.

Calling the transport protocol assigned to a wire the "SCA binding" is confusing, and an argument can be made that the SCA authors should have named it something else. In fact, the SCA binding is different than other bindings. When a service or reference is bound, the binding fixes the communications channel. That is, the remote communications protocol cannot be changed by the runtime at some later point. The SCA binding, on the other hand, does not fix the remote protocol; it is just a placeholder for one selected by the runtime when it creates a wire.

Why did the SCA authors even bother to mention the SCA binding? The answer is that there is one case where it is needed. When a reference is explicitly bound, there must be a mechanism for overriding the binding in a higher-level composite and re-placing it with a wire. This is done by using binding.sca on a promoted reference. For example, the following overrides a binding set on a reference in a composite and replaces it with a wire:

```
<component name ="CreditScoreComponent">
   <implementation.composite name="…"/>
   <reference name="auditService"
   target="AuditService">
      <binding.sca/>
   <reference>
<component>
```

Because this is a corner case, it is likely that most applications will never need to make use of the SCA binding directly. However, it is important to be aware of the differences between it and other bindings.

Summary

This chapter has covered integrating SCA services with clients and services hosted outside a particular domain using bindings. In particular, we covered interoperable communications using web services and connecting services in a domain to a message bus via JMS.

Having now covered the core SCA concepts, including services, components, composites, policy, wires, and bindings, in the next chapter, we turn to an in-depth discussion of the role the domain plays in SCA.

9

The Domain

Composites are deployed to a domain, which contains one or more runtimes that host components. The domain, however, plays a much bigger role in SCA than simply defining a set of cooperating runtimes composites are deployed to. The **domain** is the foundation of SCA and provides management facilities, resource sharing, policy administration, and the communications infrastructure for wiring services.

This chapter explores the role of the domain. It accounts for different types of domains, how to deploy to a domain, how to structure and manage a domain, and how to reuse and enforce policy in a domain.

The **domain** *is the foundation of SCA. It provides management facilities, resource sharing, policy administration, and the communications infrastructure for wiring services.*

The Role of a Domain

In the first chapter, "Introducing SCA," we introduced the concept of the domain and outlined its basic role. That role can be broken down into four functions: management, artifact sharing, policy administration, and communications. Table 9.1 provides a summary of these functions. Let's review each of those in detail.

Table 9.1   The Functions of the Domain

Function	Description
Management	■ Deploy and undeploy components ■ Change component wiring ■ Monitor, trace, and troubleshooting
Artifact sharing	■ Manage a repository of artifacts ■ Distribute artifacts to runtimes
Policy administration	■ Centralize policy definitions ■ Application of policy to services
Communications	■ Establish wires ■ Flow service invocations ■ Ensure reliability, security, and other qualities of service

Management

Most modern runtime environments allow some degree of dynamic modification. Java EE application servers, .NET service hosts, and web servers provide management interfaces to deploy and undeploy applications. It is not uncommon for advanced runtimes to support greater dynamicity, such as upgrading applications without disrupting service to end users.

The creators of SCA envisioned domains to be potentially very dynamic.

Similarly, the creators of SCA envisioned domains to be potentially very dynamic. Although some domains may be fairly static, most enterprise domains will need to evolve significantly over time as requirements change. Composites may need to be added, updated, or removed. To affect these changes, the domain has a set of operations for adding and removing composites. Because domains may vary, SCA doesn't define how those operations are manifested. Instead, SCA defines the behavior associated with these operations and leaves it to runtime vendors to decide how best to implement them. Domains may use command-line tooling, a management console, file system directory, or some other means to add and remove composites.

Although not required by the SCA, advanced domains may have the capability to change wires after components have been deployed.

Although not required by the SCA, advanced domains may have the capability to change wires after components have been deployed. Figure 9.1 depicts how a component reference may be rewired to a new service after it has been deployed.

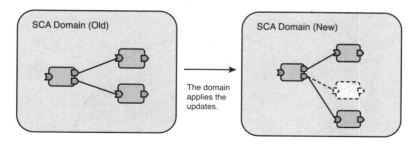

Figure 9.1   A composite is updated and the domain applies the changes.

Similarly, vendors may include additional management features, such as monitoring, tracing, and troubleshooting.

Artifact Sharing

Sharing artifacts such as Java classes or definitions found in XML files is a common requirement for applications. If different applications use the same library, referencing a single copy may be easier to manage than bundling separate copies with each application. Many technologies have been developed over the years to assist with artifact sharing in single-machine environments. Windows introduced DLLs. OSGi has the notion of bundles. Java has classpaths and, more recently, has embarked upon the specification of a module system.

In distributed environments, artifact sharing is more complicated because it potentially involves making artifacts available to a number of runtimes on different machines via a deployment infrastructure. Java EE application server clusters are a classic example. When an application archive (a WAR or EAR) is deployed to a Java EE application server cluster, it is replicated to all nodes in the cluster. Each node receives a copy of the archive and runs its contents. A common Java EE application server architecture is to have a central administration server responsible for managing the nodes in a cluster and distributing artifacts to them. This cluster architecture is illustrated in Figure 9.2.

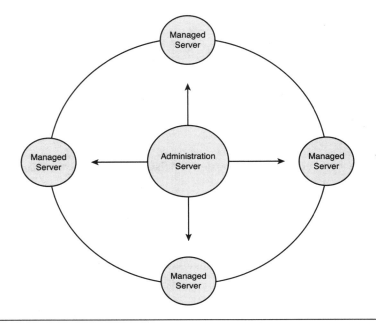

Figure 9.2   A Java EE cluster and deployment architecture

Enterprise repositories store and manage artifacts and make them available to multiple clients.

With the move to service-based applications, requirements for artifact sharing have evolved beyond the Java EE distribution model. Services are built around contracts, which often reference additional artifacts such as WSDL documents and XML schemas. These artifacts must be shared between clients and service providers that are potentially hosted on different machines. One solution to this problem is an enterprise repository. Enterprise repositories store and manage artifacts and make them available to multiple clients. Figure 9.3 provides a sketch of how this works.

Depending on the vendor, an enterprise repository might include features such as workflow and versioning.

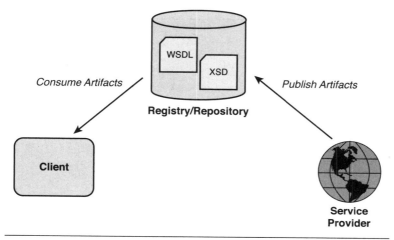

Figure 9.3   Repositories store artifacts such as WSDLs and XSDs, which can be accessed by clients.

Enterprise Repositories and Registries

An enterprise repository is responsible for managing application artifacts such as WSDL documents, XML schemas, and sometimes code. It is also common to use the term "enterprise registry" to refer to software that performs the same function. Unfortunately, the industry hasn't settled on the distinction between the two terms. To avoid confusion, we chose to stick with one term: **enterprise repository**.

The domain fills the role of an enterprise repository and deployment infrastructure: It stores and manages artifacts, as well as distributes them to runtimes. To accomplish this task, the domain uses some form of repository. Let's see how this works.

The domain fills the role of an enterprise repository and deployment infrastructure: It stores and manages artifacts, as well as distributes them to runtimes.

As we covered in the first chapter, artifacts are made available to the domain as contributions. Depending on the SCA implementation, contributions are installed in the domain using a command-line deployment tool or via more sophisticated graphical tooling, such as an IDE or management console. Figure 9.4 illustrates this process.

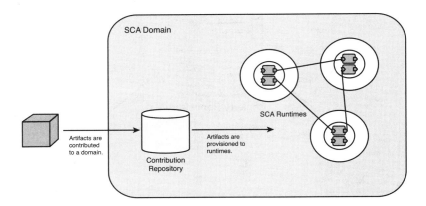

Figure 9.4   The domain stores contributions in a repository where they can be accessed.

When a contribution is installed, it is stored in a repository. As we see later, when the contribution has been installed, it can be referenced by other contributions. This enables a contribution to use artifacts in another installed contribution. After a contribution is installed, composites contained in it may be deployed. As part of this process, the domain may distribute artifacts required by components to runtime nodes where those components are hosted.

Policy Administration

Most enterprise architectures use some form of policy. In Chapter 6, "Policy," we explained that policy is a requirement placed on how a runtime must execute code. Common types of policy include security ("use encryption for remote invocations"), reliability ("provide guaranteed delivery of messages to a particular service"), and transactionality ("invoke this service in a transaction").

Both Java EE and web services provide mechanisms for declarative or configuration-based policy. Java EE allows transactional and security behavior to be declared in EJB configuration. Web services has WS-Policy and an assortment of specifications for security and reliability based on it. However, what Java EE and web services lack is a standard way to specify policy once and reuse it across applications—for example, requiring that all remotable services use a certain type of message-level encryption.

The domain is designed to address the problem of policy reuse by providing a way to uniformly apply policy across all deployed composites. The domain does this by treating policies as contributions that are installed and activated. When a policy configuration is installed as a contribution, it can be applied to services in the domain (see Figure 9.5).

The domain is designed to address the problem of policy reuse by providing a way to uniformly apply policy across all deployed composites. The domain does this by treating policies as contributions that are installed and activated.

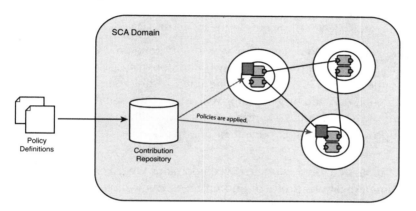

Figure 9.5   Policies are contributed to the domain and applied across runtimes.

The domain allows policy configurations to be selectively applied to services, references, bindings, and component implementations. It's the job of the domain to ensure that these policies are applied wherever they are required.

Communications

Establishing remote communications is fundamental to the domain. Because we have already spent substantial time on how a domain instantiates wires and implements bindings in previous chapters, we will not spend much time on the role of the domain as a remote communications infrastructure.

Perspective: Wiring-in-the-Really-Large

When we compared Spring with SCA in the first chapter, we made the distinction between "wiring-in-the-small" versus "wiring-in-the-large." The former involves the assembly of components in a single address space. In contrast, "wiring-in-the-large" entails component assembly across remote boundaries. Spring is about "wiring-in-the-small"; SCA deals with both.

Throughout the book, we have also discussed how wiring is done only within a domain. In other words, wires exist only between two components deployed to the same domain. This is because SCA does not define interoperable wiring between domains. There is no guarantee the two domains will support the same wire communications protocol. To communicate outside a domain—either to a non-SCA service or a service provided by a component in another domain—bindings are used.

Wouldn't it be useful if SCA enabled wiring between domains where two domains could negotiate a communications protocol and enforce policy such as security? This type of "wiring-in-the-really-large" would simplify cross-domain communication, as bindings would not have to be configured on references.

To achieve this, SCA would need to standardize an interoperable way to obtain details about the contents of a domain, and in particular, its services. Domains would advertise a set of available services and their endpoint addresses much like a component. It would then be possible to wire across domains in much the same way that wiring is done today within a domain.

Currently, the SCA specification committees have not indicated whether this is a future area of development. However, it's useful and fun (at least for people who like technology) to think about how SCA may evolve in the future.

Types of Domains

Broadly speaking, domains fit into one of three categories: local, distributed, or federated.

To use a cliché, domains come in a number of shapes and sizes. Most of the examples we have used throughout the book show distributed domains with multiple runtimes. This can lead to the impression that a domain's complex infrastructure is ill-suited for more basic needs. On the contrary, although domains can scale up, they are also capable of scaling down. A domain can be contained within a single server environment or even in an embedded device.

Broadly speaking, domains fit into one of three categories: local, distributed, or federated. Different vendors may support one or more of these domain types. Table 9.2 summarizes the different types of domains, which we explain further in this section.

Table 9.2   Domain Types

Type	Description
Local	■ Contained in a single process or server partition ■ Examples include web applications and embedded devices ■ Are not fault tolerant
Distributed	■ Spread across multiple runtimes, likely running on different machines ■ Tend to support high-end features such as fault tolerance and reliability
Federated	■ Spread across multiple different types of runtimes ■ Provide support for creating composite applications developed using multiple technologies ■ Tend to support high-end features such as fault tolerance and reliability

Local Domains

A local domain is one where the domain is contained within a single process or partition on a machine. For example, a local domain may be hosted within a single server instance. Or in server environments that support segregating code, the domain may be contained within a partition. Local domains are commonly used for embedded devices and server installations where scalability demands are limited and high availability is not needed.

A local domain is one where the domain is contained within a single process or partition on a machine.

An example of a local domain is one embedded in a web application, as illustrated in Figure 9.6.

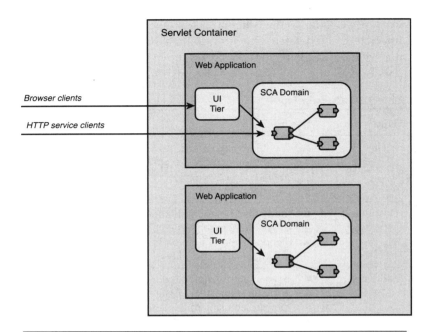

Figure 9.6   Domains embedded in web applications

This diagram illustrates how local domains can be embedded in web applications where the browser-based UI tier interacts with services and has the services exposed to nonbrowser clients via an HTTP-based binding such as web services.

Distributed Domains

A distributed domain is one where the domain is spread across multiple processes.

A distributed domain is one where the domain is spread across multiple processes. Typically, these processes will be individual runtimes running on different machines. Distributed domains are most commonly used when services need to be hosted in multiple runtimes for scalability (spread processing load), availability (provide redundancy), or security (segregate code) reasons.

An example of a distributed domain is one that is spread across an application server cluster. As we mentioned earlier, application server clusters are often managed by a specific server, sometimes referred to as the administration server. When a domain is mapped to this type of cluster architecture, the administration server is responsible for interfacing with the contribution repository and provisioning components to the cluster nodes. Figure 9.7 illustrates an application server-based distributed domain.

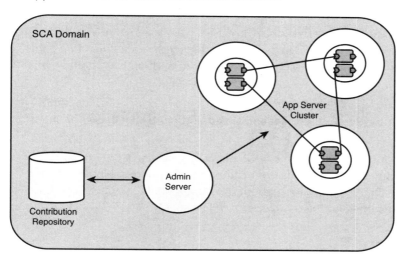

Figure 9.7   Mapping a domain to an application server environment

As shown in Figure 9.7, the administration server is responsible for deploying composites to an application server instance. If these application server instances are clustered (as seen in the figure), a composite will be deployed to all application servers in the cluster. This will enable the application server-based domain to provide service failover and load-balancing.

In some situations, an application server cluster may be overkill. In these cases, a distributed domain could be composed of small profile servers such as web servers, servlet containers, or OSGi runtimes. In this type of "lightweight" distributed domain, components are deployed to individual servers as opposed to all runtimes in a cluster. Although advanced capabilities such as failover and load-balancing may not be available, these types of distributed domains are generally more straightforward to configure and maintain.

Distributed Domain Architectures

In Chapter 5, "Composition," we described how SCA was designed to enable optimized communications in a domain. Because target services are specified in a composite, domain infrastructure can attach wires directly to endpoints without having to route through an intermediary message broker or bus.

There are two basic approaches to implementing this kind of point-to-point communication in a domain. We term these **decentralized** and **controller-based** architectures, respectively.

In a decentralized domain, each runtime node maintains a copy of the domain configuration and is responsible for making connections to other nodes. Nodes function autonomously, exchanging information about the components they are hosting so that other nodes can connect to them, as shown in Figure 9.8.

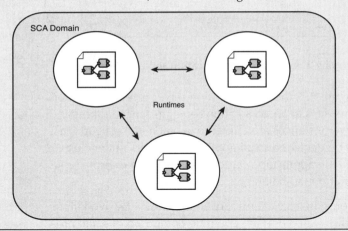

Figure 9.8   Each node in a decentralized domain maintains a copy of the domain configuration.

An advantage of the decentralized model is that it can be made very resilient. There is no single point of failure in the domain because all runtimes operate independently.

A disadvantage of the decentralized approach is handling change. If a component is undeployed or a service address is changed, all runtimes most be notified. As a domain grows, keeping the information in sync in an efficient way becomes a challenge.

In contrast, controller-based architectures centralize all domain information in an administrative server, called a controller, which is responsible for managing runtime nodes. The open source Fabric3 implementation adopts this architecture. In this model, the controller instructs each runtime regarding what components to run and how to wire them. This architecture is depicted in Figure 9.9.

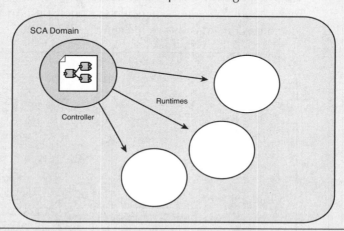

Figure 9.9   In controller-based domains, the controller maintains a central copy of the domain configuration.

The main benefit of the controller model is that each runtime need only know about a specific set of endpoints. This makes handling changes easier and scalable, as a limited number of runtimes are notified.

Another advantage of controller-based architectures is that by centralizing domain management, the controller is potentially able to make intelligent decisions about where to provision components. Because it sees the "big picture" (that is, all components in the domain and how they are wired), a sophisticated controller could decide to provision components to specific runtimes based on load or other requirements.

A disadvantage of the controller model is that it introduces a potential single point of failure. If the controller does not have a backup, the entire domain may be affected by a crash.

In the end, there is no right way to implement a domain. Each architecture has its benefits and drawbacks. In choosing among SCA implementations, it is necessary to understand the implications of decentralized and controller-based architectures and to select the one that best fits your organization's technical requirements.

Federated Domains

A federated domain is distributed and contains different types of runtimes.

Federated domains are the largest-scale domains. A federated domain is distributed and contains different types of runtimes. For example, it may include Java EE application servers, BPEL servers, servlet containers, and C++ runtimes. Federated domains are used when an organization needs to deploy composite applications that make use of many implementation technologies. An example of a federated domain is shown in Figure 9.10.

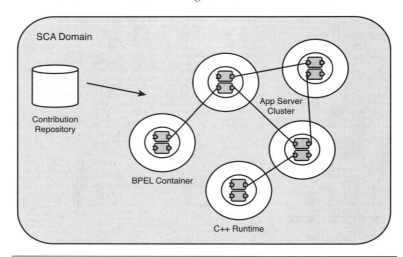

Figure 9.10   A federated domain

Federated domains are capable of wiring different implementation technologies together. Although they may be more complex to configure and maintain (for example, they require different types of runtimes to be managed), federated domains have the advantage that they provide a way to integrate services written using different technologies and manage them as a whole.

Coordinating Distributed Domains

Regardless of whether it is decentralized or controller-based, a distributed domain requires a protocol for coordinating with its runtimes. Coordination can be subdivided into two basic phases: startup and messaging. Startup is the process by which runtimes join a domain. Messaging is used to update runtimes with domain changes, such as a component deployment, undeployment, or rewiring.

A range of approaches can be used for startup and messaging. Startup can be implemented manually where runtimes are explicitly booted based on some configuration. Alternatively, runtimes may use a dynamic protocol where they start independently and then join a domain using a peer-to-peer protocol such as JXTA or UPnP. Peer-to-peer protocols may also be used to send domain change messages to runtimes. Or more traditional messaging technologies such as JMS or application server clustering may be employed.

Fabric3 can use configuration-based startup and peer-to-peer protocols such as JXTA for startup. A benefit of a dynamic, peer-to-peer technology such as JXTA is that manual setup is kept to a minimum, which can be an advantage in environments where a large number of runtimes are present.

Contributions

Getting components to run in a domain is a two-step process: installation and deployment. Components must first be installed in the domain as part of a contribution. The contribution may contain supporting artifacts such as implementation classes, schemas, WSDL documents, and libraries or depend on other contributions containing those artifacts.

Getting components to run in a domain is a two-step process: installation and deployment.

SCA specifies one contribution format that all implementations must support: the ZIP archive (which includes JAR, WAR, or EAR files, which are all based on ZIP). However, because a domain may make use of a wide variety of artifacts, an SCA implementation may allow additional contribution formats. For example, an SCA implementation can also support TAR files, RPMs, or even DLLs. Furthermore, contributions need not be archives. Nonarchive contributions such as file system directories can also be supported as contributions.

The process of installing a contribution in a domain is vendor-specific. Installation may be done using a command-line tool, management console, or by copying a contribution archive to a file system directory. After the contribution containing the components has been installed, the latter are activated by deploying a composite. This composite may also be bundled in the contribution.

In some environments, installation and deployment may be combined in a single step. For example, during development, a local domain may be configured to scan a file system directory and automatically install contributions and deploy their composites. In production environments, these steps are likely to be separate as contributions are first installed and verified and additional configuration applied prior to deployment.

The next several sections describe how to structure contribution archives and reference artifacts in other contributions. We then turn to the specifics of how composites are deployed in a domain.

Different Ways to Install and Deploy a Contribution

As domains vary significantly, the SCA authors did specify concrete ways to perform deployment. What are some of the concrete ways deployment is performed in actual SCA implementations? In practice, SCA deployment tools are likely to be similar to existing server technologies for the near future. We describe some of the more common ones here.

In a production environment, deploying to a domain is likely to be done via a management console, command-line tool, or script. These mechanisms use a proprietary vendor API to connect to the domain and make changes. Implementations built on an application server may use existing deployment tools. SCA support in WebLogic Server, for example, works in this manner. Contributions are installed and deployed using the existing WebLogic management console or command-line administration tool.

In a development environment, using the same server deployment tools would be cumbersome because they require contributions to be repackaged after every change. Fabric3 avoids this through support for "exploded" contributions. Similar to web servers, servlet containers, and application servers, Fabric3 has a file system directory where composites and their associated artifacts can be placed. Adding a composite file to the directory triggers a deployment to the domain, whereas deleting the file results in the composite being removed from the domain.

In an IDE, adding and removing files in a file system can also be awkward. Moreover, running an application in a separate server process and performing remote debugging can be slow. To address this, Fabric3 has plugins for IntelliJ and Eclipse that run an embedded domain inside the development environment. This is similar to the way current IDEs run embedded servlet containers, such as Tomcat and Jetty for testing.

It was envisioned that in the future, SCA would enable a series of new graphical tooling. These tools will automate the creation of SCDL and allow changes to the domain, such as rewiring through visual interfaces. However, given the conservative nature of many datacenters and the traditional lag between runtimes and new tooling, SCA implementations will most likely use existing deployment technologies for the near-term.

The Contribution Archive

SCA ZIP archives should include a special manifest file, sca-contribution.xml, identifying it as a contribution. This file is located in the META-INF directory under the archive root directory. It is used to identify composites available for deployment, declare imports, and export contained artifacts so that they are available to other contributions.

Back in Chapter 1, we listed the contents of a simplified version of the `LoanApplication` contribution manifest, which we repeat here in Listing 9.1.

Listing 9.1   *A Simple sca-contribution.xml Manifest*

```
<contribution xmlns="http://www.osoa.org/xmlns/sca/1.0"
xmlns:bb="http://www.bigbank.com/xmlns/lending/composites/1.0">

    <deployable composite="bb:LoanApplicationComposite"/>

</contribution>
```

Contributions may contain zero or more deployable composites. A **deployable composite** is one that is intended to be deployed directly in the domain, as opposed to used as a component implementation in another composite. As seen in Listing 9.1, the deployable composites in a contribution are identified using the `<deployable>` element. In the example, the contribution has one deployable composite, `LoanApplicationComposite`. Note that when using the deployable element, the `@composite` attribute

*A **deployable composite** is one that is intended to be deployed directly in the domain.*

refers to the fully qualified composite name, including its namespace. The actual `LoanApplicationComposite` file can be placed anywhere in the contribution. The only requirement is that the filename ends in .composite. Generally, it's good practice, though, to place deployable composites in the META-INF directory so that they may be easily identified.

Artifact Sharing

Service-based applications typically must share artifacts. At a minimum, services must make their contract definitions available to clients. Moreover, component implementations may use common artifacts such as libraries, XSDs, and classes. Sharing can be accommodated by manually copying the artifacts to different contributions. However, as the number of clients and artifacts increase, this approach tends to become unmanageable. To avoid this, SCA allows contributions to reference artifacts in other contributions. This is done via export and import entries in the sca-contribution.xml manifest. SCA defines an import/export mechanism for XML-based documents (for example, WSDLs and XSDs) and allows implementations to add additional support for other artifact types, such as Java packages. We look at each of these in turn.

Perspective: SCA and OSGi

Until recently, OSGi has received significant adoption in the Java market without much fanfare, including Eclipse (the basis of its plug-in system), embedded devices, and, more recently, in server-side runtimes. Two of the most popular OSGi implementations are Eclipse Equinox (http://www.eclipse.org/equinox) and Apache Felix (http://felix.apache.org/site/index.html).

For those unfamiliar with OSGi, it is a standard that specifies (among other things) how application modules, or "bundles," can be installed, started, stopped, uninstalled, and shared in a Java-based runtime. OSGi also specifies a component model (it calls components "services"), a service registry, and a set of standard services applications can access.

There are a number of ways SCA and OSGi can integrate. An OSGi runtime can participate as an SCA runtime in a domain. OSGi services can be accessed and used by SCA components. Further, OSGi bundles can be supported as a packaging format for contributions.

Early on when the contribution mechanism was being designed in the SCA specification working groups, OSGi (www.osgi.org) was considered for use as its packaging model. This would have entailed using OSGi's import and export mechanism directly instead of defining a new one. Given these similarities and its popularity, why was OSGi not adopted by SCA?

The primary reason OSGi was not adopted by SCA was that it is purely Java-based. Specifically, its import and export mechanism did not provide a way to reference non-Java artifacts such as XML documents. What SCA needed was a mechanism for sharing artifacts of many different kinds.

What the specification working groups came up with was a sharing mechanism that was not restricted to Java artifacts and could be extended by vendor implementations. With this approach, SCA runtimes could choose to support OSGi's sharing capabilities in addition to the standard SCA ones.

Exporting and Importing XML Artifacts

Sharing XML documents between contributions is done using the standard `<import>` and `<export>` elements in the sca-contribution.xml manifest. Listing 9.2 shows the manifest export entry for the contribution containing the WSDL documents for services belonging to the BigBank loan application.

Listing 9.2   Exporting a Namespace

```
<contribution xmlns=http://www.osoa.org/xmlns/sca/1.0>
    <export namespace="
    http://www.bigbank.com/xmlns/lending/lending/1.0"/>
</contribution>
```

Because the contribution contains only WSDL documents and no composites, there are no `<deployable>` entries in the manifest. Instead, it lists a single export for the `http://www.bigbank.com/xmlns/lending/lending/1.0` namespace. This will make all definitions in that namespace available to other contributions. For example, all `portType` definitions in WSDL documents contained in the contribution will be exported.

To use a WSDL `portType` definition, a contribution must import the `http://www.bigbank.com/xmlns/lending/lending/1.0` namespace. Listing 9.3 demonstrates how this is done using the `<import>` manifest element.

Listing 9.3   Importing a Namespace

```
<contribution xmlns=http://www.osoa.org/xmlns/sca/1.0>
    <import namespace="
http://www.bigbank.com/xmlns/lending/lending/1.0"/>
</contribution>
```

The `<import>` element is primarily a statement that some definitions for the specified namespace will not be found in this contribution. If a namespace is *not* imported, it is an error if some definition isn't found for that namespace. However, when such an import statement exists, then when the contribution is installed into a domain, that domain is responsible for matching the import to a contribution that exports that namespace (see Figure 9.11).

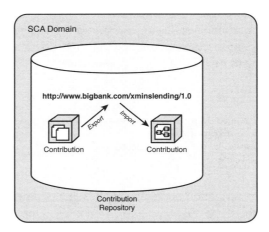

Figure 9.11   Importing a namespace

It is important to note that the actual exporting contribution is never referenced directly by the importing contribution. Providing this level of indirection enables artifacts to be repackaged without breaking importing clients.

After the domain has matched an import to the exporting contribution, specific definitions can be referred to by their qualified name as if they were contained in the importing contribution. For example, the `LoanServicePort` defined in a WSDL document contained in the exporting contribution can be referenced in a composite file contained in the importing contribution, as shown in Listing 9.4.

Listing 9.4   Referencing a Definition in an Imported Namespace

```
<composite ….>
   <service name="LoanApplicationService" promote="
LoanApplicationComponent">
      <interface.wsdl wsdlElement="http://www.bigbank.com/lending/1.0#
wsdl.port(LoanService/LoanServicePort)
"/>
      <binding.ws/>
   </service>

   …
</component>
```

It is also worth noting that the import/export mechanism requires developers to be disciplined about naming XML definitions. Because exports are global to the domain, names must be unique according to the rules of XML across all contributions in order for import statements to be so unspecific. However, unfortunately, the world of XML definitions is not always as simple as we would like, and we have to accommodate reality. If a domain needs to be able to contain two different contributions that each exports definitions from the same namespace, import statements from the contributions that use them will need to have an explicit `@location` attribute in their import statement that identifies which of the contributions to use. However, even in this case, the location attribute is merely used to identify a contribution. It is not necessary to identify specific definition documents within domains. This is because one contribution cannot export multiple conflicting XML definitions, even when the domain itself might contain conflicting definitions.

Unique Names in XML

People sometimes mistakenly assume that names must be unique within an XML namespace. Technically, speaking, this is not the case. XML namespaces are actually divided into symbol spaces, also known as namespace partitions. A name must be unique within a symbol space, not a namespace. For example, the same name can appear in both an XML Schema type definition and an element declaration. Another example is WSDL 1.1, which defines four symbol spaces where names must be unique: message, port type, binding, and service.

Symbol spaces make ensuring uniqueness in a domain less of a burden. Clashes are most likely to occur when namespaces are used incorrectly, such as when two documents inadvertently use the same namespace. In these cases, requiring proper naming practices is arguably a good thing because it forces issues to be corrected prior to an application being put into production.

Other Artifact Types

In addition to namespaces, SCA enables vendors to extend the import/export mechanism to other artifact types. The sidebar, "Fabric3 Packaging Extensions," describes how Fabric3 has done exactly this.

Fabric3 Packaging Extensions

Fabric3 introduces a number of useful packaging extensions not covered in SCA. The first is the capability to bundle third-party archives in JAR-based contributions. Often, a contribution will want to make use of third-party libraries that are distributed as one or more JARs. If those JARs are not packaged as SCA contributions (that is, they have an sca-contribution.xml manifest that exports their contained Java artifacts), there is no standard way for the contribution to access the third-party library.

Java EE web applications solve this problem by enabling third-party libraries to be included in the WEB-INF/lib directory of a WAR. All JARs bundled in the directory will be placed on the web application classpath. Fabric3 adopts a similar approach: Any JARs placed in the META-INF/lib directory of a JAR-based contribution will be placed on the contribution classpath at runtime. This provides a simple solution for bundling additional JARs with a contribution.

Fabric3 also extends the SCA contribution import/export to support OSGi classloading and bundles. Using `<export.java>` and `<import.java>`, a contribution can share classes contained in a set of packages between bundles. The following example demonstrates exporting and importing a set of packages between two contributions:

```
<contribution xmlns=http://www.osoa.org/xmlns/sca/1.0>
   <export.java package="com.bigbank.loan"/>
   <export.java package="com.bigbank.credit"/>
</contribution>

<contribution xmlns=http://www.osoa.org/xmlns/sca/1.0>
   <import.java package="com.bigbank.loan"/>
   <import.java package="com.bigbank.credit"/>
</contribution>
```

When a package is imported, the SCA runtime places Java classes contained in it on the classpath of the importing contribution.

Deployment Composites

Applications often require environment-specific configuration information when they are deployed. This is particularly the case when applications need to be first verified in a staging environment prior to being deployed in production. In SCA-based applications, for example, as an application moves into production, wires to test services may need to be retargeted to live endpoints.

One way to accommodate configuration changes is to place two or more deployable composites in the contribution archive corresponding to each deployment environment. This approach is, however, fragile and subject to error. First, there is the possibility that a deployer could select the wrong composite to deploy. In addition, if one of the deployment environments changes after a contribution archive is produced, it may require the archive to be modified so the deployable composite can be updated.

In SCA, deployers apply final configuration using external deployment composites. An external deployment composite is identical to other deployable composites except that it is not contained in a contribution archive. Rather, it is added to a contribution after it has been installed in the domain. External deployment composites enable deployers to make final changes without having to modify the original contribution archive. When it is added to a contribution, it becomes one of the contribution's deployable composites. This means it may be activated in the domain like any other deployable composite.

Let's examine how external deployment composites work by returning to the BigBank credit composite. In the current version, assume that BigBank's scoring algorithm uses a third-party credit bureau. The bureau provides two web service endpoints: one for testing and another for accessing live credit histories. As part of its testing infrastructure, BigBank has mimicked its production systems in a staging environment. The key difference between the two environments is that the staging environment only has access to a test database and third-party test services, the credit bureau's test endpoint for retrieving credit histories.

BigBank has decided to accommodate the different web service endpoints by applying the binding configuration in two deployment composites designed for each environment. This is done by first promoting the reference to the credit bureau's web service, as shown in Listing 9.5.

Listing 9.5   The Credit Composite with a Reference to Be Configured by a Deployment Composite

```
<composite ... name="CreditComposite">

   <component name ="CreditComponent">
     <implementation.java class="com.bigbank.CreditComponent"/>
   <component>

   ...
   <reference name="creditBureauService"
promote="CreditScoreComponent/ creditBureauService"/>

</composite>
```

Next, the composite and its associated artifacts are bundled in a contribution archive. When the contribution is installed in the test domain, the external deployment composite shown in Listing 9.6 is added to the contribution.

Listing 9.6   The Test Deployment Composite

```
<composite … name="TestCreditDeploymentComposite">

   <component name ="CreditComponent">
      <implementation.composite name="
http://www.bigbank.com/xmlns/loanApplication/1.0:CreditComposite"/>
   <component>
   <reference name="creditBureauService">
      <binding.ws
uri="www.creditBureau.com/services/test/CreditHistory"/>
   </reference>

</composite>
```

The deployment composite defines a `CreditComponent`, which uses the `CreditComposite` as its implementation. The `CreditComponent#creditServiceBureau` reference is configured with the web service binding and points to the credit bureau's test endpoint. In the deployment composite intended for production, the reference would be configured with the web service binding pointing to the live endpoint.

Thus far, we have not said how external deployment composites are added to a contribution. Like the other contribution operations—install, update, and remove—SCA leaves it up to domain implementations to provide proprietary mechanisms. The specification describes an abstract operation called **add deployment composite**, but there is no requirement that this correspond to a specific deployed service on the domain. The domain just needs to provide some mechanism for the user to access this functionality. Typically, vendors will provide some form of command-line tool and possibly an API for script-based deployment or a management console where the deployment composite is graphically created.

Structuring Contributions

Contributions may be structured in a variety of ways. All services for a single application can be packaged in a single contribution archive or divided by subsystem. Unlike Java EE, which mandates applications be packaged in a single archive (EAR or WAR), SCA provides the option of decomposing applications into finer-grained contributions. Whether this is appropriate or a single-archive approach is better is largely a function of the application architecture and preference.

We do, however, offer one important piece of advice: Place binding configuration in top-level composites and use deployment composites to override information. This avoids "hard-coding" endpoint addresses and environment-specific information such as JMS queues several layers deep in a composite hierarchy. It also has the effect of making external dependencies more evident in an application.

The Domain Composite

Once a contribution is installed in a domain, it may be activated or deployed. When the composite is deployed, the domain provisions its components to a runtime or set of runtimes. As part of this process, the domain will also provision required artifacts in the contribution and its imported contributions to the target runtimes. Similarly, components may be undeployed or updated. In a domain, components may come and go, wires may be added or changed, and services may be exposed at new endpoint addresses. How is change—deployment, undeployment, and updates—introduced in a domain?

Given that SCA is a component-based technology and supports the notion of composition where components are built from other components (see Chapter 5), it may come as no surprise that there is a root-level composite in a domain. This composite is called the **domain composite**. A domain composite contains all the components deployed in the domain, just as any other composite may contain child components. Change is introduced in the domain by modifying the domain composite.

Although the domain composite is like any other composite in that it has components, wires, and properties, it also has some special characteristics.

Although the domain composite is like any other composite in that it has components, wires, and properties, it also has some special characteristics. One of the most important is that the domain composite is virtual. That is, the domain composite is not defined using an XML document. Rather, it is derived or "synthesized" from all the composites deployed to the domain. Also, unlike any other composite, it does not live within a single contribution. Its components come from all the installed contributions in the domain.

Another feature of the domain composite is that it can be modified through a set of operations. Because domains may vary widely, SCA does not specify an API for doing this. Rather it defines a set of abstract operations for doing so. Each vendor implementation is free to define specific mechanisms for invoking these operations—for example, via a command-line tool, API, service endpoint, or management console. We discuss the principle domain operations in the sections that follow: adding and removing from the domain composite. Later, we provide examples of how these concrete operations are performed using the Fabric3 runtime.

Add to Domain Composite

SCA's concept of adding a composite to the domain corresponds to most people's concept of **deployment**. (Although, unfortunately, "deployment" does not have the exact same meaning throughout the software industry.) It results in activating all of its contained components. In a local domain, the activated components will be provisioned to the same runtime. In a distributed domain, the activated components may be deployed to different runtimes.

It is important to note that when a composite is added to the domain, it is *included* in the domain composite. In Chapter 5, we detailed how inclusion works. When a composite is included in another composite, its components are inlined. This means that the included composite is discarded and its contained components become direct children of the domain composite. Figure 9.12 illustrates this process.

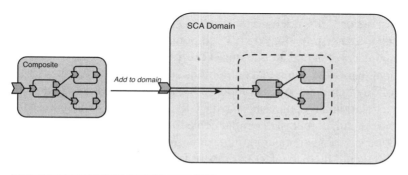

Figure 9.12   The add to domain operation includes a composite in the domain composite.

An effect of inclusion is that child components of composites deployed to the domain composite become peers. This enables components contained in separate deployed composites to be wired directly. It also provides for some interesting dynamic behavior, the most common of which we outline later in the chapter.

In addition to the fairly syntactic concept of inclusion into the domain composite, this step in the deployment process also prepares the application to be run. One of the most important parts of this preparation is assignment of URIs to services.

URI Assignment

A Uniform Resource Identifier, or URI, is defined by the IETF—one of the principle Internet standards bodies—as a way to uniquely identify a resource. A resource can be virtually anything from a web page, image, or video clip, to a file or program. Even if you have only heard the term in passing, you are already familiar with URIs. A URL, for example, is a specific type of URI. Although there are specific rules for how URIs are constructed (for example, legal characters, the meaning of various segments of the URI, and so on), the key things to remember are that URIs are a way to identify a resource and that they may be hierarchical. In other words, URIs may refer to resources contained within other resources. For example, the URI http://www.bigbank.com/loanapp/intro.html#getting_started refers to the "`getting_started`" fragment contained in the page intro.html.

SCA uses URIs as a way to identify resources in a domain.

What do URIs have to do with SCA? In short, SCA uses URIs as a way to identify resources in a domain. In the context of our current discussion, URIs are used to identify deployed components and the services they provide. When a component is deployed to the domain, it is assigned a URI. This URI is calculated from the component name. Recalling that composites are a type of component, it follows that the domain composite is a deployed component and that all domain composites have a URI. How URIs are assigned to the domain composite is implementation-specific, but it is usually done via some configuration mechanism. An example of a domain URI would be bigbank.com or loans.bigbank.com.

Because components added to the domain composite become its children, they are assigned a hierarchical URI. URIs use the / character for hierarchical parts. Consequently, the URI for a deployed component is calculated by combining the domain URI and component name, separated by a /. For example, if a component named `CreditComponent` is added to the domain composite, its URI will be loans.bigbank.com/CreditComponent. This holds for the entire composition hierarchy. For example, in Chapter 5, we showed the example where the BigBank credit scoring function was provided by a series of components contained within a composite named `CreditComposite`. If `CreditComposite` was contained in `LoanApplicationComposite`, which was added to the domain composite, the URI assigned to `CreditComponent` would be loans.bigbank.com/CreditComposite/CreditComponent. Note that because the `LoanApplicationComposite` was added to the domain, it was discarded and not used in determining the URI.

Wouldn't it be simpler if SCA had just used the component name? If that were the case, there would be no way to uniquely identify a component unless SCA required that all component names had to be unique. In large systems with several levels of composition, this would be unmanageable. Imagine if operating system file systems had not introduced the concept of subdirectories: maintaining unique names for all files with current disk storage capacities would be impractical. Similarly, guaranteeing that all component names in all composites across a domain are unique would impose an unrealistic burden. By using hierarchical URIs, name clashes can more easily be avoided and deployed components can be identified at any level in the composition structure.

Wiring at the Domain Level

Having discussed the URI-based naming conventions used by SCA during deployment, we now turn to a more detailed discussion of ways the domain composite can be modified via the add to domain composite operation.

Through the add to domain composite operation, new applications can reuse existing services that were deployed as part of another composite or set of composites. To demonstrate how this is done, we return to the BigBank application. Assume the `Credit Composite` listed in Listing 9.7 is added to the domain composite.

Listing 9.7   The CreditComposite Is Added to the Domain Composite

```
<composite … name="CreditComposite">

    <component name ="CreditComponent">
        …
    <component>

…

</composite>
```

When the operation completes, `CreditComposite` will be discarded, and `CreditComponent` will become a child of the domain composite, as shown in Figure 9.13.

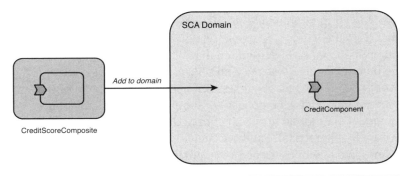

Figure 9.13   Adding the CreditComposite

Clients in other deployed composites will now have access to the `CreditService` interface, which is provided by `CreditComponent`. For example, if BigBank needed to roll out an application for a new loan offering, it could reuse the existing `CreditService` interface by wiring to it in the composite that will be added to the domain. This composite is listed in Listing 9.8.

Listing 9.8   The NewLoanApplicationComposite

```
<composite … name="NewLoanApplicationComposite">

<component name ="NewLoanApplicationComponent">
    <implementation.java
class="com.bigbank.LoanApplicationComponent"/>
    <reference name="creditService" target="CreditComponent"/>
```

```
<component>

...

</composite>
```

In the preceding composite, the
`NewLoanApplicationComponent#creditService` reference is
wired to the default service provided by `CreditComponent`, specifically the `CreditService` service. Notice that `CreditComponent`
is not defined in `NewLoanApplicationComposite`. When
`NewLoanApplicationComposite` is included in the domain
composite, it is discarded and `NewLoanApplicationComponent`
becomes a child of the domain composite. The target
`"CreditComponent"` configured on the
`NewLoanApplicationComponent#creditService` reference will
then resolve to the previously deployed `CreditComponent`. Figure
9.14 illustrates the end result.

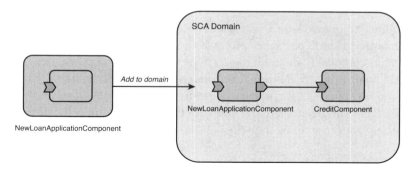

Figure 9.14   Adding the NewLoanApplicationComposite

It is also worth noting that autowire could have been used in the
preceding example instead of the explicit wire to
`CreditComponent`. If autowire had been enabled on
`NewLoanApplicationComposite` or on the domain composite
(how this is done is implementation-dependent), the
`NewLoanApplicationComponent#creditService` reference
would have been targeted to `CreditComponent/CreditService`
automatically by the domain, without the need for the
`<reference>` configuration.

Adding a Wire

Another common change at the domain level is adding a wire dynamically. To understand how this works, consider the following. BigBank has just signed an agreement to use an additional third-party credit bureau and needs to update the loan application to use the new credit service in addition to the existing ones.

In the original `LoanApplicationComposite`, the `LoanApplicationComponent#creditService` reference is wired to two `CreditService` providers, as shown in the following listing:

```
<composite .. name="LoanApplicationComposite">
   <component name ="LoanApplicationComponent">
      <implementation.java class="com.acme.LoanApplicationComponent"/>
      <reference name="creditService" target="CreditScoreComponent1
➡CreditScoreComponent2"/>
   <component>
   ...

</composite>
```

When `LoanApplicationComposite` was added to the domain, `LoanApplicationComponent` was included as a child of the domain composite. BigBank has a couple of options to update the original wiring. `LoanApplicationComposite` could be modified and redeployed. Or another composite containing only a `<wire>` element can be created and added to the domain composite. The composite containing the wire is listed in the following:

```
<composite .. name="WireComposite">
   <wire source="LoanApplicationComponent/creditService" target="
NewCreditScoreComponent"/>

</composite>
```

The sequence of steps BigBank takes in updating `LoanApplicationComponent` is illustrated in Figure 9.15. After the composite containing the new `CreditService` provider is added to the domain, the wire composite is added.

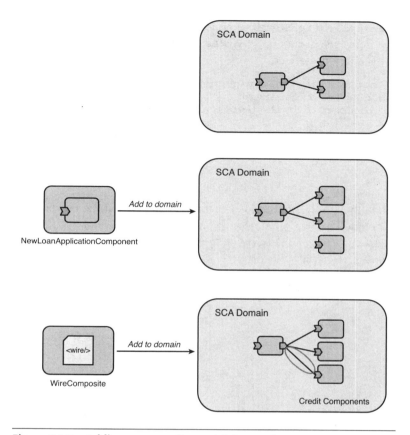

NewLoanApplicationComponent

WireComposite

Figure 9.15   Adding a composite containing a wire

When `WireComposite` is added, the domain establishes an additional communication channel between `LoanApplication`
`Component` and the new `CreditServiceComponent`. Assuming
`LoanApplicationComponent` was implemented in Java, implementation instances would be injected with a list containing three
`CreditService` interface proxies.

Adding a Bound Service

Sometimes it is desirable to expose a service at an endpoint for
external clients after its component has been deployed. This can
be done by creating a composite with a promoted service and
adding it to the domain. The following listing shows

LoanApplicationServiceComposite, which promotes
LoanApplicationComponent/LandApplicationService and
binds it to web services:

```
<composite .. name="LoanApplicationServiceComposite">
   <service name ="LoanApplicationService"
promote="LoanApplicationComponent/LandApplicationService">
      <binding.ws/>
   <service>
   …

</composite>
```

When the composite is added to the domain, the promoted service
is included in the domain composite. This has the effect of exposing
the existing LoanApplicationService as a web service endpoint.
Figure 9.16 depicts this process.

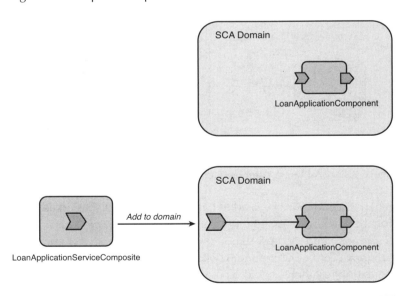

Figure 9.16   Adding a promoted service

Similarly, additional promoted services could be added that create
endpoints over additional bindings.

Remove from Domain Composite

In addition to the add operation, SCA implementations are required to provide a mechanism for removing, or undeploying, a composite. How the removal operation is performed is runtime-specific.

Deploying Policies

SCA's approach to policy depends on a separation of roles. Developers and assemblers specify minimum policy requirements through intents but don't specify the details of how those requirements will be met; policy administrators and deployers specify this. Policy administrators specify the policy sets that can be used to satisfy a policy intent under various conditions as stated in the XPath expressions in their `@appliesTo` attributes. The deployer then has the final call and can explicitly pick policies for specific services, rather than relying on the policy sets that would be chosen by the rules.

Although the `@appliesTo` attribute of `policySet` specifies the conditions under when the policy should apply, the domain provides the scope over which it applies. In other words, `policySet` applies to service and reference bindings that meet that `@appliesTo` condition throughout the domain.

New policy sets are added to the domain in the same way that other definitions are added to domains. The policy sets are defined within documents with a `<definitions>` root element. These definitions documents are packaged in contributions and installed into domains in the same way as other artifacts. One difference from other artifacts, however, is that all the policy sets (and other definitions) within a definitions document are automatically visible to all other contributions, without having to export them from the contribution in which they are written or import them into the contribution in which they are used.

Summary

This chapter has covered the main functions of the domain: management, artifact sharing, policy, administration, and remote communications. Recalling that a domain may consist of heterogeneous services—that is, services written in different programming languages—the next chapter provides an overview of using BPEL as alternative component implementation technologies.

Service-Based Development Using BPEL

Up until now, we have only seen services implemented in Java. In this chapter, we describe how components can be developed using BPEL. BPEL is very well-suited to SCA component development, because it was explicitly designed for handling long-running conversations and bidirectional interfaces.

What Is BPEL?

The first release of BPEL was called Business Process Execution Language for Web Services, with an acronym of BPEL4WS. It has since been changed to WS-BPEL, although people usually just call it BPEL (pronounced beep'uhl).

History

In December of 2000, Microsoft published its proposal for a business process language called XLANG. Four months later, IBM published its proposal, which was called WSFL. The two companies then collaborated to merge the ideas of the two languages into BPEL4People 1.0, which was published in July 2002, as a proposal from IBM, Microsoft, and BEA.

BPEL is very well-suited to SCA component development, because it was explicitly designed for handling long-running conversations and bidirectional interfaces.

In May 2003, some minor cleanups were done, and version 1.1 was published and submitted for standardization to OASIS. OASIS then worked for the next four years on WS-BPEL 2.0, which was published in April 2007.

The 2.0 version of the specification included improvements to the extensibility of the language, and added some important new features, but most important, it improved the description of the semantics of the language, which is critical to achieving the portability goal of the language. Any significant new projects built with BPEL should be based on version 2.0 of the specification.

A Language for Web Services

If you were going to design a language from scratch that was designed for use with asynchronous web services, there is a good chance you would design something very similar to BPEL.

Ignore, for the time being, the concept of business processes. If you were going to design a language from scratch that was designed for use with asynchronous web services, there is a good chance you would design something very similar to BPEL. The asynchronous qualifier in that statement is critical, but before dealing with that, the features that make it a language for web services include the following:

- Variables and parameters typed by XML Schema
- Operation signatures specified by WSDL
- Expressions and conditionals specified using XPath
- An XML syntax for the language itself

Nonetheless, if it weren't for asynchrony, the language would likely look very different. Two of the asynchronous patterns that BPEL adopts as central patterns are exactly the patterns that SCA has defined for asynchrony, as follows:

- Bidirectional interfaces, which BPEL calls partner link types
- Conversations that are embedded in BPEL's concept of a correlation set

Each of these topics, and how they are used within an SCA environment, will be dealt with in more detail later in the chapter.

Finally, there is the concept of the business process. Actually, the concept supported by BPEL is more precisely described by the term **orchestration**. It is a much more flexible form of control flow than exists in imperative languages, where the language primitives only support a single thread of control, and calls to special-purpose libraries are needed in order to introduce concurrency (such as tasks in Java). In BPEL (as in any language designed to support workflow patterns), the language supports static and dynamic forking and various thread-joining patterns. **Static forking** is where the number of new threads is known at compilation time and can be represented by transitions in a graph. **Dynamic forking** is where the number of threads is determined only at runtime, usually based on the data being handled by a business process (such as a list of part vendors). By "thread" here, we do not necessarily mean operating system thread, but rather the more general concept of a thread of control. The control flow is best understood and is typically viewed as a graphical representation, such as that shown in Figure 10.1.

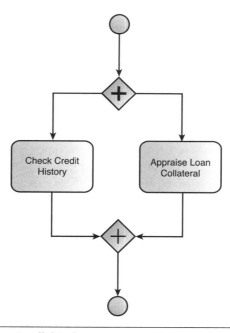

Figure 10.1   Parallel tasks

This representation of control flow is often used to represent business processes, because formal procedures that have been followed by businesses (or any organization) can be easily represented by such graphs. Think of the planning that goes on for building construction. The steps involved in construction are not typically tracked by computers, but if they were, you would need control flow constructs to support various complex forking and joining scenarios in order to accurately represent the work on the ground.

As businesses do more and more of their work as tasks on a computer, keeping track and controlling the flow of work in the business *can* be handled by a computer. This also has the advantage that tasks can change over time from being manual tasks to automated tasks (or vice versa) without having to change the fundamental business process that is controlling everything. Ultimately, this kind of workflow representation remains the best representation, even when *all* the tasks have been automated—especially when the work lasts long enough to require asynchrony (conversations and callbacks).

Using BPEL with SCA

A BPEL process definition can be used as the implementation of an SCA component.

BPEL fits very well into the world of SCA. A BPEL process definition can be used as the implementation of an SCA component. The BPEL partner links become services and references (more on this later), and the interfaces of those services and references are specified using the WSDL port types that make up the BPEL partner link types. SCA's conversational interfaces provide what BPEL refers to as **engine-managed correlation**, which removes the need for developers to specify correlating information explicitly.

What the BPEL specification lacks is exactly where the SCA assembly specification steps in. BPEL provides no mechanism for specifying *what* will provide the services at the other end of the partner links. SCA's wiring fills this need. BPEL also has no way of specifying bindings or policies for the partner links. The SCA binding specifications and policy specification provide for this. Together, the SCA specifications and the BPEL specification provide a complete answer. And because not all services make sense to be developed in BPEL, the SCA Java specifications round out a complete programming model for SOA development.

BPEL Versus Java for Conversational Services

When a Java class is used to implement a conversational service, every operation in the interface is always active. In the conversational loan service introduced in Chapter 4, "Conversational Interactions Using Java," the interface had operations for `apply()`, `getStatus()`, and `cancel()`. There is nothing in that interface or in the code that allows the system to automatically handle situations where messages arrive in an order that makes no sense, such as a `getStatus()` or `cancel()` request that arrives before `apply()`. The developer has to have code that explicitly checks that the operation has been invoked at an appropriate time for the conversation. For more complex conversations, the check is hard to do, and the result is hard to understand, because there is no single place you can go to see a representation of the acceptable sequence. By contrast, take the case in BPEL, where you have the following activities connected in a sequence:

1. Receive X from client.
2. Reply to X.
3. Receive Y from client.
4. Reply to Y.
5. Receive Z from client.
6. Reply to Z.

The acceptable order for requests from the client is clear, and an attempt to send requests in any unexpected order will generate a fault without any code on the part of the service.

Using BPEL for the Loan Service

To get a sense for using BPEL to implement a component, we will replace the Java implementation of the loan service from the application introduced in Chapter 4 with a BPEL implementation of that service.

BPEL does not define a graphical representation for processes, although the expectation has always been that a graphical representation would be the most common way for developers to work with these processes. However, the OASIS technical committee that standardized BPEL was not chartered to standardize such a representation. One common notation for business processes is the

Business Process Modeling Notation (BPMN). Its concepts don't align perfectly with BPEL, because it has a number of constructs with no equivalent in BPEL, and BPEL has constructs without a representation in BPMN. Nonetheless, it is close enough to represent the basic control flow of the process.

For the sake of this example, imagine that the process for handling new loan applications is a little bit more complicated than it was in Chapter 4; let's create a loan-approval process based on the loan-application process used as an example at the end of the BPEL specification. In this process, if the loan amount is less than some designated amount (say $10,000), a call is made to a risk assessment service, which tries to determine whether the risk is low enough to immediately approve it, or high enough to immediately deny it. If, however, the amount is larger than $10,000 or if the automatic risk assessment service can't make a clean determination, the full loan review is initiated. The process might look like that shown in Figure 10.2.

Unfortunately, BPMN has no representation of the partner links behind the communication activities. Listing 10.1 is some of the partner link declaration section of that process.

Listing 10.1   Partner Links for the Loan Application Process

```
<partnerLinks>
  <partnerLink name="customer"
    partnerLinkType="lns:loanPartnerLT"
    myRole="loanService" />
  <partnerLink name="approver"
    partnerLinkType="lns:loanApprovalLT"
    partnerRole="approver" />
  <partnerLink name="assessor"
    partnerLinkType="lns:riskAssessmentLT"
    partnerRole="assessor" />
</partnerLinks>
```

All the partner links in this process have only a single role. The partner link with myRole="loanService" is the only service offered by the process. The other two (named "approver" and "assessor") are references. The algorithm for the mapping of partner links to services and references is described in the next section.

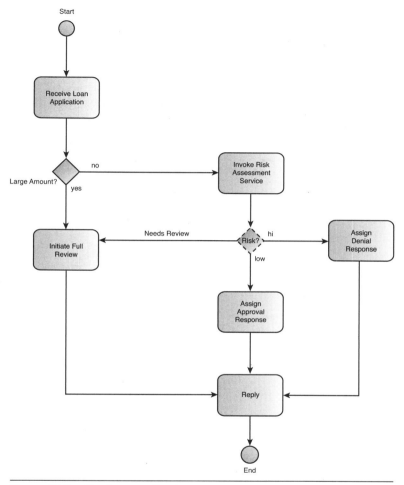

Figure 10.2   The loan application process

Because this implementation makes use of an approver and an assessor, our assembly needs a couple of additional components that existed in the composite described in Chapter 4. The new composite would look like what is shown in Figure 10.3.

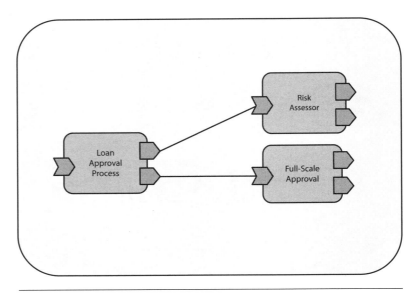

Figure 10.3   Loan application components

Partner Links Are Services and References

BPEL identifies the external services that it communicates with
through **partner links**, and like SCA services and references, they
can be bidirectional. The client may need to provide services that
can be used by the process for callbacks. A partner link's type is
specified by a **partner link type**, which consists of either one or
two port types (two if it is bidirectional).

Symmetry of Partner Link Types

There is one difference between SCA's concept of bidirectional
interfaces and BPEL's partner link types, which is that partner link
types are symmetric. An SCA bidirectional interface is made of an
interface and a **callback interface**. There is an implication that the
service provider is providing the interface and the client is providing the callback interface. However, BPEL makes no such distinction. In fact, BPEL does not refer to the two roles as "service
provider" and "client." The roles can have any name, and there is
nothing else to distinguish one role as more important than the
other.

So, what *is* the difference between a "client" and a "service provider?" With bidirectional interfaces, both roles provide services that can be used by the other role. The only difference is that the "client" sends the first message of the conversation. The direction of that first message provides the asymmetry, and then after that, there are no constraints on the messages that might be sent between the two roles.

In BPEL, even that distinction is not made. It is theoretically possible that a partner link type could be created where either role could initiate the conversation. In that case, there would be no asymmetry at all. However, although that may make the model more elegant and theoretically more powerful, in fact, almost every conversational service is designed where it is known in advance which role will send the first message. The distinction between a client and a service provider exists in the mind of the developer, so it makes sense to recognize it in the programming model.

Static Control Flow Analysis with SCA BPEL

When you use a BPEL process definition as the implementation of a component, SCA needs to be able to tell which of the partner links should be represented as services and which should be represented as references. If the partner link type has only one role, the choice is easy: The partner links with the one role as "myRole" are services and the partner links with the one role as "partnerRole" are references.

When the partner link type has two roles (that is, it is bidirectional), SCA determines which are services and which are references by depending on the fundamental asymmetry between clients and service providers described previously—figure out which role will send the first message of the conversation. The SCA BPEL specification says that this is accomplished by static control flow analysis of the BPEL process.

Partner links are used for either inbound or outbound communication. Inbound communication occurs as either a receive, onMessage, or pick activity. Outbound communication is done with either an invoke or a reply activity. The order in which the activities can occur is constrained by the sequence of activities they

SCA determines which are services and which are references by depending on the fundamental asymmetry between clients and service providers.

are in and by any links present in the process. The SCA processor can analyze each use of a partner link and determine whether the first activity for the partner link is inbound or outbound communication. If it is inbound (for example, receive), the partner link is turned into a service. If it is outbound (for example, invoke), it is turned into a reference.

According to SCA, the static analysis is not allowed to try to guess the path taken through any condition. (Although in most cases, it would be impossible anyway, but the specification disallows it so that different processors don't come up with different answers.)

In the rare case that it can't be determined which will occur first, the partner link is turned into a reference. This can happen when a receive and an invoke activity for the same partner link are in the same flow, and there is no link that causes one of the two to occur before the other.

Usually, the programmer does not need to think about any of this. The partner links that the developer thinks of as services become services, and the partner links that the developer thinks of as references become references.

Partner Link Types as Interfaces

In SCA, a bidirectional interface is defined in Java with an @Callback annotation, as we saw back in Chapter 3, "Service-Based Development Using Java" (see Listing 10.2).

Listing 10.2   Bidirectional Interface in Java

```
@Callback(CreditCallback.class)
public interface CreditService { ...  }
```

To expose the service using WSDL, port types that correspond to the Java interfaces would be created (by hand or using JAX-WS to generate them), and the component type would identify the bidirectional interface of the service by specifying both the service provider interface and the callback interface. The component type would look like Listing 10.3.

Listing 10.3   Bidirectional Interface Using WSDL

```
<componentType xmlns="http://www.osoa.org/xmlns/sca/1.0"
  <service name="CreditService">
    <interface.wsdl
interface="http://www.bigbank.com/loanapplication#wsdl.interface(Credit
➥Service)"
callbackInterface="http://www.bigbank.com/loanapplication#wsdl.
➥interface(CreditCallback)"/>
```

BPEL requires that the pairing of an interface and its corresponding callback interface be specified in a partner link type. The partner link type name is then used as the interface name. This is appropriate because the two interfaces are not really independent. They were designed to be used together, so it is appropriate that there be a name for the combination.

In BPEL, the partner link type for this bidirectional interface would be in the WSDL file (usually with the corresponding port types) and would look like Listing 10.4.

Listing 10.4   Bidirectional Partner Link Type Definition

```
<partnerLinkType name="CreditServicePLT">
  <role name="creditBureau">
    <portType="bb:CreditService">
  </role>
  <role name="creditRequestor">
    <portType="bb:CreditCallback">
  </role>
</partnerLinkType>
```

The SCA BPEL specification then states that the partner link type can be used in the component type as an alternative to the typical way of specifying bidirectional interfaces. This is done by using `<interface.partnerLinkType>` instead of `<interface.wsdl>`. Because the partner link type is symmetric, you must also specify the name of the role that is provided by the service, as shown in Listing 10.5.

The partner link type can be used in the component type as an alternative to the typical way of specifying bidirectional interfaces.

Listing 10.5   Bidirectional Interface Using a Partner Link Type

```
<componentType xmlns="http://www.osoa.org/xmlns/sca/1.0"
  <service name="CreditService">
    <interface.partnerLinkType type="bb:CreditServicePLT"
      serviceRole="creditBureau"/>
  </service>
  ...
```

SCA Extensions to BPEL

Up until now, we have seen that standard BPEL processes may be used without using any extensions, APIs, or standardized services from SCA. The business process does not need to have any reference to SCA in it at all.

There are a few capabilities that SCA provides for BPEL processes that are only available by using the SCA extension to BPEL.

However, there are a few capabilities that SCA provides for BPEL processes that are available only by using the SCA extension to BPEL. Any BPEL engine that is working within an SCA domain should understand these extensions, although careful thought should be given before they are used, because they will cause the process to be unable to run in a BPEL engine that is not running in an SCA domain.

Nonetheless, BPEL does provide a mechanism for adding extensions. SCA's extension is declared at the beginning of any process that uses it (see Listing 10.6).

Listing 10.6   The SCA Extension Declaration for BPEL

```
<extensions>
  <extension
   namespace="http://docs.oasis-open.org/ns/opencsa/sca-bpel/200801"
   mustUnderstand="yes" />
</extensions>
```

The extension is marked with `mustUnderstand="yes"` because most of the extensions affect the semantics of the process, and an engine that did not understand the extensions would generate results different from what would have been desired by the developer.

SCA Properties

BPEL has no capability to provide data that can be set by a deployer and used by the process. In other words, there is no equivalent to SCA's concept of properties. Nonetheless, properties are at least as valuable for BPEL processes as they are for any other implementation type.

Properties are at least as valuable for BPEL processes as they are for any other implementation type.

Consider the loan application process again. In that process, $10,000 was hard coded into the process in the condition for the branch that determined whether to attempt automatic loan approval based on risk assessment rules. Rather than have that number hard coded into the process, the value should be represented as a property that can be set at the place where the process is used.

SCA's extension for declaring properties provides an attribute that can be added to a variable declaration to also designate the variable as a property. If the cutoff amount for automatic processing were a property, it would be defined as shown in Listing 10.7.

Listing 10.7   An SCA Property as a BPEL Variable

```
<variable name="cutoffAmount" type="xsd:integer"
        sca-bpel:property="yes">
  <from>
    <literal>10000</literal>
  </from>
</variable>
```

The variable's initialization value will be used as the value of the variable if the property is not set in the composite file that instantiates this process. If the property is set, the process uses that property value rather than the value in the initialization expression. Just in case the initialization expression has some side effects (which would be bad practice), the SCA BPEL specification requires that the expression be evaluated before its result is ignored and the SCA property value is used instead. Any subsequent property initialization expressions that access the variable should see the SCA property value, so the replacement can't wait until after all the initialization expressions have been evaluated.

Customizing the Generated Services and References

The developer may not like the way that SCA generates service and reference definitions for a BPEL process. The automatically generated component type uses the partner link names as the names of the services and references. Because these names are not guaranteed to be unique for the process (they are only unique within a single scope), the automatically generated name might need to include a disambiguation digit at the end of the name. For example, it might have to generate "myService1" and "myService2" as service names for two partner links named "myService." If this happens, the developer may want to choose better names. The developer may also want different names if there is a convention, such as ending partner links with "PL," which he does not want to have exposed in the service or reference names.

To customize the generated name, the developer can include an attribute from the SCA BPEL extension that explicitly specifies the name. This looks like Listing 10.8.

Listing 10.8   Partner Link with Customized SCA Service Name

```
<partnerLink name="CreditServicePL"
partnerLinkType="bb:CreditServicePLT" myRole="creditBureau"
sca:service="CreditService"/>
```

Because it is theoretically possible for the static analysis to come up with the wrong choice, when determining whether a partner link should be a service or a reference, this mechanism can also be used to force a partner link that would otherwise have been turned into a service into a reference, and vice versa.

References with Multiplicity

A partner link is used to communicate with a single service. There is nothing in BPEL that corresponds to SCA's concept of a reference that has a multiplicity of "0..n" (which we will refer to as a **multireference**). Nonetheless, as with properties, this is a useful concept that should be made available to developers. Also, SCA should be able to be used with a top-down development style, where an architect designs the components and the wires without knowing what implementation language will be used for each of the components. If such an architect included any multivalued references, it should still be possible to implement that component using BPEL.

Recall that in SCA, a multireference does *not* mean that outbound messages on the reference are automatically broadcast to all the targets. Instead, it just means that all the targets are somehow presented to the component developer to do with as she wants. She may send requests to every target in parallel, to every target sequentially, to a subset of the targets, or to just one of the targets. How the list of targets is presented to the component developer is up to the programming language.

In BPEL, most references are represented as partner links. However, there is no obvious way for SCA to extend BPEL links so that they instead represent a list of targets, instead of only one. Instead, SCA has to represent the list of targets as the contents of a variable and depend on the developer using BPEL's capability to set partner link targets at runtime.

Multiplicity Example with Credit Bureaus
To see the value of multiplicity in the context of our example, imagine that the process is modified so that a credit check is made with a list of credit bureaus before the rest of the loan approval process is done by the bank. We would want the list of credit bureaus to be expandable, rather than hardcoded into the process.

We will modify our process by adding a new activity immediately after the initial receive activity for getting credit scores from credit bureaus. The fact that it is done for multiple credit bureaus is represented in BPMN by the parallel bars at the bottom of the new activity (see Figure 10.4).

The BPEL representation of this is significantly more complicated. First, we need the variable that will hold the list of targets for the multi-reference that will represent the credit bureaus. At assembly time, the reference will be wired to services for each of the credit bureaus to be used. The variable that holds these targets looks like Listing 10.9.

Listing 10.9   Partner Link with Customized SCA Service Name

```
<variable name="bureaus" element="sca-bpel:serviceReferenceList">
  <sca-bpel:multiReference partnerLinkType="pos:CreditBureauPT"
    partnerRole="bureau" />
</variable>
```

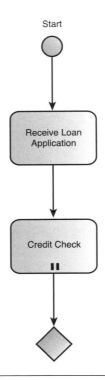

Start

Figure 10.4   The new credit check activity

This causes the "`bureaus`" variable to hold endpoint references for each service that the multireference is wired to within the composite file. The child element of the variable declaration is used to specify the type of the reference, which may be either a single-direction interface or a bidirectional interface, specified using a `partnerLinkType` and a `partnerRole`; this is analogous to the way single-valued references are typed.

At runtime, the contents of the "`bureaus`" variable will be a document that looks like Listing 10.10.

Listing 10.10   A ServiceReferenceList with Two Endpoints

```
<<sr:serviceReferenceList
  xmlns:sr="http://docs.oasis-open.org/wsbpel/2.0/serviceref"
  xmlns:wsa="http://schemas.xmlsoap.org/ws/2003/03/addressing">
  <sr:serviceRef>
    <wsa:EndpointReference>
      <wsa:Address>http://creditBureau1.com/svc</wsa:Address>
```

```
      </wsa:EndpointReference>
    </sr:serviceRef>
    <sr:serviceRef>
      <wsa:EndpointReference>
        <wsa:Address>http://creditBureau2.com/svc</wsa:Address>
      </wsa:EndpointReference>
    </sr:serviceRef>
  </sr:serviceReferenceList>
```

Next is the BPEL representation of a parallel call to each credit bureau. We take advantage of BPEL's parallel "for-each" activity to accomplish this. It looks like Listing 10.11.

Listing 10.11   Accessing All (0..n) Reference Targets in Parallel

```
<forEach counterName="idx">
  <startCounterValue>1</startCounterValue>
  <finalCounterValue>
    count($bureaus/sref:service-ref)
  </finalCounterValue>
  <scope>
    <partnerLinks>
      <partnerLink name="bureauLink"
         partnerLinkType="pos:CreditBureauPT"
         partnerRole="bureau"
         sca-bpel:multiRefFrom="bureaus" />
    </partnerLinks>
    <sequence>
      <assign>
        <copy>
          <from>$bureaus/sref:service-ref[$idx]</from>
          <to partnerLink="bureauLink"/>
        </copy>
      </assign>
      <invoke partnerLink="bureauLink"
         operation="getCreditReport"
         inputVariable="applicantSSN"
         outputVariable="creditReport">
      </invoke>
      ... do something with the credit report
    </sequence>
  </scope>
</forEach>
```

In this code sample, you can see that the forEach loop variable only maintains the variable for the index. If there are three credit bureaus in our list (that is, there were three wires), the forEach will initiate three parallel branches of control flow. Within each scope, a local partner link is defined, and that partner link is assigned one of the targets (the bold part of the preceding code). This means that in this example, three scopes will be simultaneously started, each scope will have its own partner link, and each partner link will be assigned to one of the three reference targets.

When each `invoke` completes, it now has the credit report for the applicant from one of the three credit bureaus. The next thing to do would be to add that credit report to a list of credit reports that will be given to the reviewers that come later in the process. (This part of the code was not shown in the preceding sample.)

The entire `forEach` will complete when the scope of all three of the initiated scopes have been completed. The rest of the process can then run.

Summary

BPEL is a language that was designed for orchestrating web services. It is easy to use standard BPEL process definitions as the implementation of components within SCA. It is also possible to use SCA extensions to standard BPEL to take advantage of SCA-specific features, such as properties and multireferences, or to customize things like the names of the service and references that are generated for a process definition.

11

Persistence

SCA is not intended to be a platform technology. By "platform technology," we mean a technology such as Java EE and .NET designed to cover all application development needs, from the user interface (or interfaces) to long-term data storage. Rather, SCA is concerned with what is typically referred to as the "middle-tier": the code that comprises the bulk of an application's processing logic.

All but the most trivial applications require some form of persistence, most commonly to a relational database; many applications also require some form of user interface. SCA does not offer its own set of solutions for the presentation and persistence tiers. Instead, the goal of the SCA authors was to make it easy to integrate with existing and emerging technologies in these areas.

Seen in this light, although covering significant ground, SCA is less ambitious than Java EE and .NET. A benefit of this approach is that developers don't need to learn a completely new set of technologies when working with SCA. However, a major downside is that with SCA, there is no clear consensus or one way to handle presentation and persistence needs.

Indeed, a number of approaches have been taken by vendors and open source SCA implementations. In the next chapter, we take a look at how Java EE web applications can front-end SCA services. In this chapter, we focus on persistence, and in particular, how components can use JDBC and the Java Persistence API (JPA) to transactionally write data to a relational database.

Of the various ways to persist data in Java, we chose JDBC because it is ubiquitous. Our choice of JPA, however, is based on slightly different reasons. First, JPA is emerging as the primary way Java-based enterprise applications access data in a relational database. Enterprise application developers are likely to already be familiar with JPA. In addition, it is our conviction that JPA is one of the best persistence solutions available to Java developers. JPA is a standard and, more important, is widely viewed as providing an efficient and flexible approach to persistence.

Given that SCA does not provide its own persistence API, various SCA runtimes may adopt different approaches. In this chapter, we cover how to use JDBC and JPA with Fabric3. You should be aware that some SCA runtimes might not support JDBC or JPA or do so in a slightly different way. Consequently, if application portability to different runtimes is a requirement, you will need to plan carefully. To assist with this, we note throughout the chapter when a proprietary Fabric3 feature is being used. We also begin the chapter with architectural suggestions for increasing portability in the sidebar, "Architecting for Portability."

Architecting for Portability

One of the major selling points of Java EE is application portability: Assuming a Java EE application did not use vendor-proprietary APIs, it could be deployed to any Java EE-compliant application server.

Despite the claims of avoiding "vendor lock-in," the reality has been that Java EE has had mixed success with application portability. Vendors have often interpreted the Java EE specifications differently, resulting in different runtime behaviors. Also, despite its mandate as an enterprise technology platform, long features such as clustering are not covered by Java EE. This has resulted in vendors introducing proprietary extensions in their runtimes that hinder application portability.

To be sure, over the years Java EE has improved with respect to application portability. More features are covered and the specifications have been made clearer, thereby reducing the possibility of different interpretations. However, despite these advances, Java EE application portability still requires significant effort.

In previous chapters, we mentioned that SCA goals for portability were less ambitious. Specifically, a pragmatic decision was made to focus on skills, as opposed to application portability. SCA would initially provide a reduced level of application portability but would standardize enough so that developers would be on familiar ground when working with different SCA runtimes.

Because SCA does not standardize a persistence API, persistence is an area that presents one of the biggest challenges with respect to application portability. One strategy for dealing with this is to not use runtime-provided persistence facilities at all. In this approach, the application manages its persistence needs, perhaps by using a third-party library directly such as Hibernate or the basic JDBC facilities bundled in the JDK. The major drawback to this approach is that in enterprise scenarios, the application must handle a number of complex infrastructure concerns: for example, bootstrapping the persistence technology, connection pooling, and transactional behavior.

As an alternative, we recommend isolating the use of persistence APIs with a combination of SCA composition and the Data Access Object (DAO) pattern. When an application is ported to a different SCA runtime, these isolated areas can be replaced with another runtime-specific implementation.

A Data Access Object hides persistence details from clients and presents an interface to clients consisting of operations for querying, saving, modifying, and deleting application data. As is evident from the "object" reference in its name, the DAO pattern has been a widely used pattern in object-oriented languages. In SCA, a DAO would most likely be implemented as a local service because operations are typically fine-grained. The following example illustrates a local service that persists `LoanApplication` data:

```
public interface LoanApplicationDao {

    void save(LoanApplication application);

    LoanApplication update(LoanApplication application);

    void remove(LoanApplication application);

    LoanApplication findById(Long id);
}
```

The component implementation for the `LoanApplicationDao` could use JPA, JDBC, or some other means to persist a `LoanApplication` instance. A portable application would potentially have multiple implementations that were used in different SCA runtimes.

Often, applications will include multiple DAOs to handle persistence for the various data types an application may use. These DAOs can be organized into a composite or set of composites that provide persistence services to various parts of an application. The following demonstrates a composite that promotes a `LoanApplicationDao` and a `ApplicantDao`:

```
<composite … name="JPAPersistenceComposite">

    <service name="LoanApplicationDaoService"
promote="LoanApplicationDao"/>

     <service name="ApplicantDaoService" promote="ApplicantDao"/>

    <component name ="LoanApplicationDao">
       <implementation.java
class="com.bigbank.persistence.jpa.LoanApplicationJPADao"/>
          …
    <component>

    <component name ="ApplicantDao">
       <implementation.java class="com.bigbank.
persistence.jpa.ApplicantJPADao"/>
          …
    <component>

…

</composite>
```

The previous composite configures two JPA DAOs and can be used by `LoanComposite`:

```
<composite … name="LoanComposite">

    …

    <component name ="LoanPersistenceComposite">
       <implementation.composite
name="loan:JPAPersistenceComposite"/>
    <component>

</composite>
```

Besides providing a way to clean separate persistence concerns from other component configurations in the `LoanComposite`, creating a separate persistence composite enables the JPA-based implementation to be easily replaced if the loan application needs to be ported to an SCA runtime that does not support JPA.

Using JDBC

In this section, we cover using JDBC to access relational data. The `javax.sql.DataSource` API is the primary way to obtain a database connection and perform SQL operations using JDBC. In SCA runtimes such as Fabric3 that provide JDBC support, a `DataSource` is obtained through injection. However, instead of annotating a setter method or field with `@Reference` or `@Property`, `@Resource` is used. The `@Resource` annotation belongs to the `javax.annotation` package and is defined as part of the JSR-250 specification, "Common Annotations for the Java Platform." The `@Resource` annotation is used by SCA to declare a reference to a resource provided by the runtime—in this case, a `DataSource`. Listing 11.1 shows how to inject a `DataSource` on a component setter method.

In SCA runtimes such as Fabric3 that provide JDBC support, a `DataSource` is obtained through injection.

Listing 11.1   Injecting a DataSource Using @Resource

```
import javax.annotation.Resource;
import javax.sql.DataSource;

public class LoanApplicationJDBCDao implements LoanApplicationDao {
    private DataSource loanDS;

    @Resource (name = "loanDB")
    public void setDataSource(DataSource dataSource) {
        loanDS = dataSource;
    }
}
```

In the preceding example, the `name` attribute specified on the `@Resource` annotation instructs the SCA runtime to inject the `DataSource` named `"loanDB"`. This `DataSource` is configured in a runtime-specific manner.

DataSource Configuration

In this chapter, we do not cover how to configure a `DataSource` because it is vendor-specific. Typically, a `DataSource` is configured via a management console or through a configuration file. You will need to consult the SCA runtime documentation to determine how this is done.

If the `name` attribute is not specified, the `DataSource` name will be inferred from the field or setter method according to the same rules that apply for properties and references. For example, if the `name` attribute were not specified in Listing 11.1, the inferred name would be `"dataSource"`.

The Fabric3 @Resource Annotation

Unfortunately, the `javax.annotation.Resource` annotation defined by the JSR-250 specification, "Common Annotations for the Java Platform," does not support annotating constructor parameters; that is, it does not support `ElementType.PARAMETER`. This means it is not possible to use the annotation to inject resources in a constructor similar to the way component properties and references can be. For those wanting to use constructor injection, Fabric3 provides the proprietary `org.fabric3.api.annotation.Resource` annotation, which is identical to the `javax.annotation.Resource` variant.

DataSources and Transaction Policy

Before obtaining and using a database connection object from an injected `DataSource`, it is necessary to take into account the transaction policy in effect for a given component. If you have used JDBC with a Java EE application server, this will be familiar. Recall in Chapter 6, "Policy," we covered the different transaction policies that can be applied to a component implementation:

- **Global managed transaction**—This is the most common transaction policy associated with a component implementation. When applied to a component implementation, the SCA runtime will ensure that a global transaction is present before dispatching to a method on the component. In doing so, the SCA runtime will use a transaction propagated from the invoking client or begin a new transaction depending on whether the service implemented by the component propagates or suspends transactions. If multiple resources such as `DataSources` associated with different databases are used during an invocation, they will be coordinated as part of a single transaction. Consequently, all work done will either be atomically committed or rolled back as part of the transaction. This process is often referred to as a two-phase commit, or 2PC, transaction.

- **Local managed transaction**—When a component is configured to run with this policy, the SCA runtime will suspend any active transaction context and execute the component within its own local transaction context. Upon completion of an operation, the SCA runtime will coordinate with resources used by the component to individually commit or roll back work. This means that work involving different resources will either fail or complete independently. For example, updates to two `DataSources` will be performed individually: They may fail or succeed independent of one another.

- **No managed transaction**—Components that use this transaction policy are responsible for managing transactions. In this case, the component implementation uses the JDBC APIs to manually control when a transaction commits or rolls back. This is done using the `Connection.setAutoCommit(boolean)`, `Connection.commit()`, and `Connecton.rollback()` methods.

Global and Local Managed Transactions

Let's return to the DAO that persists loan application data from previous examples. In Listing 11.2, if the DAO is configured to run as part of a global managed transaction or local managed transaction, the SCA runtime will either commit or roll back changes when the `update` operation completes.

Listing 11.2   Using a DataSource in the Context of a Global Transaction

```
import javax.annotation.Resource;
import javax.sql.DataSource;

import org.osoa.annotations.GlobalManagedTransaction;

@GlobalManagedTransaction
public class LoanApplicationJDBCDao implements LoanApplicationDao {
    private DataSource loanDS;

    @Resource (name = "loanDB")
    public void setDataSource(DataSource dataSource) {
        loanDS = dataSource;
    }

    public void update(LoanApplication application){
```

```
            Connection conn = null;
              try {
                  conn = loanDS.getConnection();
                  // … update the application
            } catch (SQLException e) {
                  // … rollback
            } finally {
                  if (conn != null) {
                  try {
                        conn.close();
                  } catch (SQLException e) {
                        // …
                  }
            }
        }
      }
    }
    // …
}
```

Because the DAO runs as part of a global transaction, it must not call `Connection.commit()` or `Connection.rollback()` because the runtime will handle that when the update operation completes successfully or throws an exception. Before returning, the only thing the DAO must do is ensure that connections are properly closed using a `try...finally` block.

The main differences between using `DataSources` in the context of local and global transactions become apparent in two cases: when multiple `DataSources` are used by the same component and when multiple DAOs are used by a client. We examine both cases in turn.

Consider the code in Listing 11.3, where two `DataSources` are accessed by the `LoanApplicationJDBCDao`.

Listing 11.3   Using Multiple DataSources in the Context of a Global Transaction

```
import javax.annotation.Resource;
import javax.sql.DataSource;

import org.osoa.annotations.GlobalManagedTransaction;

@GlobalManagedTransaction
public class LoanApplicationJDBCDao implements LoanApplicationDao {
      private DataSource loanDS;
private DataSource auditDS;

      @Resource (name = "loanDB")
```

```
public void setLoanDataSource(DataSource dataSource) {
     loanDS = dataSource;
}

@Resource (name = "auditDB")
public void setAuditDataSource(DataSource dataSource) {
     auditDS = dataSource;
}

public void update(LoanApplication application){

     Connection loanConn = null;
     Connection auditConn = null;
     try {
          loanConn = loanDS.getConnection();
          auditConn = auditDS.getConnection();
          // … update the application using loanConn
          // … insert an audit record using auditConn

} catch (SQLException e) {
          // … rollback
     } finally {
          //… close connections
     }
   }
}
// …
}
```

Because the implementation in Listing 11.3 is configured to use a global transaction, the update to the loan database done using the loanConn connection will be performed in the same transaction as the audit record insert done with the auditConn connection. Consequently, the update and insert will succeed together or be rolled back. On the other hand, if the LoanApplicationJDBCDao were annotated with @LocalManagedTransaction, the update and insert would be performed individually. In other words, they would succeed or fail independently. In this case, it would be possible for the loan application update to commit while the audit record insert is rolled back by the runtime due to an exception.

Another case where the differences between global and local managed transactions become apparent is when a client accesses two DAOs that use the same DataSource. Suppose the BigBank application has two DAOs: a LoanApplicationJDBCDao to persist loan application data and an `ApplicantJDBCDao` responsible for persisting applicant information. Both DAOs use the same `DataSource` and are invoked by `LoanComponent`, which is configured to use a global managed transaction, as shown in Listing 11.4.

Listing 11.4   Invoking Multiple DAOs in the Context of a Global Managed Transaction

```
import org.osoa.annotations.GlobalManagedTransaction;
import org.osoa.annotations.Reference;

@GlobalManagedTransaction
public class LoanComponent implements LoanService {
     private LoanApplicationDao loanApplicationDao;
     private ApplicantDao applicantDao;

     public LoanComponent(@Reference LoanApplicationDao
loanApplicationDao, @Reference ApplicantDao applicantDao) {
          this.applicantDao = applicantDao;
          this.loanApplicationDao = loanApplicationDao;
     }

     public LoanResult apply(LoanRequest request) {
          LoanApplication application = //… create the application
from the request
          LoanApplicant applicant = //.. create the applicant from
the request
          loanApplicationDao.save(application);
          applicantDao.save(applicant);
     }

     // …
}
```

If the `LoanApplicationJDBCDao` and `ApplicantJDBCDao` implementations are configured to use a global managed transaction, the calls to `loanApplicationDao.save(..)` and `applicantDao. save(..)` in Listing 11.4 will be performed in the same transaction context. That is, they will succeed or fail together. If, however, the DAO implementations are configured to use local managed transactions, each call will be performed independently. Figure 11.1 illustrates the difference.

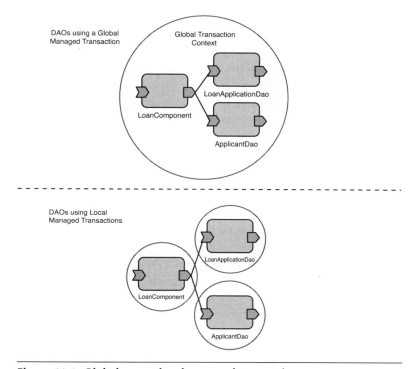

Figure 11.1 Global versus local managed transactions

How does an SCA runtime guarantee "atomicity" across `DataSources` and components when a global managed transaction is in effect? In other words, how does it ensure that persistence operations are handled as a single unit? An SCA runtime enforces atomicity by associating a database connection object with the transaction context through the use of a transaction manager. If a global transaction is in effect, the SCA runtime will associate the JDBC `Connection` object returned from the first call to `DataSource.getConnection()` with the active transaction. Subsequent calls to `DataSource.getConnection()`—whether from the same component instance or other components—will return the same `Connection` object as long as the transaction is active. In addition, when the `Connection` object is returned, the runtime will enlist it with a transaction manager. If multiple `DataSources` are used during a transaction, their `Connection` objects will be enlisted with the transaction manager. Upon completion of the transaction, the transaction manager will coordinate commits across all enlisted connections, known more generally as "resources." If an exception is encountered, the transaction manager will coordinate rollbacks across the enlisted resources. Fortunately, this work is handled transparently by the runtime. Application code does not need to worry about connection management, resource enlistment, or performing coordination.

No Managed Transaction

Component implementations may also be configured to run without a managed transaction. In this case, the implementation is responsible for managing its own transaction demarcations boundaries. This involves either setting `Connection.setAutoCommit (boolean)` to `true`, which results in all SQL statements being executed and committed as individual transactions. Otherwise, application code must explicitly call `Connection.setAutoCommit (false)` followed by `Connection.commit()` or `Connection. rollback()`, as shown in Listing 11.5.

Listing 11.5   Manually Managing Transaction Boundaries with a DataSource

```
import javax.annotation.Resource;
import javax.sql.DataSource;

import org.osoa.annotations.NoManagedTransaction;

@NoManagedTransaction
public class LoanApplicationJDBCDao implements LoanApplicationDao {
     private DataSource loanDS;

     @Resource (name = "loanDB")
     public void setLoanDataSource(DataSource dataSource) {
          loanDS = dataSource;
     }

     public void update(LoanApplication application){
          Connection conn = null;
          try {
               conn.setAutoCommit(false);
               //… update the application
               conn.commit();
          } catch (SQLException e) {
               try {
```

```
                    conn.rollback();
            } catch (SQLException e2) {
                    //… log the exception
            }
        } finally {
            // … close connection
        }

    }
    // …
}
```

As seen in Listing 11.5, given the added complexity associated with application managed transaction boundaries, it is generally advisable to use either globally or locally managed transactions.

Perspective: When to Use Different Transaction Policies

Global transactions involving two-phase commit (2PC)—for example, when multiple DataSources are used in a transaction—will entail a performance penalty. This is because the runtime transaction manager must coordinate commits across multiple resources.

As a way to avoid this performance penalty, it is often suggested to use local managed or no managed transactions. Using local managed transactions will result in persistence operations being performed independently, thereby saving the overhead of 2PC resource coordination. The drawback of this approach is that atomicity is lost as the persistence operations may fail independently.

Using no managed transactions places the burden of committing or rolling back work for a particular database Connection on the application. As with local managed transactions, this approach avoids the overhead of 2PC. However, it is generally not recommended, as managing connections directly greatly complicates application code.

Fortunately, most modern transaction managers perform optimizations that make using global transactions generally the best option. A common optimization is to avoid 2PC coordination if only one resource is enlisted in a transaction. For example, if a component (or set of components) uses a single DataSource for a given transaction, the runtime transaction manager can dispense with 2PC coordination. Some transaction managers also implement more sophisticated optimizations (such as the "last agent" optimization, or WebLogic Server's "last logging resource" optimization) that circumvent part of the 2PC process.

Given the capability of modern transaction managers to perform these optimizations, managed global transactions are generally the best choice. In cases where an optimization cannot be performed and where atomicity is not a strict requirement, local managed transactions may result in performance improvements. However, as with all performance tuning, it is best to quantify performance requirements upfront and tune based on actual measurements.

Using JPA

Instead of JDBC's result set model where data is presented in rows and columns, JPA deals directly with Java objects and provides facilities for mapping them to relational database tables.

Having covered the lower-level JDBC API, we now turn to how to use JPA with SCA components. Even though JPA was developed in response to the deficiencies of EJB Entity Beans, its object/relational mapping (O/R) approach to persistence is particularly effective in building loosely coupled, service-based architectures. Instead of JDBC's result set model where data is presented in rows and columns, JPA deals directly with Java objects and provides facilities for mapping them to relational database tables. Although we assume some familiarity with JPA, we list its main benefits here:

- **Less code**—By working with objects and automating much of the mapping process to relational tables, JPA results in less application code than JDBC.

- **Less complexity**—JPA handles tasks such as unique ID generation, versioning (that is, guarding against overlapping updates of the same data by different clients), and entity relationships that typically require complex application code with JDBC.

- **Portability**—Most JPA implementations have built-in features for handling the idiosyncrasies of various databases, making code more portable.

- **Performance gains**—Despite the "mapping overhead," JPA implementations can actually improve performance by supporting advanced optimizations, such as delayed flushing and operation batching, that would require complex manual coding if done using JDBC.

In this section, we will not delve into the intricacies of working with JPA. Rather, we concentrate on the specifics of using JPA with SCA, and in particular stateless services, transaction policy, and conversational interactions.

More on JPA

This chapter assumes basic familiarity with JPA or an Object/Relational Mapping (O/R) tool such as Hibernate (www.hibernate.org). If you are not familiar with JPA or want to learn more, we highly recommend the very thorough book by Christian Bauer and Gavin King, *Java Persistence with Hibernate* (Manning, 2006).

The Basics: Object Lifecycles and the Persistence Context

In JPA, an object that is persisted to a database such as a `Loan Application` is referred to as an "entity." The `EntityManager` API provides operations for querying, saving, updating, and deleting entities. Similar to a `DataSource`, an `EntityManager` is injected on a component instance. However, instead of using the `@Resource` annotation, the `@PersistenceContext` annotation from the `javax.persistence` package is used. (Why it is called "PersistenceContext" will become apparent later.)

Listing 11.6 demonstrates how the `LoanComponent` uses an `EntityManager` to persist a new `LoanApplication`, resulting in a database insert.

Listing 11.6   Using the EntityManager API to Persist a LoanApplication

```
import javax.persistence.PersistenceContext;

public class LoanComponent implements LoanService {

    private EntityManager entityManager;

    @PersistenceContext
    public void setEntityManager(EntityManager entityManager) {
        this.entityManager = entityManager;
    }
    // ...
```

```
public LoanResult apply(LoanRequest request) {
    LoanApplication application = new LoanApplication();
    // … populate the application with data from the request
    entityManager.persist(application);
}

}
```

EntityManager instances are associated with a **persistence context**, which is essentially an in-memory cache of changes before they are written to the database. When a component adds, modifies, or removes an entity, the entity is tracked as part of a persistence context before the changes are written to the database.

Entities can be in one of four states: new, managed, removed, or detached. A new entity is an object that has been instantiated (using the Java new operator) but has not been persisted; in other words, it exists only in memory and has not been inserted into the database. A managed entity is one that has been associated with a persistence context, typically by invoking EntityManager.persist() or retrieving it into memory via a query. A removed entity is one that is scheduled for deletion in the database. Finally, a detached entity is one that is disassociated from a persistence context.

How does an entity become detached? Consider the case of LoanComponent. When a LoanRequest is received, the component instantiates a new LoanApplication and populates its fields with values from LoanRequest. At this point, LoanApplication is considered to be in the new state. After the component invokes EntityManager.persist(), LoanApplication is associated with a persistence context and placed in the managed state. After the component has finished operating on LoanApplication and the unit of work has completed, the persistence context is closed and LoanApplication is placed in the detached state. The component may still access and manipulate the LoanApplication object, but its data is not guaranteed to be synchronized with the database. Later, the LoanApplication object may become associated with a new persistence context using the EntityManager.merge() operation. When changes tracked by the new persistence context are sent to the database, updates made to the

`LoanApplication` object while in the detached state will be written as well.

Entity detachment and reattachment are illustrated in Figure 11.2.

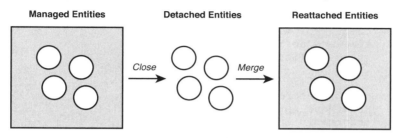

Managed Entities   **Detached Entities**   **Reattached Entities**

Close   Merge

Figure 11.2   Detachment and merging

Detachment occurs when either `EntityManager.close()` is explicitly called or a transaction completes. In JPA, this is referred to as a "transaction-scoped" persistence context. Fabric3 also supports extended persistence contexts that remain active for the duration of a conversation.

Transaction-Scoped Persistence Contexts

When injecting `EntityManager`, the default behavior of an SCA runtime is to associate it with a persistence context for the current transaction, commonly referred to as a "transaction-scoped" persistence context. This has two main effects. First, in the case where a client invokes local services in the context of a global transaction that is propagated, the local service providers will share a persistence context. Second, the persistence context will be flushed (that is, changes written to the database) and closed when the transaction completes. At that point, entities will be detached.

To see how this works, let's return to the `LoanComponent` example. Suppose it uses two JPA-based DAOs to persist `LoanApplication` and `LoanApplicant` information. Because the DAOs abstract the use of JPA, the `LoanComponent` implementation remains unchanged from Listing 11.4. It uses a global transaction and invokes each DAO in turn. The implementation is listed again in Listing 11.7 for convenience.

When injecting `EntityManager`, the default behavior of an SCA runtime is to associate it with a persistence context for the current transaction, commonly referred to as a "transaction-scoped" persistence context.

Listing 11.7   The LoanComponent Remains Unchanged When Using JPA-Based DAOs

```
import org.osoa.annotations.GlobalManagedTransaction;
import org.osoa.annotations.Reference;

@GlobalManagedTransaction
public class LoanComponent implements LoanService {
      private LoanApplicationDao loanApplicationDao;
      private ApplicantDao applicantDao;


      public LoanComponent(@Reference LoanApplicationDao
loanApplicationDao, @Reference ApplicantDao applicantDao) {
            this.applicantDao = applicantDao;
            this.loanApplicationDao = loanApplicationDao;
      }

      public LoanResult apply(LoanRequest request) {
            LoanApplication application = //… create the application
from the request
            LoanApplicant applicant = //.. create the applicant from
the request
            loanApplicationDao.save(application);
            applicantDao.save(applicant);
      }

      // …
}
```

The main change will be in the two DAOs, which use injected `EntityManagers` (see Listing 11.8).

Listing 11.8   The Two JPA-Based DAOs

```
@GlobalManagedTransaction
public class LoanApplicationJPADao implements LoanApplicationDao {
      private EntityManager entityManager;

      @PersistenceContext
      public void setEntityManager(EntityManager entityManager) {
            this.entityManager = entityManager;
      }

      public void update(LoanApplication application){
entityManager.persist(application);
      }
}
```

```
@GlobalManagedTransaction
public class ApplicantJPADao implements ApplicantDao {
      private EntityManager entityManager;

      @PersistenceContext
      public void setEntityManager(EntityManager entityManager) {
            this.entityManager = entityManager;
      }

      public void update(Applicant applicant){
entityManager.persist(applicant);
      }
}
```

Because a global transaction is propagated from LoanComponent to the DAOs, the runtime will associate the same persistence context with each injected EntityManager. Changes made by one DAO will be visible to others sharing the same persistence context. Assuming the global transaction begins when LoanComponent. apply() is invoked and ends when the operation completes, the persistence context will be flushed and changes written to the database after the method returns.

Another item to note is that because the SCA runtime manages EntityManagers, application code must take care not to call JPA APIs for transaction demarcation—in particular, EntityManager. getTransaction() or any of the methods on javax. persistence.EntityTransaction.

The Persistence Context and Remotable Services
The examples thus far have dealt with interactions between local services. This is because persistence contexts are not propagated across remotable service boundaries. Persistence contexts are only shared between local services participating in the same global transaction.

Although it is possible to marshal detached entities across remote boundaries and merge them into another persistence context, this often has the effect of introducing undesired coupling between remotable services as it exposes the internal domain model (that is, the set of entities). Moreover, entities are best designed as fine-grained Java objects, which in many cases do not translate well into interoperable data types, in particular XML schema. For example, it is common to create entities that model one-to-many relationships using Java generics, as shown in Listing 11.9.

Listing 11.9   An Entity

```
@Entity
public class LoanApplication {

    @OneToMany
    private Set<Options> options = new HashSet<Options>();

    public Set<Options> getOptions() {
        return options;
    }

    //...
}
```

Unfortunately, Java generics, as shown in Listing 11.9, do not map well to XML schema types. This may lead to problems with interoperability if the LoanService provided by the LoanComponent is exposed as a web service endpoint. To avoid these mapping and coupling issues, entities should be translated into a format more appropriate for remote marshalling—for example, JAXB types.

JPA and Conversational Services

Using JPA with conversational services is only slightly different than with nonconversational ones. When doing so, it is important to account for detached entities. Remember, as shown back in the first listing in the sidebar "Architecting for Portability," a persistence context is closed and associated entities detached when a transaction completes. Depending on how transaction boundaries are defined, a conversation may start and end within the span of a single transaction, or (the common case) it may be longer-lived and exist over multiple transactions. Figure 11.3 and Figure 11.4 depict short- and long-lived conversations.

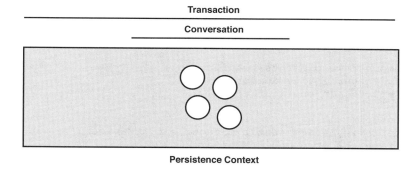

Figure 11.3   A short-lived conversation

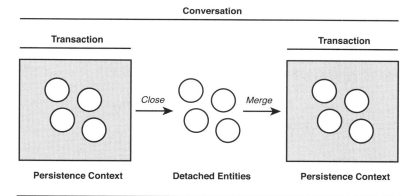

Figure 11.4   A long-lived conversation

In short-lived conversations that do not span a transaction, the persistence context outlives the conversation lifetime. Consequently, component implementations need to handle detached entities.

However, with longer-lived conversations, component implementations have to take special care to reattach entities to a new persistence context. Suppose `LoanService` was conversational, with `apply` and `updateContactInfo` operations. Further, for illustration purposes, assume `LoanComponent` implementing the service persists `LoanApplication` entities using JPA directly instead of DAOs. If each operation was called in the context of a different transaction, `LoanComponent` must ensure that `LoanApplication` was merged with the persistence context, as shown in Listing 11.10.

Listing 11.10   Merging Persistence Entities

```
@Scope("CONVERSATION")

public class LoanComponent implements LoanService {
        private EntityManager entityManager;
        private LoanApplication application;

        @PersistenceContext
        public void setEntityManager(EntityManager entityManager) {
                this.entityManager = entityManager;
        }

        public LoanResult apply(LoanRequest request) {
                application = new LoanApplication();
                // … populate the application with data from the request
                entityManager.persist(application);
        }

        public updateContactInfo(Info info) {
                // update the application
                application = entityManager.merge(application);
        }

        public end() {
                // perform some processing
        }

        //…

}
```

After `apply` is called, `entityManager` will be flushed and changes (that is, the new loan application) applied to the database. In addition, the persistence context will be closed and the `application` object detached. Subsequent calls to `updateContact` will therefore need to reattach the `application` object by calling `EntityManager.merge()`. When `updateContact` returns, the runtime will flush and close the persistence context.

Extended Persistence Contexts

In conversational interactions, it is often desirable to extend the scope of the persistence and have it remain active for the duration of a conversation.

In conversational interactions, it is often desirable to extend the scope of the persistence and have it remain active for the duration of a conversation, as opposed to the lifetime of a transaction. Persistence contexts tied to the lifetime of a conversation are termed "extended persistence contexts." Figure 11.5 depicts an extended persistence context.

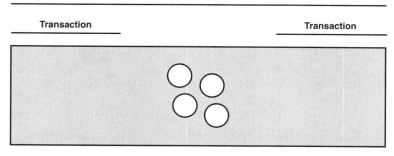

Figure 11.5   Merging persistence entities

The main benefit of extended persistence contexts is that reattachment does not need to be done. This simplifies code and saves the
expense of a merge operation. Extended persistence contexts are
specified by setting the `type` attribute of `@PersistenceContext` to
`javax.persistence.PersistenceContextType.EXTENDED`.
Listing 11.11 shows how this is done. Note also that the call to
`EntityManager.merge()` from Listing 11.10 has been removed
because it is no longer needed.

Listing 11.11   An Extended Persistence Context

```
@Scope("CONVERSATION")

public class LoanComponent implements LoanService {
    private EntityManager entityManager;
    private LoanApplication application;

    @PersistenceContext (type = PersistenceContextType.EXTENDED)
    public void setEntityManager(EntityManager entityManager) {
        this.entityManager = entityManager;
    }

    public LoanResult apply(LoanRequest request) {
        application = new LoanApplication();
        // … populate the application with data from the request
        entityManager.persist(application);
    }

    public updateContactInfo(Info info) {
```

```
        // update the application
}

public end() {
        // perform some processing
}

//...
}
```

If each operation (for example, `apply` and `updateContactInfo`) were invoked in different transaction contexts, the persistence context would be flushed multiple times as each transaction completed. However, the persistence context would remain open. Assuming the end operation was annotated with `@Ends Conversation`, the extended persistence context would be closed only when it was invoked.

Accessing the `EntityManagerFactory`

To access `EntityManagerFactory` instead of an `EntityManager`, a component implementation can use the `@PersistenceUnit` annotation. For example, the `LoanApplicationJPADao` can be rewritten to use the `EntityManagerFactory`, as shown in Listing 11.12.

Listing 11.12   Injecting an EntityManagerFactory

```
import javax.persistence.PersistenceUnit;
import org.osoa.annotations.GlobalManagedTransaction;

public class LoanApplicationJPADao implements LoanApplicationDao {
      private EntityManagerFactory emf;

      @PersistenceUnit(unitName="loanApp")
      public void setEntityManagerFactory(EntityManagerFactory emf) {
          this.emf = emf;
      }

      public void update(LoanApplication application){
          EntityManager entityManager = emf.createEntityManager();
          entityManager.persist(application);
      }
}
```

Accessing the Hibernate API with Fabric3

At times, it is useful to be able to access the proprietary APIs of a JPA provider. As an alternative to `EntityManager`, Fabric3 provides access to the Hibernate `org.hibernate.Session` object. To utilize it, use the `@PersistenceContext` annotation, substituting `Session` for `EntityManager.getDelegate()`, as shown in the following excerpt:

```
import org.osoa.annotations.GlobalManagedTransaction;
import org.hibernate.Session;
import org.javax.persistence.EntityManaget;
import org.javax.persistence.PersistenceContext;


@GlobalManagedTransaction
public class LoanApplicationJPADao implements LoanApplicationDao {
     private Session session;

     @PersistenceContext
     public void setSession(EntityManager em) {
          this.session = (Session)em.getDelegate()
     }

// ...
}
```

Summary

This chapter has dealt with one of the most important aspects of application development: persistence. In particular, we have covered how to effectively use JDBC and JPA with SCA. The next chapter completes this application development picture by explaining how SCA integrates with Java EE web technologies, specifically servlets and JSPs.

12

The Presentation Tier

SCA does not offer an alternative presentation-tier technology. When it comes to user interfaces, SCA's mantra is integration. Service tiers built with SCA can be integrated with a variety of client technologies, including Swing and rich-clients built using Adobe Flex, AJAX, and web frameworks, such as Struts and Java Server Faces (JSFs).

Instead of a cursory overview of how SCA integrates with a wide variety of presentation-tier technologies, this chapter focuses on how Java EE web applications are used as front-ends to SCA services. Specifically, we cover how servlets and Java Server Pages (JSPs) access SCA services. With this knowledge, it is possible to integrate SCA services with more sophisticated presentation-tier technologies, including the myriad of web frameworks that exist today.

Web Components

As a component-based technology, it may not be surprising that SCA has the notion of a web component. Web components are Java EE web applications configured as components. What does this mean? In a nutshell, it is the way servlets and JSPs can be wired to SCA services. This brings SCA protocol abstraction benefits to the presentation tier; similar to Java-based components, servlets and JSPs can invoke services without having to resort to low-level, transport-specific APIs.

Web components are like any other SCA component in that they may have references wired to remotable services.

Web components are like any other SCA component in that they may have references wired to remotable services. Returning to the BigBank loan application from previous chapters, BigBank may decide to offer a consumer-facing web application that offers loans directly to customers. In this case, a Java EE web application will provide the user interface and interact with the `LoanService` for processing. Listing 12.1 illustrates this scenario.

Listing 12.1   A Web Component Wired to the LoanService

```
<composite ..>

    <component name="lending">
        <implementation.web/>
        <reference name="loanService" target="LoanComponent"/>
    </component>

    <component name=" LoanComponent ">
        <implementation.java ../>
    </component>
</composite>
```

Using a web component, implementing a servlet that collects loan application information and submits a request to the `LoanService` is fairly straightforward. In fact, the servlet resembles a typical Java-based component, as shown in Listing 12.2.

Listing 12.2   A Servlet That Accesses the LoanService

```
public class BigBankLoanServlet extends HttpServlet{

    @Reference
    protected LoanService loanService;

    protected void doPost(HttpServletRequest req, HttpServletResponse
➥resp) throws ServletException, IOException {
        // …
    }

}
```

In Listing 12.2, take note of the @Reference annotation. As with Java-based components, this instructs the SCA runtime to inject a proxy to a service. When injected, the servlet can invoke the proxy, which may forward the request to a component hosted on a remote runtime. The specific transport used—for example, web services, JMS, or RMI—is conveniently abstracted from the servlet code.

Having seen the essentials of how a web component is implemented, let's now look in more detail at how one is configured.

Configuring a Web Component

In the preceding example, we implemented a servlet with a single reference to the LoanService. This reference is wired by configuring a web component in a composite. Web components are designated using the implementation.web element. Listing 12.3 presents the BigBank web component.

Listing 12.3   Defining a Web Component

```
<composite ..>

    <component name="BigBank">
        <implementation.web/>
    </component>

</composite>
```

As with other component types, when the web component is deployed to a domain, the SCA runtime is responsible for injecting reference proxies—in this case, on the servlet.

Often, more than one servlet in a web component may need to access the same service. In this case, each servlet defines a reference (using the @Reference annotation) with the same name. In the composite, the reference only needs to be configured once: The SCA runtime will inject a reference proxy into each servlet with an @Reference declaration. For example, if the BigBank web component contained two servlets with references to LoanService, the component definition would be the same as in Listing 12.3.

Packaging and Deploying a Web Component

Web components are packaged as Java EE web archives (WARs).

Up to this point, we have not discussed how web components are packaged and deployed to a domain. In Chapter 9, "The Domain," we detailed how SCA defines a portable packaging format for contributions, namely a ZIP-based archive, but allows for alternative packaging formats. In line with this, web components are packaged as Java EE web archives (WARs). This has several advantages. Most notably, WARs are familiar to most enterprise Java developers. In addition, existing tooling may be used to package web components.

When packaging a web component as a WAR, the composite file that defines the web component must be located in the WEB-INF directory and named web.composite. It is worth noting that in addition to the web component, the composite may define additional components and include other composites. For example, web.composite may configure several Java-based components used by the web application.

In addition to the web.composite file, a WAR-based contribution also must contain an sca-contribution.xml manifest file located in the META-INF directory. As with standard SCA contributions, this manifest file may specify imported contributions, export artifacts, and declare deployable composites. For example, a web component may reference artifacts such as WSDLs or schemas contained in another contribution, in which case it would import that contribution. However, a WAR-based contribution would typically not contain deployable composites other than the one defined in the web.composite file.

One important feature provided by WAR-based contributions is that classes placed in the WEB-INF/classes and jars in the WEB-INF/lib directories are accessible to servlets and JSPs contained in the archive. This is a useful and necessary feature—because Java EE defines this behavior, if SCA did not support it, many web applications would not work when deployed to an SCA runtime.

As we explained in Chapter 9, SCA does not define a standard way to deploy contributions to a domain. A runtime may use a command-line tool, a file directory, a GUI environment, or some other mechanism. However, SCA does define specific behavior for what

happens when a composite is deployed to the domain:
Components are included as top-level components in the domain
composite. Consequently, when web.composite is deployed to a
domain, its child components become domain-level components,
as illustrated in Figure 12.1.

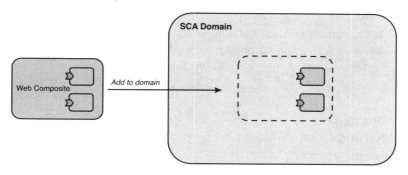

Figure 12.1   Deploying a web component to the domain

In the case of the BigBank web component, its reference is wired to
the `LoanService` offered by the domain-level `LoanComponent`.
This is shown in Figure 12.2.

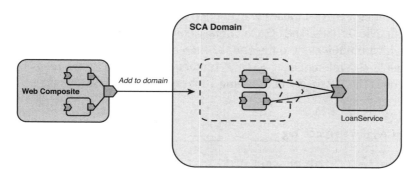

Figure 12.2   Deploying the BigBank web component

Embedding an SCA Domain in a Web Application

In enterprise architectures, SCA domains will commonly span multiple runtimes. For more modest applications, some SCA runtimes such as Fabric3 support the capability to embed a domain entirely within a web application deployed to a servlet container. This enables web components to be conveniently packaged with other services in a single WAR. For more information and examples of embedding an SCA domain in a web application, see the Fabric3 site (www.fabric3.org).

Properties

Web components may also have properties used for configuration. To access a property, a servlet declares a field or setter with the `@Property` annotation. When the web component is instantiated by the SCA runtime, it injects the property values specified in the web component entry.

Java Server Pages and the SCA Tag Library

SCA defines a JSP tag library for accessing services from JSPs. Tag libraries are the standard way defined by Java EE to add custom behavior to JSPs. The SCA tag library contains the `reference` tag, which is equivalent to the `@Reference` annotation for servlets: It declares a reference, its service contract, and a name for the reference. The JSP fragment in Listing 12.4 demonstrates how this is done.

Listing 12.4   Using the SCA JSP Reference Tag

```
<%@ page contentType="text/html;charset=UTF-8" language="java" %>
<!-- body of the JSP -->
<sca:reference name="loanService" type="bigbank.LoanService"/>

<!-- … -->

<%
    LoanApplication application = …
    loanService.apply(application)
%>
```

In the preceding JSP fragment, the `<sca:reference>` tag declares the `loanService` reference, with a service contract as defined by the `bigbank.LoanService` Java interface. Using the tag has two effects. First, it declares a reference for the web component that is wired in the web.composite file. Assuming this JSP and the servlet from the earlier example both declared the `loanService` reference, the web.composite file would remain the same as in Listing 12.3. In other words, the web component definition would contain only one `<reference>` entry. When the web component is deployed to the domain, the SCA runtime will ensure that reference proxies are available to all servlets and JSPs that declare it. The second effect of the JSP `<sca:reference>` tag is that it makes the reference proxy available in the JSP page context using `loanService` as the variable name. As seen in Listing 12.4, the reference proxy can be invoked using inline Java.

Generally, using inline Java in JSPs is considered bad practice as it mixes rendering logic (HTML and JavaScript) with application logic. An example that would align more closely with JSP best practices would use other tags to access the reference proxy. Because the reference proxy is made available in the JSP page context, it can be accessed using JSP expressions. For example, assume BigBank has another JSP that displays current rates using `RateService`. The current rates returned from the service can be iterated and displayed using built-in JSP tags and the JSP expression language, as shown in Listing 12.5.

Listing 12.5   Accessing a Reference Proxy Using JSP Tags

```
<%@ page contentType="text/html;charset=UTF-8" language="java" %>

<%@ taglib prefix="c" uri="http://java.sun.com/jsp/jstl/core" %>
<%@ taglib prefix="sca" uri="http://www.osoa.org/sca/sca.tld" %>

<sca:reference name="rateService" type="bigbank.RateService"/>

<html>
   <body>
    <table>
       <c:forEach items="${rateService.rates}" var="rate">
          <tr>
             <td>${rate.type} at ${rate.percentage}% and ${rate.apr}
            ➥APR</td>
          </tr>
```

```
        </c:forEach>
    </body>
</html>
```

To use the `reference` tag, you need to include the tag library jar in the web component WAR under the WEB-INF/lib directory. SCA runtimes that support web components (for example, Fabric3) make this tag library available as part of the runtime distribution or development kit. After you have obtained the tag library, it must be declared in a JSP using the `taglib` directive, as shown in Listing 12.6.

Listing 12.6   Using the Taglib Directive with the SCA Tag Library

```
<%@ page contentType="text/html;charset=UTF-8" language="java" %>
<%@ taglib prefix="sca" uri="http://www.osoa.org/sca/sca.tld" %>
<!--jsp contents -->
```

Asynchronous Interactions

At times, it is useful to avoid blocking on a request before returning a response to a browser client. In these situations, servlets can use non-blocking operations on SCA services. Assuming the `LoanService.apply(..)` operation is marked with the `@OneWay` annotation and is long-running, the servlet in the example shown in Listing 12.7 will return a response to the client before the service provider has completed processing.

Listing 12.7   A Servlet Invoking a Non-Blocking Operation on an SCA Service

```
public class BigBankLoanServlet extends HttpServlet{

    @Reference
    protected LoanService loanService;

    protected void doPost(HttpServletRequest req, HttpServletResponse
➥resp) throws ServletException, IOException {
        LoanApplication application = // …
        loanService.apply(application); // returns immediately as the
➥call is non-blocking
    }

}
```

Asynchronous invocations can improve scalability because the runtime does not need to hold open client connections while processing is being done. This is particularly the case when operations may require a significant amount of time to complete. The main drawback to using asynchronous invocations in servlets is that error handling becomes more difficult. For example, if an error occurs while processing the loan, the user will not receive immediate feedback because the servlet will have already returned a response to the client. Instead, error handling would need to be done by `LoanComponent` (that is, the component providing `LoanService`), with possibly a notification sent to the user via email or some other communications channel.

Although servlets and JSPs may invoke non-blocking operations, they cannot receive callbacks. If a service is bidirectional (that is, it specifies a callback service), it must be accessed from an intermediary service that implements the required callback interface. To understand how this works, let's return to the `CreditService` callback example we introduced in Chapter 3, "Service-Based Development Using Java." The `CreditService` and `CreditServiceCallback` interfaces are defined in Listing 12.8.

Listing 12.8   The CreditService and CreditServiceCallback Interfaces

```
import org.osoa.sca.annotations.OneWay;
import org.osoa.sca.annotations.Callback;

@Remotable
@Callback(CreditCallback.class)
public interface CreditService {

    @OneWay
    void checkCredit(String id);
}

@Remotable
public interface CreditCallback {

    @OneWay
    void onCreditResult(CreditScore score);
}
```

Because the `CreditService` requires the client to provide a call-back service, it cannot be invoked from a servlet. Instead, an intermediary service would need to be wired to the servlet, which in turn would have the `CreditService` wired to it. The intermediary would be responsible for handling the callback. The SCDL for setting this up is provided in Listing 12.9.

Listing 12.9   Bidirectional Wiring with Web Components

```
<composite ..>

    <component name="lending">
        <implementation.web/>
        <reference name="creditServiceIntermediary" target="
CreditServiceIntermediary"/>
    </component>

    <component name="CreditServiceIntermediary">
        <implementation.java ../>
  <reference name="creditService" target="CreditService"/>
    </component>
</composite>
```

Accessing Conversation Services

Up to this point, we have discussed how to access non-conversational services from servlets and JSPs. Doing so is fairly straightforward, particularly because client servlets or JSPs do not need to take threading issues into account, even though web components are by nature multithreaded—that is, they may receive more than one simultaneous request. If the SCA service accessed by a servlet or JSP is implemented by a stateless component, the SCA runtime will guarantee that only one web request will have access to it at a time, as illustrated in Figure 12.3.

In this case, the servlet or JSP and component implementation does not need to take any special care, such as synchronizing field access. When a service is implemented by a composite-scoped component, it is up to it to manage concurrent access (perhaps by not using field variables or synchronizing access to them), as all requests will be dispatched to the same instance (see Figure 12.4).

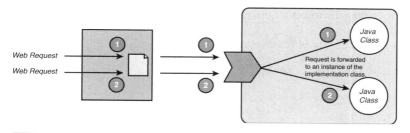

Figure 12.3   Dispatching multiple requests in a web component to a stateless component

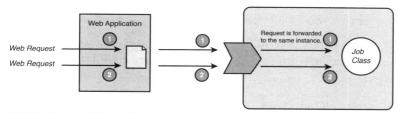

Figure 12.4   Dispatching multiple requests in a web component to a composite-scoped component

When invoking a service provided by a composite-scoped component, the servlet or JSP does not need to regulate concurrent access because the service provider handles it internally in the component implementation.

If a service is conversational, servlets and JSPs will need to take special care with concurrent access. To guard against inadvertently having two or more clients access the same conversational service instance through a servlet or JSP, web components associate references wired to conversational services with the HTTP session. This means that conversational services *cannot* be injected on a servlet field using the `@Reference` annotation. For example, assuming that `MyConversationalService` is marked as `@Conversational`, the code in Listing 12.10 will result in an error when the contribution containing the web component is installed.

Listing 12.10   Attempting to Illegally Inject a Conversational Service

```
public class MyServlet extends HttpServlet{

    // this reference will result in an error
    @Reference
    protected MyConversationalService myService;

}
```

If the preceding code were legal, because servlets handle multiple simultaneous requests, it would result in every client accessing the same instance of the `MyConversationalService` instance—something that is most likely not intended.

There are two options for accessing conversational services from a servlet. The first is to use the `ComponentContext` API, as shown in Listing 12.11.

Listing 12.11   Using the ComponentContext API

```
public class MyServlet extends HttpServlet{

    @Context
    protected ComponentContext context;

    protected void doPost(HttpServletRequest req, HttpServletResponse
➥resp) throws ServletException, IOException {
        MyConversationalService service =
➥context.getService(MyConversationalService.class, "myService");
        // …
    }

}
```

The `ComponentContext` instance—which is threadsafe—is injected on the servlet using the `@Context` annotation. When the `ComponentContext.getService(..)` API is called, passing the expected interface type and reference name, a reference proxy is returned. This proxy will always dispatch invocations to the same instance for the current HTTP session. If two requests associated with different HTTP sessions are received by the servlet, the code in Listing 12.11 will dispatch to two different instances of the `MyConversationalService`. If, however, two requests associated with the same HTTP session arrive, they will be dispatched to the same instance. Figure 12.5 illustrates this dispatching.

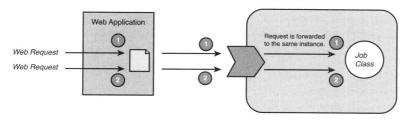

Figure 12.5   Dispatching to conversational services

The second option for accessing a conversational service is to use the Servlet `HttpSession` API. Listing 12.12 shows how this is done.

Listing 12.12   Using the Servlet HttpSession API to Access a Conversational Service

```
public class MyServlet extends HttpServlet{

   protected void doPost(HttpServletRequest req, HttpServletResponse
➥resp) throws ServletException, IOException {
      HttpSession session = request.getSession();
      MyConversationalService service = (MyConversationalService)
➥session.getAttribute("myService");
      // …
   }

}
```

As seen in Listing 12.12, the SCA runtime makes reference proxies available from the HTTP session by reference name. Which way is better: using `ComponentContext` or `HttpSession` API? Whatever method is chosen is largely a matter of personal preference. The important thing to remember is not to attempt to store reference proxies in member variables, as doing so will expose a conversational instance to all web component clients.

Defining a Component Type

Previously, we mentioned that the SCA runtime will scan the contents of a web component for `@Reference` annotations and `reference` JSP tags when it is installed to determine the set of wireable references.

What happens when there are no @Reference annotations or reference tags used in a web component? This could happen if a web component contains servlets that only use the ComponentContext API. In this case, the runtime has no way to determine the set of references for a web component by introspecting its servlets and JSPs.

When this happens, a special file called a web.componentType file must be created and placed in the WEB-INF directory of the WAR. The componentType file is an XML file that defines services, references, and properties for a component implementation. We haven't mentioned the componentType file previously because it is generally not needed—in Java, annotations can be used instead.

An example of a web.componentType file that defines a single reference is shown in Listing 12.13.

Listing 12.13   A web.componentType File

```
<componentType xmlns="http://www.osoa.org/xmlns/sca/1.0">

    <reference name="loanService">
        <interface.java interface="bigbank.LoanService"/>
    </reference>

</componentType>
```

It is possible to use a combination of @Reference annotations, reference JSP tags, and a web.ComponentType file. The SCA runtime will combine all three sources when calculating the wireable references for a web component.

Summary

This chapter has provided an introduction to integrating SCA services with presentation tiers built using Java EE web applications. It has covered using web components to wire from servlets and JSPs to services. With this knowledge, you should have a thorough understanding of the basics to build user interfaces that front SCA services.

Index

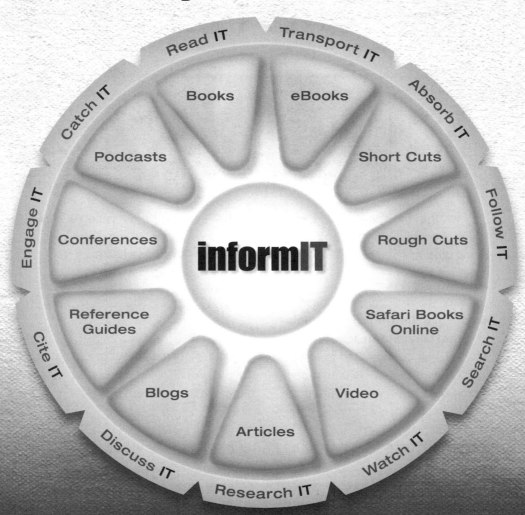

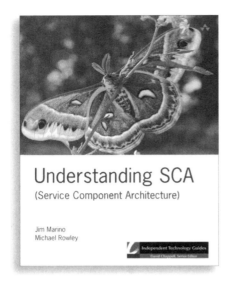

FREE Online Edition

Your purchase of **Understanding SCA (Service Component Architecture)** includes access to a free online edition for 45 days through the Safari Books Online subscription service. Nearly every Addison-Wesley Professional book is available online through Safari Books Online, along with more than 5,000 other technical books and videos from publishers such as Cisco Press, Exam Cram, IBM Press, O'Reilly, Prentice Hall, Que, and Sams.

SAFARI BOOKS ONLINE allows you to search for a specific answer, cut and paste code, download chapters, and stay current with emerging technologies.

Activate your FREE Online Edition at www.informit.com/safarifree

STEP 1: Enter the coupon code: YKGOZBI.

STEP 2: New Safari users, complete the brief registration form. Safari subscribers, just log in.

If you have difficulty registering on Safari or accessing the online edition, please e-mail customer-service@safaribooksonline.com